D1309147

Family Evaluation in Custody Litigation

REDUCING RISKS OF ETHICAL
INFRACTIONS AND MALPRACTICE

G. ANDREW H. BENJAMIN
AND JACKIE K. GOLLAN

AMERICAN PSYCHOLOGICAL ASSOCIATION
WASHINGTON, DC

Published by
American Psychological Association
750 First Street, NE
Washington, DC 20002
www.apa.org

To order
APA Order Department
P.O. Box 92984
Washington, DC 20090-2984

Tel: (800) 374-2721; Direct: (202) 336-5510
Fax: (202) 336-5502; TDD/TTY: (202) 336-6123
On-line: www.apa.org/books/
E-mail: order@apa.org

In the U.K., Europe, Africa, and the Middle East, copies may be ordered from
American Psychological Association
3 Henrietta Street
Covent Garden, London
WC2E 8LU England

Typeset in Goudy by EPS Group Inc., Easton, MD

Printer: Data Reproductions Corporation, Auburn Hills, MI
Cover Designer: Berg Design, Albany, NY
Technical/Production Editor: Casey Ann Reever

The opinions and statements published are the responsibility of the authors, and such opinions and statements do not necessarily represent the policies of the American Psychological Association (APA). Statements made in this book neither add to nor reduce requirements of the APA Ethics Code. Nor can they be definitively relied upon as interpretations of the meaning of the Ethics Code standards or their application to particular situations. Each ethics committee or other relevant body must interpret and apply the Ethics Code as it believes proper, given all the circumstances.

Library of Congress Cataloging-in-Publication Data
Benjamin, G. Andrew H.
   Family evaluation in custody litigation : reducing risks of ethical infractions and malpractice / by G. Andrew H. Benjamin and Jackie K. Gollan.
       p. cm.—(Forensic practice guidebook)
Includes bibliographical references and index.
   ISBN 1-55798-953-2 (hardcover : alk. paper)
   1. Custody of children—Law and legislation—United States.   2. Psychology, Forensic —United States.   3. Child psychologists—Malpractice—United States.   4. Custody of children—Psychological aspects.   I. Gollan, Jackie K.   II. Title.   III. Series.

KF505.5 .B46 2002
346.7301'73—dc21

2002015078

British Library Cataloguing-in-Publication Data
A CIP record is available from the British Library.

Printed in the United States of America
First Edition

CONTENTS

FOREWORD TO THE SERIES

When the American Psychological Association (APA) launched its *Law and Mental Health Professionals* book series in 1993, it broke new publishing ground by offering clinicians comprehensive reviews of the law that affects them in each jurisdiction. This review of the relevant law is essential for practitioners so that they can understand how that law controls their professional practice; specifies situations in which the legal system needs their assessment, therapeutic, and administrative services; and affects clinical services when patients become involved in legal entanglements.

What is not covered in that series is the clinical information that will help mental health professionals practice ethically and competently in forensic situations. APA's *Law and Public Policy: Psychology and the Social Sciences* book series partially addresses this need by publishing volumes that consider the science underlying law-related mental health practice. *Violent Offenders: Appraising and Managing Risk* by Vernon L. Quinsey, Grant T. Harris, Marnie E. Rice, and Catherine A. Cormier (1998) and *Treating Adult and Juvenile Offenders With Special Needs* edited by José B. Ashford, Bruce D. Sales, and William H. Reid (2000) are excellent examples of this type of book. Although the information contained in these volumes is critical for mental health professionals to understand if they plan to provide, or are providing, forensic services, the volumes tend to be lengthier because of this series' concern with scholarly and scientific comprehensiveness.

Experience teaches that clinicians also have a need for guidebooks that will accurately convey, with brevity and clarity, how to participate in the myriad forensic practice areas. That is the purpose of the *Forensic Practice Guidebooks* series. Over time, volumes in this series will cover all topics for which clinicians may be asked to provide services to clients enmeshed in the law or to provide services to a legal system (e.g., the courts, social

services, corrections) to aid in the administration of the law. The overarching goal of the *Forensic Practice Guidebooks* series is to help clinicians
engage in forensic practice ethically and competently in today's changing
professional environment.

Bruce D. Sales, PhD, JD
Series Editor

PREFACE

This book speaks with a single voice in addressing a major problem of contemporary society that has at least three facets: Our first and most compelling purpose is to reduce the damaging stresses that are imposed on children who, through no fault of their own, are embroiled in the struggles and passions of high-conflict divorce and custody litigation. Our second purpose is to make available to the courts to which these cases are assigned the best resources of the mental health professions. Psychologists have amassed powerful bodies of technique and practice in serving the needs of families beset by conflicts they cannot resolve on their own. Our third purpose is to provide a unique toolbox of proven methods that puts psychologists on an equal footing with practitioners of law and medicine, outside the domain of the health care system, in rendering important services to the community that the community appropriately respects and rewards.

Although our book speaks with a single voice, as authors we come to the work with different backgrounds. That is why we have each chosen to make separate prefatory comments in welcoming readers to this work.

From Jackie Gollan:

I trained with Andy Benjamin in the Parenting Evaluation Treatment Program (PETP) from 1994 to 1996 as a clinical psychology PhD graduate student at the University of Washington. Following this, for a brief time in 1997, I coordinated the PETP program. Working clinically and administratively to untangle the psycho–legal complexities in these cases was intriguing work and among the highlights of my graduate career. These experiences inspired my pursuit of postdoctoral work with litigating families at Massachusetts General Hospital/Harvard Medical School (MGH) and the Boston Family Courts. While working in the Seattle and Boston courts, it was apparent that the PETP protocol structured a process that was often confusing and chaotic. The evaluation procedures suggested how to avoid malpractice hotspots, resolve ethical issues, push through evaluation delays, and reduce parental anxieties. This textbook describes a standardized assessment methodology that produces a comprehensive and well-considered evaluation for the court. With attention to empirical approaches, ethical principles, and legal standards, we hope that the PETP procedures enhance the well-being of legal participants in family courts.

From Andy Benjamin:

When I first joined the University of Washington as an assistant professor in the mid-1980s, it became apparent that many of my colleagues in mental health were often confused, frightened, or disturbed by their interactions with lawyers and the courts. These feelings seemed the result of limited education about how mental professionals could work well with the legal system. I discussed this phenomenon with several of my colleagues. Jack Carr, PhD, the acting chair of the Department of Psychiatry and Behavioral Sciences, encouraged me to develop a forensic training program for mental health professionals. I kept two facts in mind during the program's development and early stages of implementation. First, the department was involved in training psychology interns and psychiatry residents. Both sets of trainees had vastly different abilities to conceptualize and write fluently. Second, our courts in Washington were filled with very competent forensic experts for most of the areas of practice. This was not true for family law (divorce or paternity cases in which the parenting plans for the children of the parents were being contested) and dependency cases (cases in which the state was removing the children from a family because of alleged abuse or neglect).

It appeared and still seems true that most mental health professionals have difficulty sustaining practice in this area because of the emotional intensity of working with children and parents of such families. In addition, word was already spreading that the highest risk for ethics complaints arose during work with family law litigants. As a result of these two concerns it became apparent that a forensic training program was needed in the area of family law and dependency evaluations. The procedures for conducting such evaluations needed to be standardized and thorough so that a diversely trained group of professionals would not make mistakes that would lead to any denial or loss of their licensing as practitioners or as supervisors.

The following book is an outgrowth of my having developed and run the forensic PETP for 14 years (we refer interested readers to the Web site: http://depts.washington.edu/petp/). I am pleased to report that PETP's procedures have withstood the tests of time and clinical exposure. After having supervised hundreds of cases, I have revised and streamlined PETP's procedures. Based on these experiences and the emerging research literature, the resulting evaluation processes produce comprehensive evaluations that the courts and the parties (the litigants who have filed lawsuits) view as thorough and fair.

Series editor Bruce D. Sales, PhD, JD, specifically requested that I write this book. He and I have worked together since I was his first student at the University of Arizona. We both believe that mental health professionals can serve in critical roles as experts who provide the courts with valid and reliable evidence about the psychological issues of each case. This book is an effort to prepare mental health professionals for such a role. Although this book is written for novices, it contains helpful tips for even the most expert forensic mental health professional. This book is a clinical text that combines conceptual and historical exposition with hands-on presentations of interviewing and report-writing strategies. We also added many forms and an evaluation report to help readers visualize how to design and write a parenting evaluation that would be relevant for court personnel. We hope that publishing this book will result in increasing our abilities as evaluators. Our clients—the children of family law cases —will benefit as we become even more proficient as evaluators.

ACKNOWLEDGMENTS

We have different and partially overlapping constellations of mentors and colleagues to whom we would like to express our appreciation for their assistance in helping us complete this book.

From Andy Benjamin:

I would like to acknowledge Stephen Feldman, PhD, JD; Marsha Hedrick, PhD; Stuart Greenberg, PhD; and Molly Reid, PhD, for their assistance in helping to develop and continuing to nurture the Parenting Evaluation Treatment Program. Many colleagues provided editorial support that strengthened the manuscript. Jackie and I are very thankful to Eric Drogin, PhD, JD; Robert Kinscherff, PhD, JD; Sandra McPherson, PhD, JD; Joti Samra, PhD; and Joan Sullivan, JD. Bernard Z. Friedlander, PhD, have provided invaluable assistance in bringing the project to a successful conclusion. We also thank Phuong Huynh, our development editor at APA Books, who competently and cheerfully guided our manuscript through the editorial process.

Finally, on a personal note, my wife of 25 years, Nan Herbert, deserves the leading acknowledgment. This book has been an enormous project that she has endured tolerantly. Her warm, loving support has made a great difference in my life.

From Jackie Gollan:

With any effort of this sort, there are numerous mentors and colleagues without whose insight and guidance I could not have co-written this book. Special thanks to Bruce Sales, PhD, JD; Neil Jacobson, PhD; Kenneth Herman, PhD, JD; Robin Deutsch, PhD; Mira Levitt, PhD; Peggie Ward, PhD; Lauren Wakschlag, PhD; and Bennett Leventhal, PhD. These individuals have taught me that the interdisciplinary areas of the family and the law are inspiring and diverse. By their example, I have learned that remaining connected to research will help the field finalize a clearly specified and satisfactory approach to evaluating parental capacity in family litigation.

Finally, on a more personal note, I also thank my colleague and husband, Eric Gortner, PhD, JD, and my family for their support, encouragement, and humor while writing this book.

Family Evaluation in Custody Litigation

INTRODUCTION

We have divided the text into three parts. Part I describes the preparatory work that should be accomplished before conducting evaluations. We briefly discuss the context of family litigation, the incidence and nature of separation and divorce, and the tremendous impact of divorce on parents and children. We also review the kinds of cases that present for evaluation in family litigation. Because these evaluations are subject to legal liabilities, we also discuss the legal evidentiary standards used in the court system with regard to psychological testing, scientific evidence, and expert witness testimony. To ensure adherence to the highest standards of practice, we discuss relevant ethical guidelines and review how to achieve both adherence and competence in conducting parenting evaluations.

Part II focuses on the assessment procedures in conducting court-appointed or -stipulated evaluations (these are evaluations that are agreed to by both parties and their lawyers). We discuss the pre-evaluation procedures to avoid both the appearance of conflict of interest and perceived bias by the parties. We also discuss the parameters of confidentiality and fee agreements. We then outline the phases of the multiparty evaluation, offering practical advice about assessment strategies that lead to efficient, thorough, and fairly perceived data collection. The structure of parent–child observation visits to family homes, review of collateral reporter records, and solicitation of third-party collateral interviews are delineated.

Finally, we discuss methods of data integration, report writing, and court presentation. We also outline practical information about appropriate data collection and management. This protocol provides an objective approach that enables fair and thorough evaluations of developmental and attachment issues, cultural family dynamics, and nontraditional families. We describe the ethical and legal concepts and procedures relevant to family law custody proceedings, and we suggest how evaluators may maintain professionalism with court personnel and litigants.

Part III contains a sample case with two discussion and recommendation sections so that readers can experience the scope of a comprehensive evaluation.

THE PROCESS BEFORE US

Child custody disputes involve cases in which the parties, usually the parents, may disagree about residential schedules, decision-making about the children, and myriad other issues. Typically, neither party believes the other party should have much contact and access to the children. These situations generate divisive issues regarding parental rights and developmentally appropriate access and care of children. They require guidelines for measuring parental fitness and ascertaining the best interests of the children. The law in most states requires a judge to arrive at decisions about the welfare of the children in family law cases. To do so, the judge must weigh and balance multiple pieces of evidence about the child's circumstances that include the adjustment to the two different homes, among other issues. Family court judges, who aim for expedient and careful review of these family situations, have limited access and resources to examine the key components of family functioning. As a result, many family court judges now regularly appoint mental health professionals who have been training in law and psychology to evaluate the family dynamics and patterns, with a specific focus on protecting the physical and psychological well-being of children. When done competently, parenting evaluations provide key psychological evidence that allows judges to adjudicate cases in ways that maximize the best interests of children (Gould, 1998).

From a social policy perspective, having one neutral mental health professional conduct a comprehensive evaluation with all family members supplants the duplicative efforts of multiple experts who may be prone to act as "hired guns" rather than as educators. From the judicial perspective, contested custody cases require professional consultation to identify the nature and health of the family relationships and the needs and capacities of children and their caretakers. When conducted competently, mental health professionals can provide psychological evidence that is necessary for the judge to understand the needs of the children and the parental capacity of both parties.

Conducting forensic evaluations in child custody is technically difficult and contentious work. It is also a highly satisfying endeavor. As we describe in this book, conducting parenting evaluations requires a strong foundation with graduate and professional education in many areas, including psychology, psychiatry, and law. Specialized clinical training in child, adolescent, family, and adult work as well as nonspecific clinical proficiency also is helpful.

Given the complexity of the law, the stakes and money involved in these cases, and the specificity of some questions asked, it is professionally risky to begin forensic evaluation without specific training and supervision with the scientific and legal aspects of the judicial process and psychiatric and psychological issues regarding health and illness. Unfamiliarity with, or disregard for, the guidelines outlining the procedures for evaluating these families increases the likelihood of committing ethical and malpractice infractions (in the arenas of law, psychiatry, or psychology; Greenberg & Shuman, 1997). Moreover, incompetence increases the rate of error, which introduces predictive uncertainty and potential injury to family members.

We aim to describe a methodology of family forensic evaluation based on the most recent guidelines promulgated by the American Psychological Association (APA). The conceptual underpinnings of this evaluation protocol are founded on available psychiatric and psychological research from numerous areas. Examples include clinical and experimental research on healthy family process, child development, custody and divorce, child dependency, psychological testing, family forensics, adult and child psychopathology, parenting, and stress. We were attentive to studies that had been published in peer-reviewed journals. Because only a handful of studies have focused on the process and outcome of custody evaluations, we also included survey research that may inform readers about proficient practice.

We encourage use of assessment procedures with acceptable psychometric properties, such as internal consistency, interrater reliability, and validity. The benefits of using an empirically derived assessment approach for custody evaluation, however, extend beyond the ideal of scientific integrity. Use of empirically validated tools enhances professional acumen and reduces the risk of ethical or malpractice claims.

Reducing ethical infractions speaks to our second goal in writing this book. We have developed an evaluation approach that aims to meet the guidelines established by the APA, the professional organization that has published the most thorough principles and standards. Although current research reveals substantive information about dimensions of the best interest of the child, we are years away from using actuarial prediction to inform courts about what factors ultimately predict successful child outcomes. As a result, competent custody evaluators continue to use informed and conservative clinical judgment in formulating conclusions and recommendations. Given the high stakes of custody proceedings, we suggest careful adherence to standardized procedures and practice to generate ethical work. We have written this book with the hope of continuing to develop a child custody assessment protocol that appropriately protects children and parents through predictable and consistent methodologies. Survey research shows that careful adherence to methodology and ethical guidelines reduces the risk of licensing board complaints concerning custody evaluators (Gourley & Stolberg, 2000; Kirkland & Kirkland, 2001).

This book also aims to outline the guidelines of child custody assessments while incorporating the evaluative goals defined by legal standards. Child custody evaluations are essentially psychological consultations for the court, addressing issues that protect and enhance the well-being of children caught in parental conflict and litigation. Our approach toward these evaluations is based on the idea of "empirically derived" therapeutic jurisprudence (Wexler & Winick, 1996). The concept of *therapeutic jurisprudence*, introduced in the early 1980s, refers to a process of addressing family-based legal and social problems through legal intervention to evoke changes that enhance psychological and family health. This concept is particularly relevant for litigating parents in custody disputes, who both may be capable parents, but appear to require legal intervention to parent cooperatively. We embrace the idea that therapeutic jurisprudence with families in custody disputes should be based on an empirical foundation derived from controlled, experimental, and survey psychological research. And as such, we have tried to include that literature here.

In this book, we focus on custody cases, partitioning out issues pertaining to dependency or child protection cases. We do this partly because the issues that arise from dependency or child protection cases differ from those involved in child custody cases. Moreover, the court assumes a different role in child custody cases than it does in dependency or child protection cases. For example, in custody cases, the legal system negotiates between caretakers, both of whom may be fit to parent the children. If parents are unable to settle on a parenting agreement out of court, a family court intervenes and determines a resolution that is designed to cultivate each child's best interests. The *best-interests standard*, which we describe in detail later, is a legal concept that attends to the child's general and specific needs to promote healthy development (Hall, Pulver, & Cooley, 1996). Likewise, the court legally intervenes in child protection cases that may also include custody issues to protect children from injurious or neglectful behavior by a parent or guardian. These kinds of cases are different from custody cases because the focus is on adjudicating the parent's custodial rights to their children who have deteriorated in the parent's custody.

Given the complications of such litigation and the risks attendant in working with the parties and lawyers involved, evaluators must be well prepared. In fact, according to APA's 2002 *Ethical Principles of Psychologists and Code of Conduct*, psychologists are to "provide services . . . with populations and in areas only within the boundaries of [our] competence, based on [our] education, training, supervised experience, consultation, study, or professional experience" (2.01a). In addition, "psychologists undertake ongoing efforts to maintain [our] competence" (2.03). Clearly such standards are critical to follow in the task at hand.

I

UNDERSTANDING THE CONTEXT

1

CONTEXT OF CUSTODY LITIGATION

The number of divorces has increased steadily since the early 1960s, with approximately half of all marriages ending in divorce (National Center for Health Statistics, 2001). An even higher percentage of relationships that include children will break up, with as many as 64% of all relationships that produce children ending in disruption (Castro, Martin, & Bumpass, 1989; Centers for Disease Control and Prevention, 1995; Montemayor, 1984). With an estimated 1.4 million divorces in the United States in 2001 (National Center for Health Statistics, 2001), an increasing number of children are experiencing parental separation (Bramlett & Mosher, 2001). Moreover, many of these children are growing up in families in which parental hostility during separation and divorce is the norm. During the past 20 years, an estimated 2 million children have entered family or probate court as a consequence of custody disputes (Johnston & Roseby, 1997).

Experts estimate that about 10% of these families are unable to design and settle a parenting agreement and instead go to court to resolve their differences (Maccoby, Mnookin, Depner, & Peters, 1992; Melton, Petrila, Poythress, & Slobogin, 1987). Approximately one quarter to one third of divorcing couples report such hostility and discord about the daily care of their children following mediated resolution that results in an adversarial conflict (Maccoby et al., 1992; Wallerstein & Lewis, 1998). A subset of couples resorts to legal maneuvers, court hearings, delayed negotiation, and eventually a trial to resolve the parenting arrangement. Despite many legislative and judicial efforts to improve the family environment, most parents who pursue litigation in the family court report negative experiences even years after the divorce (Pearson & Thoennes, 1985; Wallerstein, 1986).

To ease the emotional and financial cost of divorce for families, the legislative and judicial branches have made numerous efforts to reduce the legal proceedings in family and probate court litigation (some states try family law cases in probate courts). Legislative reforms supported the advent of no-fault divorce, outlined the equitable distribution of assets, mandated sufficient child support payments, and championed joint custody arrangements. Increasingly, the legal system has encouraged families to use alternative dispute resolution approaches, such as mediation, to settle child custody and visitation disputes (Beck & Sales, 2001). Alternative dispute resolution is aimed at relieving the high emotional and financial costs of litigation for families and the burden of increased litigation for the courts. Indeed, results from several well-designed studies suggest that the hardship of divorce is partially mitigated through swift dispute resolution and agreement on a parenting plan that places the best interests of the child first (Emery, 2001). Mediation works for some families but not for high-conflict parties who tend to negotiate unsuccessfully (Emery, 1982; Emery, Matthews, & Kitzmann, 1991; Magana & Taylor, 1993). Moreover, mediation may not attend directly to the best interests of the children if the power balance between the parents is skewed because of domestic violence and personality aberrations (Grillo, 1991; McEwen, Rogers, & Maiman, 1995).

Custody evaluations may provide an effective alternative method to reach settlement. If an arrangement about the parenting of the children cannot be approved, these evaluations offer further psychological evidence to help the court make more thorough decisions in arriving at an order that will serve the best interests of the children. In divorce custody research, few factors discriminate between families who negotiate a parenting arrangement and those who choose to litigate (Johnston & Roseby, 1997). However, greater personal maladjustment during the marital separation may increase the likelihood of pursuing litigation. Numerous psychological processes affect the capacity and skill with which each party navigates through divorce, and these processes influence psychological adjustment. Incapacitation can result from grief, psychiatric illness, poor coping, substance use, interparental conflict, and economic strain. Moreover, important components of family functioning, including stability, flexibility, power roles, and cohesion, are disrupted. Negotiating a settlement may be complicated by the adversarial nature of the legal process (Ash & Guyer, 1986; Halon, 1990). As a result, these situations can be complex and volatile: Evaluators may encounter highly emotional and combative individuals, overinvolved lawyers, and distressed children.

EMPIRICAL FINDINGS ABOUT HIGH-CONFLICT FAMILIES

No significant demographic differences exist between high- and low-conflict divorcing couples (Maccoby et al., 1992). Differences exist, however, in the family environments of custody disputes (Maccoby et al., 1992). For example, families in custody disputes exhibit higher levels of hostility, as well as poorer communication skills, ineffective problem-solving abilities, and more misattributions than do intact families. Well-controlled research suggests that parents involved in high-conflict custody disputes are not characteristically hostile, aggressive, vindictive people. Rather, they are interpersonally sensitive and watchful for any criticism (Johnston & Roseby, 1997). Their problem-solving abilities are impaired by idiosyncratic and simple cognitive styles (Ehrenberg, Hunter, & Elterman, 1996). Such couples are reactive and hostile and, not surprisingly, express contempt and criticism toward the other parent. Their interparental disagreements center on the absence of parental capacity, readiness, and ability of the other parent rather than specific objections about parenting decisions regarding the children's religion, education, health care, and daily activities. These couples typically allege that the other parent has restricted access to their children. Allegations may include domestic violence and, in particular, child neglect, abuse, and abandonment.

IMPACT OF DIVORCE ON CHILDREN AND ADOLESCENTS

The potential for emotional and behavioral maladjustment among children who are going through parental divorce is controversial (Amato & Keith, 1991; Hetherington, 1999; Wallerstein, 1991). A substantial number of children, however, who experience parental separations and divorces adjust to this transition without significant and long-term developmental consequences (Hetherington, 1989). Moreover, children who are securely attached to one or both parents demonstrate greater resilience and better coping to divorce-related stress. Children with higher self-esteem appear more secure, tend to develop attached relationships outside of the family, and show fewer psychological difficulties (Hazelton, Lancee, & O'Neil, 1998; Hetherington, 1989). Adjustment for adolescent children is strongly related to whether parental conflict is expressed, either directly or indirectly, through the children (Buchanan, Maccoby, & Dornbusch, 1991).

Child outcomes appear to be related to parent behavior. For example, parents who make efforts to negotiate child-related issues raise children who exhibit greater prosocial play and self-esteem (Camera & Resnick, 1989; Whiteside, 1998). Psychological and physical health before divorce dramatically affect the relationships among family members that may influence the probability of adjustment after divorce. Behavioral problems among children of divorced parties have a higher likelihood of developing before the divorce. Indeed, parental behaviors such as substance use, mental illness, and domestic violence that existed long before the divorce substantially increase the risk of a poor child outcome (Block, Block, & Gjerde, 1986; Shaw, Emery, & Tuer, 1993).

To complicate matters, child-related factors interact with parental and family characteristics to generate synergistic influences on the adjustment of the parties and their children. The characteristics of the child (e.g., age, gender, temperament) and parents (e.g., psychological health, impulse control) influence the family interaction (e.g., conflict resolution skills, communication patterns, child-rearing practices) to affect adjustment before, during, and after the divorce. Myriad parental or child factors and their interactions, therefore, may lead to poor adjustment for the children following divorce (Johnston, Gonzalez, & Campbell, 1987; Kelly, 2000).

The costs and perils are great for all parties involved, especially for the children caught up in a custody dispute. Those children, who are exposed to ongoing parental conflict before, during, and after divorce, face higher risks of emotional and behavioral disturbances (Hetherington, Cox, & Cox, 1985; Sorenson & Goldman, 1990). Interparental conflict produces situations of low social support and financial insecurity. In addition, disruptive changes in routines, schools, and residences exacerbate poor transitions. Disagreements between parents about child rearing, discipline, parental access, and visitation arrangements may interfere with maintaining positive attachments between parents and children.

Longitudinal studies have indicated that divorce conflict produces negative problems that persist across the life span, from childhood into young adult years (Frost & Pakiz, 1990; Long, Slater, Forehand, & Fauber, 1988). Even highly educated, middle-class parents who separate amicably may experience a diminished capacity to parent during divorce or separation, and such parents may inadvertently jeopardize their children's well-being in numerous ways (Kalter, Kloner, Schreier, & Okla, 1989). Parents may have less parental time with children, be less emotionally and physically responsive, mete out discipline inconsistently, infantalize or parentify children, and confuse child needs with parental needs.

Parental capacity is further diminished by interparental conflict that often precedes poorly timed or inadequate interactions between parents and their children. Indeed, Kalter and colleagues (1989) demonstrated that the length of time expected for significant recovery of members from highly conflicted families is longer, and postdivorce adjustment considered to be more stressful, than had been predicted by earlier research. The legal, financial, and emotional impact of high-conflict divorce increases the risk of trauma to the children, who are frequently drawn into the middle of disputes even when parents have the best intentions of protecting them.

Many children of this type of parental relationship also may be subjected to physical or sexual abuse, domestic violence, or the emotional and physical impairment of a parent before, during, or after a divorce (Block, Block, & Gjerde, 1986; Deed, 1991; Shaw et al., 1993). During the initial period following divorce, children from these families, as compared with those from intact families, present greater behavioral problems, show less prosocial behavior, experience greater adjustment problems, and exhibit lower self-esteem (Camera & Resnick, 1989; Guidubaldi & Perry, 1985). It is more than the nominal act of divorce that results in such difficulties.

Parental conflict that involves family violence clearly affects child and parent adjustment. Since the 1970s, research has documented the serious effects associated with victimization, including a variety of psychiatric problems, substance abuse, and medical health problems in adult and child survivors of physical and sexual abuse (Briere, 1992; Kendall-Tackett, Williams, & Finkelhor, 1993; Pagelow, 1990; Sonkin, 1987; Watkins & Bentovim, 1992). Moreover, the risk that parents who witnessed and experienced violence as children will abuse their own children is also established (Johnston, 1994). Careful psychological assessment of extended family history of violence and forms of abuse through a comprehensive custody evaluation would likely further the best interests of children. Such assessments provide evidence about the effects of witnessed and experienced domestic violence on women (Pagelow, 1992) and children (Pagelow, 1990).

Attention to child factors in these cases is important particularly in light of research showing the increased likelihood of child behavioral problems and distress (Jaffee, Wolfe, & Wilson, 1990). Further, exposure to domestic violence in childhood increases the likelihood of problems in adulthood (Fortstrom-Cohen & Rosenbaum, 1985; Henning, Leitenberg, Coffey, Turner, & Bennett, 1996). A review of the research on child witnesses of domestic violence (Kolbo, Blakely, & Engleman, 1996) concluded that there is a positive correlation between witnessing violence and children's developmental problems in behavioral, emotional, social, cognitive, and physical realms. Emotional functioning among child witnesses suggests that there are significant differences in emotional functioning between witnesses and comparison groups. Child witnesses also experience more cognitive problems. With regard to physical health, evidence has suggested that witnesses experience more somatic complaints (Henning, Leitenberg, Coffey, Bennett, & Jankowski, 1997). Research has shown that long-term psychological adjustment to witnessing interparental violence produced negative effects for children that required professional assistance, particularly when the parent of the same gender was being injured. It also was found that the problems with adult adjustment were worsened by decreased parental caring and warmth during childhood (Famularo, Fention, & Kinscherff, 1994), and witnessing domestic violence was one of three predictors of posttraumatic stress disorder in children. Custody evaluations can delineate specific parental weaknesses to be remedied through domestic violence treatment, sexual deviancy therapy, individual or group counseling for victims, and supervised visitation or case management services.

CONCLUSION

In conclusion, it is typical in the field of divorce litigation to find parents (or caretakers) who allege that the other parent has injured them and their children. Allegations include physical (e.g., no parent hugging or cuddling of the child), medical (e.g., failure to provide prescribed medications to the child), or emotional neglect; physical, emotional, or sexual abuse; and alienation of the child's affections for the other parent. Equally important allegations include withheld access to the children; infliction of domestic violence (including the threat of imminent physical or sexual assault by one household member on another); and emotional or physical impairment of the other parent (including substance use or dependency). The conflict and lack of clear communication between divorcing parties may, however, foster overinterpretation and misunderstanding that, in turn, generate allegations that are not wholly accurate. Having a competent mental health professional evaluate allegations and offer recommendations about how to reorganize family relationships to promote child adjustment —rather than simply resorting to divorce litigation—may offer a productive alternative form of dispute resolution.

2

EVIDENTIARY STANDARDS AND RULES OF EVIDENCE

Understanding the differences between the legal and mental health professions is an important first step to minimizing ethical and professional infractions and generating constructive and relevant reports for the court. Different principles and methodologies in the fields of mental health and the law produce a complicated arrangement between custody evaluators and legal professionals. On a theoretical level, mental health professionals subscribe to scientific principles and standardized assessment methodologies. Conceptual issues such as achieving test validity and reliability and minimizing error biases in clinical judgment are imperative in psychological assessment. In contrast, the legal model emphasizes legal precedents established by *common law* (cases that have been appealed to a higher court with a written decision establishing the law), as well as *evidentiary standards* (standards by which the judge determines the weight of the evidence) and *rules of evidence* (rules that a judge applies to determine what evidence can be considered) established by *statute* or *rule* (laws created by the legislature or administrative bodies created by the legislature). Information is presented and "tested" through legal argument and ultimately judged by the *triers of fact* (e.g., in most states, by judges).

Significant differences between mental health and legal professionals are found in the approaches toward data collection and synthesis of information. Mental health professionals gather information from semistruc-

17

tured clinical interviews, psychological testing, self-report measurement, direct observations of family members, third-party collateral reports, and relevant records. These data are transformed into a cohesive summary that guide recommendations about how to restructure the family to promote child adjustment. Unlike legal professionals, mental health professionals are not required to follow legal rules of evidence governing the use of information during the evaluation. The common law and statutes or rules establish the standards of proof and the rules of evidence to be used in the courtroom. The legal professionals must frame their work within these judicial and legislative standards.

These differences translate into important practical considerations for the mental health professional conducting custody evaluations. Application of scientific values in psychological assessment is one of the highest priorities in evaluations, but it is important to ensure that the information gathered for these assessments is obtained within the constraints of the legal rules. Access to, and use of, data must both meet the ethical guidelines of the mental health professional while also attending to the *constraints of legal rules* (e.g., accessing the treatment records of children requires not only a parental signature but, in some states, permission from the court). Finally, understanding the *prevailing legal standards* (e.g., many states have defined by statute or rule the parenting factors that a judge should weigh more heavily in determining the residential placement of the children) is critical for mental health professionals because the broad definitions of these standards may prompt judges to rely on the refined judgments and conclusions of mental health experts. The more that mental health professionals discuss the findings of an evaluation by using the *terms of the substantive law* (e.g., the legal standard about which parenting factors receive greater weight) to organize the recitation of the findings, the more helpful legal professionals find the discussion. Indeed, psychology's ethical guidelines call for our exercising such knowledge: "When assuming forensic roles, [we] are or become reasonably familiar with the judicial or administrative rules governing [our] roles" (APA, 2002, 2.01f).

To facilitate understanding about the primary legal and scientific considerations in conducting evaluations, this chapter highlights both the legislative and judicially crafted standards used in child custody cases and the scientific considerations in conducting psychological evaluations for custody disputes. The first section briefly tracks the history of custody and divorce law up to the current legislative and judicial efforts to make decisions that rely on the prevailing "best interests of the child" standard. We then discuss the transformation from adversarial efforts to alternative dispute resolution approaches. We then move from a discussion about the legal criteria that govern the admissibility of scientific evidence in custody evaluations to a discussion about the psychometric considerations of psychological tests and the limits of expert clinical judgment.

CUSTODY AND DIVORCE LAW

The foundation of custody and divorce law in the United States derives from British Common Law. In the 19th century, children were considered property and were routinely awarded to their divorcing fathers (*Hernandez v. Thomas*). The relationship between parent and child at that time was primarily functional where children were used for labor for the family (Mason & Quirk, 1997). Unable to own property, divorced women were denied access to children. Emphasis on the critical influence of maternal nurturance generated new legislation in the 1880s, the "Tender Years" doctrine. With this statute, mothers were awarded custody of children younger than age 12. If the mother was an inappropriate custodian, custody shifted to the father.

With the advent of "no-fault divorce"; equitable division of assets and property; a resurgent interest in fathers' rights in the 1960s; and, most important, findings from psychological research about the deleterious effects of divorce on children, legislative and judicial thinking evolved from the presumption of maternal custody to a more child-oriented position. As a result, legislative reforms focused on ways to both minimize the impact of the divorce for minor children and to promote the welfare and growth of children. States outlined and adopted guidelines, modeled on the 1979 Uniform Marriage and Divorce Act and outlined the primary tenet that the court will determine custody in accordance with the best interests of the child (Krauss & Sales, 2000).

BEST INTERESTS OF THE CHILD STANDARD

The Uniform Marriage and Divorce Act (1979, § 402) established guidelines that were applied to develop the best interests of the child standard, which is now the prevailing legal standard in most of the 50 states. Typically the state laws provide greater weight to evidence that is presented in the following realms:

1. the wishes of the parents of the children;
2. the wishes of the children about their preferred custodian, assuming that they are sufficiently mature to form such an informed preference;
3. the interaction and interrelationship of the children with their parents, siblings, and other people who may significantly influence the child's best interests;
4. the child's adjustment to his home, school, and community; and
5. the mental and physical health of all individuals involved.

Most states do not permit review of custodian behavior that is not directly associated with the child (Uniform Marriage and Divorce Act, 1979). Currently, legal rights of both parents continue to take precedence, but the focus is on generating an agreement of coparenting that facilitates child well-being and growth. Although yet to be legislated, the judicial position appears to be moving toward using a model of shared parenting arrangement and equal division of responsibilities (Beck & Sales, 2001).

Most jurisdictions in the United States govern child custody determinations through a derivation of the best-interests standard. Statutory factors describing the child's best interests vary widely across states and continue to be broad and indeterminate. For instance, some jurisdictions list factors pertaining to each parent's capacity and skills, including personal habits and psychological stability, ability to tend to the child's emotional and physical needs, and ability to cooperatively coparent and support each child's attachment to each parent. As a result, jurisdictions differ widely in the application of the best-interests standard. No factor is dispositive (i.e., singularly definitive), although some factors may be weighted more by the legislative or the common law. In addition, many jurisdictions enforce important limitations on custody rights because of the histories of spousal violence, mental illness, and child abuse. In most jurisdictions, however, the fact finder (usually a judge; in some jurisdictions, a jury) is allowed wide discretion in configuring the factors and deciding in what form they should be combined to create a resolution for the child's best interest. Krauss and Sales published a good review article about these issues (2000).

Evaluators must know how their jurisdiction applies the best interests of the child standard—a state standard or a local court standard might apply. A comprehensive evaluation of the child's current developmental status, attachment, and special needs, along with an evaluation of the parenting capacities and reserves and the quality and nature of the relationships between parents and children can then frame these data within the best-interests standard of the jurisdiction.

Many people considered the advent of the best-interests standard a marker of significant progress. Its development was embraced by the feminist and "fathers' rights" movements, but for different reasons. The feminist response was initially enthusiastic because the standard allowed for reconfiguration of gender norms: Women would be able to work and shift some of the parental responsibility to their partners. The initial enthusiasm was tempered, however, by a growing recognition that the standard did not adequately recognize that women, who handled most of the parenting, were not able to maintain the same degree of parenting access to their children after divorce. As a result, the best-interests standard was viewed as destabilizing women's bargaining power in custody situations, prompting a call for using an alternative standard called the *primary-caregiver standard* (Scott, 1992), or *least-detrimental-alternative standard*. This standard allows for the historical primary care provider to maintain the same access and care to the children to promote environmental and parental consistency for children. From the perspective of observing parental rights of fathers, the best-interests standards were viewed as less discriminatory against men. Fathers' rights were protected because the best-interests standard allowed for individualized and case-sensitive analyses of the needs of children and parents.

At times, however, the best-interests standard has functioned in reality as the "best-parent" standard. The intention and language of the best-interests standard are child focused, but its breadth allows for a review of parental attributes. For instance, parenting evaluations under the best interests standard typically review mental health status and personal and psychosocial history (Halon, 2000). Parents strive to elucidate their upstanding character while maligning the abilities of other parties. If this becomes the primary focus of the evaluation, the report is likely to present a collection of subjective allegations, leaving the courts no option but to evaluate the character of each parent and to determine how his or her character influences the child's development. Although unintended, the current best-interests standard sometimes leads parents to think that they are fighting about the relative merits of their characters. All too often, custody evaluations are viewed as another venue to extend emotional and fiscal control and extortion. The evaluator should remain aware that parents are typically uninformed about the criteria and process for evaluating parenting abilities and, because of the high stakes, may campaign hard for the evaluator's vote of confidence.

Naturally, the strengths of the best-interests standard also provide opportunities for criticism. For instance, the breadth and apparent flexibility of the standard allow for variable interpretation during divorce. The variable nature of the judicial application of the best-interests standard may result in inefficiencies through overlitigation during the divorce process. In addition, even parenting experts disagree about what specific parental characteristics are crucially related to a child's best interest (Krauss & Sales, 2000). Aside from widespread agreement that a child's best interests are served by an absence of physical and emotional abuse and limited exposure to parental conflict, parenting researchers continue to refine the constellation of skills. The focus of the research should be to empirically differentiate factors that predict parental success from lack of parental success. Although the psychological literature is replete with concepts of nurturance and support as hallmarks of good parenting, it is important to move carefully from abstract concepts to descriptions of specific behaviors.

ALTERNATIVE DISPUTE RESOLUTION

The alternative dispute resolution movement in the United States represents a substantive shift from the traditional adversarial approaches to resolving family cases. Based on a cooperative conflict resolution model, mediation actively deters parties from the adversarial stance via the pursuit of the "best-interest" standard in family litigation and aims to empower each party to collaborate with each other. This approach, which emerged from confluence of social and legal changes during the past two decades, has been shaped by the social and cultural ideals of self-determination and conflict reduction. Historical shifts toward recognizing the importance of gender equality, no-fault divorce decrees, and therapeutic jurisprudence (enhancing well-being through the legal process) has supported the idea of helping parents pursue alternative means of organizing post-divorce family functioning.

In addition, from a functional perspective, mediation has emerged as a practical solution to reduce overscheduled and delayed hearings in family courts and to harness party cooperation in coparenting arrangements and post-divorce parenting activities. The legal community has begun to recognize that family litigation, which is typically expensive and slow, elicits frustration for both court personnel and parents. Moreover, adversarial means of resolving family disputes have often increased family tension, produced dissatisfaction with the court process and outcome, and inflated the probability of failing to comply with court plans. As a result, mediation has become a popular alternative for resolving custody disputes in lieu of litigation (Beck & Sales, 2001).

Mediation represents a qualitatively different approach to resolving disagreements regarding divorce and custody arrangements. Tethered to the principles of self-determination and conflict reduction, mediation promotes three goals, including educating parties about skills in communication and conflict resolution, facilitating cooperation and negotiation of disagreements, and outlining a practical and workable agreement. With these agenda items, mediation is time limited, involves both parties, and occurs at a neutral site. The work is tailored to elucidate and determine cooperative agreements to reduce disagreements pertaining to the custody and visitation arrangements.

Types of mediators vary, but they are usually professionals with both (a) an advanced degree in either the legal or mental health professions, or both, and (b) have obtained specialty training in family and couples conflict and dispute resolution approaches. The tasks of a mediator, therefore, are to carefully ascertain areas of disagreement, educate parties regarding constructive communication and productive conflict resolution, and formulate an agreement via consensus that promotes the best interests of all parties. The overarching goal is to develop a plan that attends to the best interests of the children while also outlining a way to resolve future disagreements.

Advantages of mediation include the emphasis on confidentiality, reliance on full disclosure and active participation by all parties, flexibility to include lawyer consultation, and direct encouragement to help parties assume responsibility for their decisions. An in-depth review of the structure and results of family mediation in both voluntary and mandatory court-annexed programs, however, reveals that family mediation is limited in several ways (Beck & Sales, 2001). For example, mediators and parties cannot compel partners to be active or to disclose information regarding finances and potential parenting problems. Moreover, mediation cannot offset subtle intimidation and other activities associated with power imbalances and domestic violence. Finally, individuals who choose to pursue mediation and forgo legal representation potentially overlook their legal and financial rights (Hysjulien, Wood, & Benjamin, 1994).

Mediation is one option for couples to promote the best interests of their children. It is noted, however, that systematic research has not fully demonstrated if mediation offers a more cost-effective and superior method of resolving conflicts compared to litigation. To understand the context of alternative dispute resolutions, we recommend readers to a literature review of the use and efficacy of mediation (Beck & Sales, 2001).

RULES OF ADMISSIBILITY OF SCIENTIFIC EVIDENCE

In this section, we review three primary considerations, including (a) the legal criteria that often govern the admissibility of scientific evidence in custody evaluations, (b) the court's attention to the psychometric properties of these methods, and (c) the limits of expert clinical judgment.

The rules governing the admissibility of psychometric evidence have become more comprehensive over time but differ markedly among jurisdictions. Significant legal tests include the *Federal Rules of Evidence* (FRE, 1992), the Frye test (*United States v. Frye*, 1923), and the Daubert standard (*Daubert v. Merrell Dow Pharmaceuticals*, 1993). Briefly, the FRE stipulate that evidence is admissible if it is considered relevant (Rule 401). Under Rules 402 and 403, not all evidence that is relevant is admissible. For instance, FRE 403 states,

> Although relevant, evidence may be excluded if its probative value is substantially outweighed by the danger of unfair prejudice, confusion of the issues, or misleading the jury, or by considerations of undue delay, waste of time, or needless presentation of cumulative evidence.

This standard was fairly liberal and was designed to give judges latitude to decide about the admissibility of evidence.

More recently, developments in scientific testing and knowledge led to the promulgation of the Daubert standard. In 1993, the U.S. Supreme Court instituted the Daubert standard and eliminated the use of the Frye standard in the federal courts in an effort to establish a standard for the admissibility of scientific evidence that could be implemented with greater consistency and uniformity while limiting the discretion of judges. Most of the states have adopted this standard. Daubert interpreted FRE 702, which states,

> If scientific, technical, or other specialized knowledge will assist the trier of fact to understand the evidence or to determine a fact in issue, a witness qualified as an expert by knowledge, skill, experience, training, or education, may testify thereto in the form of an opinion or otherwise, if (1) the testimony is based upon sufficient facts or data, (2) the testimony is the product of reliable principles and methods, and (3) the witness has applied the principles and methods reliably to the facts of the case.

The Daubert standard is firmly grounded on legal relevance and scientific validity, reliability, method, and procedure. Courts that use the Daubert standard consider the following four factors in reviewing the admissibility of scientific evidence:

1. the theory or technique can be empirically tested using scientific methodology to determine possible falsifiability;
2. the evidence was adequately subjected to peer review and published in peer-reviewed journals;
3. there is a known or potential rate of error of the controls and standards, where the standards outline the technique of test administration as well as the methodology for generating interpretations and conclusions; and
4. there is general acceptance within the relevant scientific community.

The Daubert standard varies across states because each state has sovereignty and has developed its own application of the standard. Some states —including Arizona, California, Florida, New York, and Nebraska—have even rejected the Daubert standard and continue to rely on the Frye test. These jurisdictions still hold that general acceptance from the relevant scientific community is a major criterion in determining the admissibility of scientific evidence.

Heilbrun (1992) has outlined criteria for the characteristics of psychological tests in forensic settings as they pertain to the admissibility of psychological evidence in court (Krauss & Sales, 2000; Shuman & Sales, 1999). Heilbrun (1992) described a series of guidelines for determining whether a test should be used in a custody evaluation. The guidelines state the following: First, the psychological test should be commercially available and adequately documented with a manual that describes psychometric properties and administrative procedures, and the test should also be listed and reviewed in *The Mental Measurements Yearbook* (2001) and other authoritative texts. Second, reliability should be established with a coefficient of .80, or with an explanation for lower coefficient. Within testing theory, *reliability* refers to the consistency and stability of repeated observations. Within scientific studies, statistical analyses of interrater agreement (e.g., kappa coefficients or intraclass correlation coefficients) are the benchmarks for the reliability of a psychological test. Within the context of child custody evaluations, reliability refers to the likelihood of obtaining similar data based on independent observations by different evaluators. "High" reliability results from empirical work that shows that the psychological test, when used accurately, measures an objective phenomenon independent of the evaluator's input.

Reliability is a precursor of, but not commensurate with, validity. Validity is the second critical component of the scientific method of testing and procedure. *Validity* refers to the likelihood that a certain procedure or test measures the concept of interest. Within the context of child custody evaluations, the concept of validity refers to the probability that a psychological test accurately captures the relevant concept of "personality functioning" or "adjustment" in accordance with governing legal standards. Third, the psychological tests used in custody should have a standard method of administration, preferably in an appropriate testing environment, to obtain the best possible measurement (e.g., no distractions, comfortable surroundings). Fourth, the test should have validation research published in a peer-reviewed publication reporting validity data and the description of the population for which the test was designed. Fifth, objective tests and actuarial data are preferred, but there should be a method of interpreting results within the context of the individual's response style. This offers the flexibility to validate the results if the test taker's approach was honest. It also allows for invalidation of the tests if the individual uses a malingering, defensive, or irreverent test-taking response style. That is, the test provides separate information about the individual's reporting style. Sixth, and finally, selection of the test is specifically guided by the referral question.

If courts in various states apply these guidelines when considering the Daubert standard, it appears that few psychological tests could be used in the family law context. However, exceptions exist. For instance, the Minnesota Multiphasic Personality Inventory, second edition (MMPI–2), exemplifies a psychological test that satisfies Heilbrun's tests. It also likely meets the Frye and the Daubert standards. The MMPI–2 test, along with a manual of the standardized administrative procedures and psychometric properties, is commercially available. The reliability of the MMPI has a coefficient above .80 (Butcher, Dahlstrom, Graham, Tellegen, & Kaemmer, 1989). In fact, more than 200 articles investigating the psychometric properties of the MMPI have been published in peer-reviewed journals, documenting forms of test reliability and validity. Specific information about relevant dimensions of reliability, including internal consistency and interrater and test–retest reliabilities, are also high on the MMPI–2. In addition, the MMPI–2 has been studied with the child custody population (Otto & Collins, 1995). Further, the MMPI–2 is considered a valid measure that differentiates between state and trait factors and partitions out response style. The test is generally accepted in the field of clinical psychology; it is one of the more popular psychological tests in custody evaluations and extensive empirical support exists. Indeed, survey research on the professional practices attests to the stature of the MMPI–2 in child custody proceedings. It is considered one of the most used psychological tests for adults (Ackerman & Ackerman, 1997; Hagen & Castagna, 2001; Keilin & Bloom, 1986; Siegel, 1996).

Results from a landmark study Keilin and Bloom conducted in 1986 indicated that, of the 82 mental health professionals participating, all conducted interviews with both parents and 75% used psychological tests with parents and children (within this group, 70% used the MMPI, and 38% used the Thematic Apperception Test and Rorschach). Ackerman and Ackerman (1997) replicated this study with a national sample of 201 evaluators from 39 states. Approximately 92% of the evaluators used the MMPI–2, 48% used the Rorschach, and 43% used intelligence testing. Finally, Hagen and Castagna's (2001) reanalyses of Ackerman and Ackerman's (1997) data indicate that, in a national sample of child custody evaluators, the MMPI was used by 84% of custody evaluators and the Rorschach by 31%. In evaluations of children, intelligence tests and the Bricklin perceptual scales were administered by a fourth of the evaluators.

Given the emerging legal rules governing the admissibility of psychological evidence, custody evaluators should select their psychological tests carefully. The election of specific psychological measures should tap into the psychological constructs of interest. An important consideration is how psychological tests provide an impression to clinicians, lawyers, and judges that they can then use to objectively evaluate psychological functioning. Few psychological tests are suited to address the primary assessment questions in custody disputes (Otto & Collins, 1995; Garb, 1998). We urge evaluators to select the psychological tests on the basis of relevance to custody work rather than on the evaluator's familiarity and experience with the test (Heinze & Grisso, 1996).

Finally, although Daubert considered the admissibility of scientific evidence, a later case (1999), *Kumho Tire v. Carmichael*, has considered the admissibility of technical and other specialized expert testimony. A critical question remains to be answered by the federal courts and the majority of state courts (which have adopted Daubert in some form): Will the various courts classify/treat proffered psychological testimony as scientific or specialized knowledge? The answer has important consequences for the admissibility of psychological evidence as proffered by experts in custody cases and eventually will be answered by each jurisdiction.

CLINICAL JUDGMENT

In his review of the literature, Garb (1998) made a compelling case for not depending on clinical judgment as a significant measure in arriving at findings about forensic questions. Instead, he urged that evaluators rely on valid assessment data, such as comprehensive and standardized interviews, that would focus on "explicitly and systematically" ruling in and out alternative hypotheses. He embraced the notion of corroborating findings through multiple forms of measurement and behavioral assessments such as child–parent observations while not depending on the results of psychological tests (he specifically argued against the use of projective instruments because of validity and reliability problems).

Nevertheless, clinical judgment is the primary tool that mental health experts deploy in parenting evaluations. The clinical interviews of parents, parent–child observations, and collateral source interviews are the defining procedures of most parenting evaluations. All such data are readily affected by clinical judgment. This is not surprising, given that training in the mental health field stresses the value of clinical judgment in assessing the relative attributes and deficiencies of clients. In the therapeutic context, clinical judgment remains the gold standard for effective assessment and intervention. Reliance on clinical judgment, however, is potentially less damaging in psychotherapeutic settings than in forensic settings. Objective truth has less relevance within a therapeutic than in a custody evaluation setting, where truth is disputed in the courtroom. In a treatment setting, the client's own perspective and framework is often the target of intervention and, importantly, errors in clinical judgment are more correctable than in a forensic setting.

Despite its ubiquity, clinical judgment remains fallible (Borum, Otto, & Golding, 1993; Garb, 1998; Grove & Meehl, 1996). Results from meta-analyses using 136 studies showed that actuarial methods were equal to or superior to the clinical method. The classic citation and seminal work in the area of clinical judgment versus actuarial methods are written by Paul Meehl (1954/1996). In this work, he asserted that actuarial methods, on which the MMPI and bulk of scientific knowledge are based, are superior to clinical judgment for predicting just about anything. Additional reviews of studies on the validity of clinical judgments have suggested that validity is generally unrelated to professional experience (Garb, 1989, 1998). Works documenting common cognitive errors include errors of clinical judgment that range from inaccuracies because of overreliance on memory, limitations in complex configural analyses, underuse of base rates, confirmatory and hindsight bias, and overreliance on unique data (Garb, 1998).

The child custody context is particularly conducive to the liabilities highlighted above regarding clinical judgment. Further, the vagaries of the best-interests standard allow for a range of clinical judgments regarding parenting ability that may in fact have little to do with true parenting abilities. Furthermore, high-conflict custody cases are commonly infused with allegations of domestic violence and child abuse that require complex judgments about credibility and other areas in which clinical judgments are susceptible to error. Nevertheless, in our view, a trained forensic mental health professional can learn to make these difficult judgments about credibility by relying on converging evidence and a cautious approach to reaching findings and interpretations.

A series of APA guidelines reinforces this conclusion. The APA *Specialty Guidelines for Forensic Psychologists* (1991) hold: "Forensic psychologists realize that their public role as 'expert to the court' or as 'expert representing the profession' confers upon them a special responsibility for fairness and accuracy...." Indeed, using the multiple measured approach of gathering data and documenting important facts and opinions remains the best approach at arriving at a fair evaluation (APA, 1994). Finally, the APA *Ethical Principles of Psychologists and Code of Conduct* (2002) 9.01(b) affirms that "psychologists provide opinions of the psychological characteristics of individuals only after they have conducted an examination of the individuals adequate to support their statements or conclusions. When, despite reasonable efforts, such an examination is not practical, psychologists document the efforts they made and the result of those efforts, clarify the probable impact of their limited information on the reliability and validity of their opinions and appropriately limit the nature and extent of their conclusions or recommendations."

Of all the professionals involved with high-conflict families in the family law context, a trained mental health expert is the best candidate to provide additional evidence to the finder of fact. In short, the error rates for clinical judgment are high enough to create a level of uncertainty that should increase caution in generating conclusions in custody evaluations. We encourage mental health experts to become knowledgeable about the scientific literature documenting the problems with clinical judgment to appropriately temper how they reach their findings and interpretations.

3

ETHICS, COMPETENCE, AND TRAINING

CODE OF ETHICS

In Principle D (Justice) of the APA *Ethical Principles of Psychologists and Code of Conduct* (2002), "Psychologists exercise reasonable judgment and take precautions to ensure that their potential biases, the boundaries of their competence, and the limitations of their expertise do not lead to or condone unjust practices." Not surprisingly, though, child custody evaluations continue to be the domain that generates the most ethical complaints faced by psychologists (Glassman, 1998). The emotionally charged atmosphere of child custody battles undoubtedly contributes to the high volume of ethical complaints. Independent of any ethical transgressions by mental health experts, the current binary win–lose framework of custody disputes inflates the probability that one party will feel disgruntled with the outcome. As discussed above, there remain significant reasons for parents to be concerned about bias or outright incompetence in the performance of mental health experts in this arena (Garb, 1998).

Although no mandated procedures or methods used by parenting evaluators exist, many guidelines do exist. However, some variability in the application of ethical guidelines by custody evaluators can occur. For instance, until explicit direction by the APA to the contrary, it was usual for parenting evaluators to make custodial recommendations based on an evaluation of only one of the parents (the APA's *Guidelines for Child Custody Evaluations in Divorce Proceedings*, 1994). Not applying this guideline led many evaluators, including *guardians ad litem* (court-appointed lawyers, mental health professionals, or trained laypeople who represent the interests of the children and who investigate allegations and report their findings to the court), to fail to interview mothers regarding domestic violence allegations, to issue reports stating there was no evidence of domestic violence, and to recommend joint custody with the fathers. (We refer readers to additional readings, including guidelines outlined by the American Academy of Psychiatry and Law [1995] and the Association of Family and Conciliation Courts [1994]).

Ethical lapses are, unfortunately, not limited to the guardians ad litem investigating child custody cases. For instance, it has been common for psychologists or other mental health providers to provide psychotherapeutic and evaluative functions within the same case, despite the resulting conflicts of interest or the appearance of conflict generated by combining therapeutic and forensic roles (Strausburger, Gutheil, & Brodsky, 1997). Since 1994, such multiple relationships were to be avoided (per APA, 1994). Recent changes in the APA *Ethical Principles of Psychologists and Code of Conduct* (2002, 3.05) clearly reaffirm that such multiple relationships should be ended: "A psychologist refrains from entering into a multiple relationship if the multiple relationship could reasonably be expected to impair the psychologist's objectivity, competence, or effectiveness in performing his or her functions...." The best work of child custody evaluators remains circumscribed and clear, providing information about the psychological dimensions of the family while also pointing out the limitations of methodology and predictive validity of the evaluation's results (APA, 2002, 9.01, 9.06). The concrete and relevant information that the professional has been able to uncover as it relates to the issues at hand is useful to the court. Problems occur, however, when mental health professionals do not fulfill and stay within their roles (Myers & Erickson, 1999).

The evaluation approach described below in great detail meets the APA guidelines. All of these guidelines proffer direction about the specific role of the evaluator, avoidance of dual role relationships, and the necessity of maintaining an objective stance. These guidelines establish the specific roles of the evaluator during data collection and integration and presentation to the court.

Section 9 of the APA *Ethical Principles of Psychologists and Code of Conduct* (2002, 2.01, 9.01, 9.02) describes broad ethical principles that the best evaluators aspire to follow while conducting evaluations. Evaluators have knowledge of, and competence with, the populations they evaluate. These principles call for evaluators to rely on techniques that produce information that can be substantiated, evaluate individuals directly before statements and conclusions can be offered, and disclose the limits of the data collection techniques and scope of opinion (9.01, 9.06). Additional principles include maintaining clear roles and identifying the constraints of confidentiality in legal proceedings (4.02). Further, principles of truthfulness and candor are promulgated to encourage forthright presentation to parties and legal professionals about the information in evaluation reports and during testimony (Principle C: Integrity; Principle D; 9.10). Such guidelines suggest that evaluators pursue appropriate actions to ensure that their professional objectivity is not compromised. Finally, the guidelines call for familiarity with the laws that govern the specific roles of evaluators in court and for resolution of potential conflicts with the legal system by informing the court about the professional responsibilities to follow the ethical guidelines (2.01f, 3.11).

Specific guidelines about custody evaluations are delineated in APA's *Guidelines for Child Custody Evaluations in Divorce Proceedings* (1994; Ackerman, 1994; Ackerman & Ackerman, 1999). These guidelines were designed to complement the earlier version of the APA *Ethical Principles of Psychologists and Code of Conduct* (1992) described above. The first section outlines the purpose of the child custody evaluation. The guidelines begin with a statement that the primary purpose is to evaluate the primary psychological needs of the children and the best interests of the children. The evaluator is to focus on parental capacity, the psychological and developmental needs of the children, and the resultant "fit" with the respective parents. The guidelines recognize that personal and societal biases (e.g., race and cultural issues, gender issues) are possible and urge evaluators to strive to overcome them and avoid multiple relationships. The more specific procedural guidelines promulgate the idea that evaluations are defined by the referral questions; that informed consent is obtained from all participants, including children; and that the psychologist informs participants about the limits of confidentiality and the disclosure of information to legal professionals. Multiple methods of measurement and data collection are to occur, and the converging data are to be treated conservatively in making conclusions. The limits of the psychological expert opinion are disclosed to the court, and the recommendations should focus on the best interests of the child. Finally, all financial information is to be disclosed, and written records must be kept, in accordance with the APA *Record Keeping Guidelines* (1993) and statutory guidelines.

PROFESSIONAL GUIDELINES

During the many years of practice conducting parenting evaluations, we have developed several guidelines to increase the professionalism of the evaluations. Although practical in nature, they naturally fit with many of the APA *Ethical Principles of Psychologists and Code of Conduct* (2002). If these guidelines are accomplished before and during the evaluation, many of the emotional and financial costs associated with mismanaged evaluations will be avoided. Custody evaluations are designed for the legal system and function to aid the trier of fact in determining legal outcomes for families in conflict. Toward this end, and to meet the guidelines mentioned above, the evaluator accomplishes the following tasks that will be delineated in greater detail in Part II of this book:

1. clarifies the limits of confidentiality and explains the nature of evaluation;
2. writes about and speaks to each party, focusing on descriptions of the relevant behaviors, not diagnoses, and operationalizes how the behavior may affect parenting;
3. acknowledges subjective opinions while upholding the objective facts;
4. reveals only that which is relevant and does not make recommendations about unrelated issues;
5. uses all available data to ensure that findings and interpretations result from multiple measure corroboration to obtain convergent validity;
6. accepts no contingency fees; and
7. withdraws from cases when countertransference interferes with objectivity.

Both parties should agree to join in the evaluation (by written stipulation) or the court with jurisdiction of the case should order both parties to participate. Unless one evaluator is able to conduct a broad-based, multiple-measured evaluation of both parties, biased reporting may affect the reliability and validity of widely used psychometric tests and the valid interpretation of all evaluation evidence (Weissman, 1991). With both parties participating fully during the process, and their fees for the evaluation paid in advance, the evaluator will be more likely to arrive at objective conclusions that are confirmed by multiple measures. Psychology may borrow from the law: The evaluator is most likely to perceive the truth about the legal issues more accurately if both parties are able to raise allegations and to defend themselves in light of those allegations. As mentioned above, both parents tend to present themselves in the best possible way, and they compete to deconstruct parenting strengths and skills to reveal deficits with the other.

The evaluator should seek written instructions from both lawyers about the allegations either party raises that, if true, would affect healthy parenting and would lead, under the law of the jurisdiction, to restricted parental involvement with the children. The custody evaluation should then delineate and provide psychological evidence about the specific parental strengths and weaknesses, and findings about the allegations based on the psychological evidence. Findings should be made only if multiple measures, physical evidence, or both have corroborated their existence. As parenting evaluators primarily interact with legal professionals, thorough and concise writing, as well as effective verbal communication, is imperative.

Given the findings of the evaluation, unless the law of the jurisdiction states otherwise, the evaluator should offer recommendations about residential placement of the children, access and visitation schedule, allocation of the decision-making authority, dispute resolution process for future disagreements, and counseling or skills-building approaches that the parents and children should pursue. The discussion section should list the findings of the evaluation under the substantive standards by which the jurisdiction organizes its evidence to determine the residential schedule of the children and the allocation of the decision-making authority of the parents. High-conflict cases often will require follow-up with therapy for victimization, substance abuse treatment, domestic violence treatment, and parenting skills training. For each area requiring treatment, the evaluator should list three health care providers (along with current telephone numbers) who have a demonstrated record of working well with high-conflict parents and their psychological and substance abuse issues. In those jurisdictions, the report and testimony should reflect this standard.

Because research suggests that treatment is rarely pursued following settlement or after litigation (Simons, Grossman, & Weiner, 1990), a guardian ad litem, case manager, or coparenting counselor (one therapist who specializes in working with high-conflict parties who will work with each party separately to develop healthier communication skills and remediate parenting deficits) should be recommended in high-conflict cases to monitor the court-ordered requirements. Residential placement and visitation schedules should be contingent on the parties complying with their treatment recommendations. If either party fails to comply, the guardian ad litem, case manager, or coparenting counselor can report his or her findings as part of the subsequent alternative dispute resolution process (so that quick, inexpensive resolution of impasses occurs). Such an arrangement can further the coordination and participation of both law and mental health professionals in settling future conflicts (also see Herman, 2001, for informative discussion about clarifying the role of parenting coordinators).

Finally, because the work takes place in a legal arena, the evaluator must prepare to be challenged. Although most jurisdictions offer protection from liability for this type of expert work, lawyers will attempt to place the evaluator in an adversarial position. The evaluator should avoid being drawn into the conflict. It is possible that one side will be better represented and prepared, and it is likely that the evaluator will feel buffeted by such an imbalance—so much so that, on occasion, such apparent unfairness may provoke the evaluator to advocate for a position. In fact, lawyers try to evoke defensiveness among experts on the stand to belie their apparent neutrality. As the evaluation proceeds, the commitment should be to produce a comprehensive evaluation; the challenge is to maintain an objective point of view throughout the process.

EDUCATION, TRAINING, AND COMPETENCE

Custody evaluations require extensive education to be conducted fairly and thoroughly. Clinicians typically have completed graduate education in child, adolescent, and adult mental health. Preparation includes formal class work in child psychological development and psychopathology, adult psychological development and psychopathology, and family therapy. Additional class work includes psychological assessment of children and adults; normal and abnormal developmental psychology; family psychology; psychopathology of children and adults; research theory and policy of divorce; social sciences research and legal research on child custody; and family issues including domestic violence, parental alienation, and abuse (Gindes, 1995). Survey research measuring the assessment practices of child custody evaluators reports that custody evaluators have developed specialized experience and training on which they base their skills. The most recent study (Bow & Quinnell, 2001) evaluated a national sample of mental health professionals and found that most had obtained primary training with adults, adolescents, and children, reporting an average of nine years in clinical work and two years in forensics before starting child custody evaluations.

To complement this academic training, evaluators need supervised and practical experience with both child and adult populations. Postgraduate training ideally focuses on the evaluation and treatment of child, adolescent, and family psychiatric or psychological problems. Formal training in forensic psychiatry and forensic psychology, particularly in child custody protection and custody litigation, may also be pursued. Because testing will be used in evaluations, evaluators need specialized training in psychological testing or how to use psychologists as consultants. Beyond the basic training, some states now regulate the appointments of custody evaluators to assure professional competence. When an evaluator is needed, judges review a list of individuals who have the specialized education, training, and experience. To receive referrals from the court, the evaluator needs to demonstrate that she or he has participated in certain graduate training curricula and has completed a set of reports supervised by a credentialed child forensic expert.

Clinicians may pursue additional training with the APA. Workshops also are offered through the American Bar Association and the American

Academy of Forensic Psychology and at annual conferences offered by state associations of guardians ad litem. State family law conferences and the national American Family Conciliation Court Review (recently renamed the Association of Family Court and Community Professionals) conferences are also forums for learning about the latest research and practice guidelines for custody determinations. Many jurisdictions have established educational organizations that serve as interdisciplinary forums for professionals serving the courts as guardians ad litem.

If clinical work and supervision through existing training programs remain unavailable for mental health professionals who want to develop forensic skills, local court personnel can identify clinicians, often housed on location in the court clinic, who have demonstrated competence in conducting custody evaluations. During the initial year of practice, ongoing consultation should be sought from one or more of these individuals who can serve as a consultant. Much of the skill building for the readers of this book will occur during their work on the cases and subsequent consultations. The clinician in training is urged to audiotape or videotape their clinical interviews and observations of their initial cases for later consultation purposes only. Following the immediate review by the consultant, the tapes should be erased. The clinician's written disclosure process should specifically delineate this possibility of consultation and that the tapes will be erased once consultation occurs (APA, 2002, 4.03); a model disclosure form for custody evaluations can be found in Appendix A). This prevents the opposing counsel from using contemporaneous material out of context during a later cross-examination at deposition or trial. Ethical or malpractice liability may not extend to such consultants in most jurisdictions.

Courts may require other specific training for evaluators in this role, so clinicians in training should check with the local courts to ensure that the training model will meet the expertise qualifications. Maintaining clinical expertise in conducting custody evaluations is also important (APA 2002, 2.03), particularly in a field that will require continual updates about the emerging knowledge related to child and adult mental health issues and family law. Maintaining knowledge about the law remains particularly challenging given the relevant legal standards and judicial shifts that influence and regulate custody law. Competence also requires familiarity with local court rules that govern the adjudicative process and how a case progresses (APA, 2002, 2.01f). Attending state continuing legal education training workshops and conferences keeps evaluators informed about the most recent developments in family case law. In addition, watching colleagues testify, attending supervision or consultation groups to discuss forensic cases, and volunteering at local law schools for expert witness training exercises (usually held in trial advocacy classes) may increase the evaluator's knowledge base.

II

CONDUCTING EVALUATIONS

CONDUCTING EVALUATIONS: INTRODUCTION

This section focuses on the assessment procedures in conducting court-appointed or stipulated evaluations. We explain how pre-evaluation procedures are designed to avoid the appearance of conflicts of interest, perceived bias, and parameters of confidentiality and fee agreements. We then outline the phases of multiparty evaluation, offering practical advice about assessment strategies that lead to efficient, thorough, and ostensibly fair data collection. Operationalizing assessment findings so that they meet the evidentiary requirements of the legal system is also discussed. We elucidate how to structure parent and child observations, how to review collateral reporter records, and ways to incorporate third-party collateral information. And finally, we discuss methods of data integration, report writing, court presentation, and maintenance of professionalism with court personnel and litigants throughout the evaluation process.

We encourage readers to review the appendices as they are mentioned within the text of each section. They represent examples of how to conduct aspects of the evaluation process and will illuminate the points of the text.

4

PHASE 1: PRE-EVALUATION PROCEDURES

Before the evaluation begins, the evaluator establishes clear professional boundaries and provides adequate notice of the evaluation procedures with the parties (e.g., caregivers in the custody dispute). The following procedures are implemented as described in detail below:

1. Obtain authority to conduct evaluation.
2. Screen for inappropriate cases.
3. Implement a tracking system.
4. Communicate the fee retainer policy.
5. Collect the first fee retainer.
6. Distribute and receive back disclosure form and testing materials.
7. Schedule the first appointments.

1. OBTAIN AUTHORITY TO CONDUCT EVALUATION

Referrals for a custody evaluation should occur through both opposing attorneys by stipulated agreement or by court order from judicial commissioners or judges of the family, probate, or juvenile courts (local court rules specify what particular court has jurisdiction over family law matters). The request for the evaluation may have been initiated by one or more parties, their attorneys or, less often, by a social services agency. In many jurisdictions such a stipulated agreement or court order provides protection from malpractice liability. Many jurisdictions hold that expert witnesses are immune from liability so that they will not be chilled from stating their forthright opinions. Immunity is granted as long as the expert acts in good faith (e.g., *Bruce v. Bryne-Stevens & Associates Engineers, Inc.*, 1989). In addition, the evaluator is more likely to establish her or his authority as an expert from the onset of the case if a stipulation or court order is in place. Check with your own lawyer or with the professional association practice directorate or your profession's ethics committee in your jurisdiction to learn about the extent of professional immunity and how to proceed as an expert to establish such immunity.

If a potential client approaches an evaluator about conducting the evaluation, the evaluator should suggest that the party contact their lawyer, or the evaluator could contact the lawyer directly. The lawyer will negotiate with opposing counsel a stipulated agreement or seek a court order establishing the evaluator as the person who will conduct the comprehensive custody evaluation. Without such an arrangement being developed at the onset, it is likely that the opposing party will believe that the other party has prejudiced the evaluator. Objectivity and fairness remain primary considerations in conducting all interactions with the parties and their lawyers if the evaluation's results are to lead to a settlement rather than to trial and an outcome that will best serve the interests of the children. As a result, the evaluator should not be viewed as pursuing the advent of an evaluation, and her or his behavior is directed by this overarching concept. In fact, this impartiality requires evaluators to withdraw from cases if either party cannot accept such a neutral role for the evaluator (such an approach is designed to meet the requirements set forth in the APA *Guidelines for Child Custody Evaluation in Divorce Proceedings*, 1994, guideline 4).

Many parties referred to child custody evaluations have attempted and failed court-ordered mediation or less formal means of compromise, so the initial impression the evaluator creates will influence the process of evaluation. Therefore, any initial contact with a party before the stipulated agreement or court order is entered should remain brief, and an appropriate explanation about objectivity should be given.

The stipulated agreement or court's appointment of a custody evaluator identifies the nature and purpose of the appointment, as well as information about when the evaluation and the final report are due, and financial logistics of the evaluation (such an approach is designed to meet certain requirements set forth in the ethical standard 3.07 in the APA *Ethical Principles of Psychologists and Code of Conduct*, 2002). The judge and lawyers are encouraged to outline the issues that they want to have examined and addressed during the evaluation. Issues may include an assessment of each adult's capacity for parenting, an assessment of the psychological functioning and developmental needs of each child, and an evaluation of the relative ability of each parent to meet the needs of the child. If the court or attorneys fail to delineate the evaluator's role specifically, the evaluator urges the attorneys for both parties to clarify the unresolved party allegations that have prevented settlement (such an approach is designed to meet certain requirements set forth in the APA *Guidelines*, 1994, guideline 8). In fact, the bulk of the evaluation will explore unresolved party allegations. The quicker all of the allegations are identified, the more likely it is that the evaluator will collect sufficient data to address each allegation.

Although questions under the purview of child custody evaluations range in scope depending on the concerns of the parties and trier of fact (in most jurisdictions, a judge rather than a jury), throughout the evaluation process the evaluator ensures that the issues are framed in a manner that will provide evidence to meet the needs and standards of the appropriate legal context (such an approach is designed to meet certain requirements set for in the ethical standard 2.01f of the APA *Ethical Principles of Psychologists and Code of Conduct*, 2002). A deadline for the completion and submission of the evaluator's report also is sought. Information about who will pay for the evaluation is clarified before it is started (such an approach is designed to meet certain requirements set forth in the APA *Guidelines*, 1994, guideline 15). Finally, the appointment establishes that the evaluator can contact professionals and collaterals who have knowledge of the family (such an approach is designed to meet certain requirements set forth in the APA *Guidelines*, 1994, guideline 11).

2. SCREEN FOR INAPPROPRIATE CASES

On occasion, the evaluator will encounter issues about which he or she lacks specific knowledge and training. The evaluator should consult with an expert so that he or she can develop a sufficient background to properly assess the impact of such an issue (such an approach is designed to meet certain requirements set forth in the ethical standard 2.01c of the APA *Ethical Principles of Psychologists and Code of Conduct*, 2002 and APA *Guidelines*, 1994, guideline 5C). The consultant may suggest literature to review, family law case precedents within the jurisdiction, or ongoing consultation through videotape or audiotape. Such an approach may not be sufficient for all cases in which physical evidence suggests that a child is the victim of sexual abuse. Unless the mental health provider has participated in specialized training in evaluating sexual misconduct, an outside sexual abuse and sex deviancy specialist investigates the allegations before the parenting evaluation is conducted. Many jurisdictions, in fact, require

PRACTICE TIP 1
Ex Parte Communication

Throughout the process, the evaluator minimizes *ex parte* communication (e.g., contact with only one of the professional legal people involved in the case). Such contact may lead to the appearance of unfairness or prejudice. Therefore, any contact with either lawyer is preferably expressed in a posted or faxed letter or by a voice mail message before or after business hours. The same message is provided to all lawyers and the guardian ad litem (GAL), if one has been appointed in the case. (GALs function in a variety of ways in the context of custody evaluations. They commonly are appointed to protect the interests of the children; sometimes the court may also appoint a GAL for a parent who is so emotionally or cognitively impaired that he or she cannot meaningfully participate in the court's process.) When the evaluator leaves a message by voice mail, the date and content of the message are documented in the evaluation record. Both lawyers are informed about the same information in a parallel manner. If either lawyer requests a conversation with the evaluator, a conference call with both attorneys (and GAL) occurs. Descriptions of the conversation and decisions from that conference call are written up by one or both attorneys and faxed to the evaluator and all attorneys. If a litigant is a *pro se*, that is, someone who is representing himself or herself legally in the proceeding, the letter will be sent directly to the party.

that sexual misconduct evaluators be licensed or certified. The evaluator will need to integrate the findings of the specialized evaluation so that the comprehensive parenting evaluation proceeds after the specialized evaluation. The evaluator informs the parties, the lawyers, and the court that the custody evaluation will proceed after the specialized evaluation report is received. If a criminal prosecution is to occur, the evaluator may also wait to conduct the evaluation, with the permission of the court, until the matter of sexual abuse is adjudicated.

A court order or a stipulated agreement that requires the evaluation to be completed in an unrealistically short period of time should also be refused. If the trial date is less than 8 weeks away, we suggest that the evaluator consult with both attorneys about the viability of getting an extension. If they cannot gain approval of the extension from the court, the evaluator should decline to evaluate the case because of the time needed to perform the many tasks of a comprehensive evaluation. This type of evaluation is fraught with ethical and malpractice risks and should not be conducted with the undue stress of limited time.

3. IMPLEMENT TRACKING SYSTEM

Armed with a stipulated agreement or a court order, the evaluator has clear authority to conduct the assessment and seek a retainer. On receipt of the stipulated agreement or court order, the evaluator notifies both attorneys that the following must be submitted to the evaluator before the

PRACTICE TIP 2
Declaration of Noncompliance

Evaluators proceed to the next phase of the evaluation only when both parties have completed the same phase. If either party fails to complete a phase and the party has failed to act after a warning, a declaration of noncompliance (see Appendix C) is sent to both attorneys. Such a declaration is a sworn statement written by the evaluator that one or both attorneys can use to move for contempt. A contempt motion typically will motivate a noncompliant party to continue with the evaluation. If a judge holds that the party is in contempt, a fine or a jail sentence or both can be meted out until the party complies with the judicial order. By completing the evaluation process in a parallel manner, neither party can later complain that the different timing of the evaluation procedures affected the outcome of the evaluation.

---

assessment will begin: the names, current addresses, and all telephone and fax numbers of the parties and a copy of the stipulated agreement or court order (once the second lawyer sends a copy of the stipulated agreement or court order, the evaluator can be assured that the second lawyer is adequately informed about the impending evaluation and her or his client's responsibilities). A reasonable processing fee is sought, in an amount sufficient to offset the costs of the following: processing the initial correspondence; copying and mailing the parenting history questionnaires; and preparing a declaration of noncompliance if one or both parties fail to comply with the evaluation process.

On receipt of the court order or stipulated agreement to conduct the evaluation, the evaluator also prepares a tracking system that notes, at minimum, the following information (see Appendix B): the docket number of the case, the name of the case, the date of appointment, the name of the judge making the appointment, whether the judge wants to be notified when the final report is filed, names and contact information of all attorneys, names of probation officers and the GAL, due date of the final report, extension date (if assented to by the lawyers and granted by the judge), dates of a pretrial discovery cutoff, and trial date.

4. COMMUNICATE FEE RETAINER POLICY

Three fee retainers are secured from the parties of the case on separate occasions (such an approach is designed to meet certain requirements set forth in ethical standard 6.04 in the APA *Ethical Principles of Psychologists and Code of Conduct*, 2002 and APA *Guidelines*, 1994, guideline 15).

The first retainer covers the initial correspondence to the parties and mailing of the Parenting History Survey (PHS; Greenberg & Humphreys, 1998). Neither the initial correspondence nor the testing is sent to the parties until both parties have paid this retainer. If any of the information stated above or the first fee retainer (it can be viewed as a processing fee) is not obtained from both parties, a declaration of noncompliance is sent to both lawyers (see Appendix C) if a voice mail reminder fails to gain compliance.

Once both parties return the initial PHS to the evaluator, a second fee retainer is obtained to cover the clinical work of a comprehensive evaluation and the report writing. The retainer fee will fluctuate depending on the number of the adults being evaluated during the comprehensive evaluation. Both parties should be instructed to bring their second retainer to their first clinical interview at the time their initial appointment is scheduled. If either party fails to pay this second retainer, the evaluation process is halted for both parties, and a declaration of noncompliance is sent out (see Appendix C). The evaluation should not continue until the balance is paid.

A third fee retainer is collected if either party engages in discovery, deposes, or calls for the expert testimony of the evaluator at trial. The party who is calling for additional services during discovery or at trial pays this retainer fee, unless the jurisdiction mandates another approach.

5. COLLECT FIRST FEE RETAINER

Collecting three separate fee retainers will avoid bookkeeping and collection problems if the evaluation becomes unnecessary at any point in the process. For instance, at the beginning of the evaluation process, one party may fail to comply with filling out and returning the testing, and a court may issue a contempt order based on the noncompliance of the party with the evaluation process. The case may settle or end by court order because of this noncompliance. Collecting retainers will also increase the evaluator's credibility if the party does not owe money during the evaluation or during deposition or courtroom testimony. A lawyer cannot accuse the evaluator's judgment of being affected by the lack of fee payment.

6. DISTRIBUTE AND RECEIVE BACK DISCLOSURE FORM AND TESTING MATERIALS

The parties are mailed a written disclosure form (see Appendix A) and an additional document that details steps of the entire evaluation process (see Appendix D). The disclosure form specifies the inability to protect any confidences, the fee arrangements, and licensing-board-required information that will differ in each jurisdiction (see Appendix A; before using this form, or any of the forms within the appendices, the evaluator alters it to meet the requirements of the licensing laws of the jurisdiction for the mental health professional. In addition, a review by the evaluator's attorney can ensure that all disclosure requirements of the jurisdiction are listed.) By providing the parties with the disclosure form in advance of any meeting, the evaluator gives them an opportunity to review it with their attorney. Along with the disclosure form and the document that details the steps of the evaluation of the process (such an approach is designed to meet certain requirements set forth in APA *Guidelines*, 1994, guidelines 9, 10), each party receives the initial testing to complete. The initial testing is conducted by mail. The PHS (Greenberg & Humphreys, 1998) is a 32-page, 107-item self-report questionnaire requesting detailed information about demographics, family history, areas of parental conflict and hostility, mental health and substance abuse issues, and each parent's strengths and weaknesses. Some questions that focused on allegations and parental behaviors are constructed in checklist form. Other questions are designed to provide opportunities for written description about the various issues. Questions range from identifying adult- and child-related concerns in the custody dispute, to involvement of third parties in child care, to expectations about the coparenting relationship in the future. This instrument is primarily used to collect a breadth of data efficiently. It is the most thorough instrument of its kind that we know of, and it is inexpensive to create and use. This questionnaire is copyrighted and commercially available at a small cost from our colleague Stuart Greenberg.

7. SCHEDULE THE FIRST APPOINTMENTS

Evaluators should schedule the parties' appointments on separate days for two reasons. First, neither party is served well by unnecessary contact with the other party. Such contact is likely to lead to conflict. One of the central tasks of conducting a comprehensive parenting evaluation is to diminish conflict and avoid fueling conflict (APA *Guidelines*, 1994, I. Orienting Guidelines: Purpose of a Child Custody Evaluation). Second, the workload of the evaluation is such that, to create sufficient time for the clinical work, the evaluation report is written as the assessment process unfolds. Unless the evaluator works on the evaluation report following each party contact, many of the narrative details and nuances of party behavior will be forgotten. Writing the report as the evaluation unfolds is an essential step of the evaluation process to limit the various forms of error variance that affect clinical judgment. Scheduling the parties' appointments for separate days provides the evaluator with the opportunity to maintain this routine.

When calling or writing each party to establish the date and time of the first appointment, evaluators should specify that the party will need at least four hours for testing and interview time, and should remind the party

PRACTICE TIP 3
Writing Immediately After the Party Interviews or Observations

On the day that the evaluator interviews or observes a party, he or she should set aside at least two hours for every hour of party contact to write the evaluation report. Unless the evaluator works on the evaluation report following each party contact, many of the narrative details and nuances of party behavior will not be integrated into the evaluation. Too much time is wasted recalling the details that emerge from very complicated story lines if the writing is left to the end of the evaluation. The task of pulling together all the data without ongoing writing is too daunting for most evaluators and leads to significant frustration and struggle if left undone to the end. Moreover, the delay in writing will lead to mistakes in clinical judgment. Retrospective writing is subject to a number of forms of error variance and may increase the risk of an ethical or malpractice complaint being filed (Garb 1998).

to bring the fees and any written documents that might be relevant to the allegations. Evaluators should encourage each party to highlight the segments of the documents that they think are noteworthy and caution them against providing documentation from people that have not observed first-hand the parenting behavior or alarming behavior that might affect parenting. Both of these steps will lead to a more efficient review of collateral records.

If either party attempts to discuss any issue with the evaluator, the party should be asked to write down any issue(s) and bring them to the first interview. Evaluators should minimize all out-of-office contact with the parties throughout the case. The evaluation report will specify the dates and hours of contact with each party. This approach permits the evaluator to testify, if necessary, that only incidental contact occurred with the parties and attorneys of the parties on all other occasions. The evaluator takes every opportunity to illuminate the objectivity of the evaluation. Maintaining parallel process while conducting the evaluation reinforces the objectivity in the minds of the parties.

5

PHASE 2: FIRST CLINICAL INTERVIEW

The following procedures are implemented during this phase and described in detail below:

1. Prepare for the first clinical interviews.
2. Review and modify the structured interview for each party.
3. Provide nonconfidentiality warnings, and complete the disclosure process.
4. Administer psychological testing.
5. Administer the semistructured interview.
6. Prepare the release-of-information forms.
7. Obtain records for later review.
8. Fill out an allegation form as an example.
9. End Phase 2 with a parent–child observation.
10. Integrate data immediately afterward.

1. PREPARE FOR THE FIRST CLINICAL INTERVIEWS

The evaluator schedules separate appointments with each parent, typically on different days. A four-hour block of time is reserved to complete the tasks of this first appointment. The following procedures occur during this block of time: Complete the disclosure process; conduct psychological testing; conduct an elaborate, structured psychosocial interview; complete

49

releases of information; and schedule the next appointment. The bulk of the time is spent conducting a clinical interview. The interview includes questions about the family of origin, school history, work history, and previous and current relationships. Details about the relationship history of the parties, including how they met, courted, decided to marry or cohabitate, and decided to have children, emerge during the process. Questions about childbirth, parenting, events leading to the separation, and the present custody dispute follow. Answers to these questions demonstrate the individual's insight, level of health, ability to communicate, and consistency as an informant (when the answers are compared with subsequent statements, e.g., responses to the Parenting History Survey [PHS]). The answers also allow the evaluator to begin forming clinical judgments about the party's parenting strengths and weaknesses. In preparing for the clinical interview, the evaluator has read the PHS of each party and compared the responses, item for item. Such analyses permit the development of hypotheses about the parenting capacity of each parent, the psychological and developmental needs of the children, and the resulting fit between these two constructs (such an approach is designed to meet certain requirements set forth in guideline 3 of the APA *Guidelines for Child Custody Evaluation in Divorce Proceedings*, 1994).

2. REVIEW AND MODIFY THE SEMISTRUCTURED INTERVIEW FOR EACH PARTY

The evaluator will administer a semistructured interview (developed in large part by our colleague Marsha Hedrick; see Appendix E). The standardized form of the interview is modified before meeting with each party based on the information gleaned from the PHS forms. The modifications are targeted to clarify allegations made by both parties and to test hypotheses generated during the review of the PHS measures.

3. PROVIDE NONCONFIDENTIALITY WARNINGS, AND COMPLETE THE DISCLOSURE PROCESS

On arrival in the clinic, each party reads and signs the disclosure form (Appendix A) that establishes that the party has consented to the confidentiality waiver and agrees to proceed with the evaluation. Although the party has seen this disclosure form at the time of receipt of the PHS, in most jurisdictions, further clarification of party questions and in-person attestation occur for formal consent to be upheld as a matter of law. Such a practice represents the best practice guideline regardless of what the law states (such an approach is designed to meet certain requirements set forth in guidelines 9 and 10 of APA *Guidelines*, 1994).

The form includes an explanation of the purpose of the evaluation, procedures used in the evaluation, inability to protect any party confidences, and right to decline to respond to any questions. In most jurisdictions, parties have no confidentiality protections concerning the evaluator's impressions and findings of a court-ordered evaluation during the pendency of a family law case, and the evaluator emphasizes nonconfidentiality to prevent any party from being surprised. Therefore, the evaluator states directly to each party that all parties, their lawyers, and the judge will have access to all of the information gathered during the evaluation. Moreover, the information gathered from all sources through the evaluation may be presented in verbal or written form to the court. This warning is given before collecting information from the parties, their children, and individuals who serve as collateral sources. The evaluator says something akin to the following statement outlined in Massachusetts state law (see *Commonwealth of Massachusetts v. Lamb*, 365 Mass. 265, 270, 1974) to both children and adults.

> I am a psychologist, and I am conducting an evaluation ordered by the court. The judge asked me to talk with you and to help him (or her) sort out how to arrange custody and visitation for your children. Did your attorney tell you about this evaluation? [Wait for party response.] I want to tell you about some details that you have read in the disclosure statement and the document that laid out the process of the evaluation I sent in the mail. Perhaps your lawyer also may have gone over some of the details. In all of the interviews we have together, you do not have to answer any questions I will ask you. You do not have to answer questions on the forms I give you. If you do answer, what you say will *not* be kept confidential or private between you and me. I may use what you tell me in the evaluation report, or I may repeat it in court in front of the judge. In addition, the lawyers, the judge, and the other party in the case will read the evaluation report. Do you understand all that I have said? [Wait for party response.] Can you tell me in your own words what I just said? [Wait for party response; restate if the party's response does not reflect understanding about nonconfidentiality and freedom to decline answers.] Finally, we can stop this interview at any time if you need a break or want to end. Any questions? [Wait for party response.]

In the report, the evaluator will insert a statement reflecting that the warning of nonconfidentiality was provided, such as the following:

> All parties to this evaluation were informed at the onset of all interviews that the data collected from clinical interviews, records, and collateral contacts would be used for this report to the court, or verbal testimony, or both. The parties indicated that they understood that no

information would be kept confidential. The parties were aware that it was within their right to refuse to answer a question or line of questions. All parties acknowledged that they understood this information.

In some instances, a party may refuse to sign the consent agreement because of an objection to one or more of the terms of the agreement. If the party seeks advice from the evaluator about signing the disclosure form or asks for an interpretation of the legal significance of the disclosure form, the evaluator refers the party back to his or her lawyer. If necessary, the Phase 2 appointment may require rescheduling when the evaluator cannot obtain informed consent. The evaluator points out that the agreement is nonnegotiable. If the party contends that she or he will only sign the informed consent agreement under protest, the evaluator cancels the Phase 2 appointment. At this point, the evaluator informs the party that a letter, called a declaration of noncompliance, will be sent to both attorneys involved in the case so that the judge can decide whether the evaluation should proceed. This statement is delivered matter-of-factly while the evaluator tells the party that no deviations from the standardized evaluation process are possible. Throughout the disclosure process, no matter what the provocation, the evaluator remains poised, and courteous and speaks matter-of-factly to the party. The initial interactions with a party will set the tone and tenor of the evaluator's later behavior. Such a measured stance remains critical at the onset of the evaluation and, once established, will be easier to maintain throughout the evaluation. Particularly with a suspicious or difficult party, the evaluator should maintain firm and reasonable boundaries. Otherwise, the evaluator will collude with the high-conflict tactics of a party and limit the efficacy of the process.

On occasion, the parties may agree through their attorneys to changes in the disclosure agreement without consulting with the evaluator first, or a judge may order changes in the disclosure agreement. If the changes will result in exposing the evaluator to violating practices described below that deter ethical complaints (e.g., the lawyers alter the disclosure agreement so that psychological testing and collateral interviews are precluded), the evaluator should decline to conduct the evaluation.

In certain jurisdictions, the confidentiality safeguards and psychotherapy privilege of the child must be specifically waived before the parenting evaluator can access the information. In Massachusetts, for example, a guardian ad litem (GAL) must be appointed by the judge to evaluate whether the psychotherapy privilege of the child can be waived. Evaluators seek consultation about the family law statutes to ensure that they comply with the law. If the law calls for a waiver, the evaluator may have to ask the lawyer to submit a motion to appoint such a GAL if the issues in the case warrant it (as seen below, often direct interviews of the children in the case are unnecessary).

4. ADMINISTER PSYCHOLOGICAL TESTING

The party then takes a computer-administered Minnesota Multiphasic Personality Inventory–Second Edition (MMPI–2; Butcher, Dahlstrom, Graham, Tellegen, & Kaemmer, 1989). At the onset of the testing, the evaluator assesses whether the party understands the directions on the MMPI–2. If the evaluator doubts the party's cognitive capacity to respond in a valid manner, cognitive testing may be necessary. Evaluators will receive very few referrals in which one or both of the parties lack cognitive capacity. In most instances, such cases are easily managed by the legal system. Attorneys are likely to settle cases in which one party lacks sufficient capacity long before an evaluation is ordered.

Research about standardized testing of high-conflict parties suggests that the results of such measures are of questionable validity and reliability (Bagby, Nicholson, Buis, Radovanovic, & Fidler, 1999). Divorced parents are highly motivated to present themselves as favorably as possible. In their effort to do so, they may produce invalid or minimized profiles. Studies reviewing MMPI normative data on child custody litigants among private practices in California (Bathurst, Gottfried, & Gottfried, 1997) suggest that individuals minimized their difficulties. As a result, best practices dictate using data from psychological testing only to generate hypotheses about response sets (whether some party approaches test taking openly and honestly or in a guarded, rigid, and prevaricating manner) and possible personality traits that can impair effective parenting. No personality test results should stand on their own as findings in the report. Please note the disclosure statement within the report, in the testing section of the sample evaluation report (Part III of this book), that describes the limited value that readers should attribute to personality test results.

One advantage of conducting MMPI–2 testing before the interview is that the party generally becomes fatigued, because of the time it takes to complete standardized testing under the controlled conditions of the office setting, and tends to be less defensive during the interview. Although the evaluator may wish to use other psychological tests, nonexistent or poor validity and reliability results for most other measures suggest that the evaluator's time is better expended using other evaluation procedures (see Garb, 1998). The other measures of the evaluation must corroborate any hypothesis generated by psychological test results before a finding is made.

5. ADMINISTER THE SEMISTRUCTURED INTERVIEW

After testing is completed, the evaluator administers a semistructured interview (Appendix E). The purpose of the interview is to collect a detailed social history of the parties using procedures that establish and reinforce the objective role of the evaluator. The evaluator asks open-ended questions, takes detailed notes, and minimizes eye contact and other empathic contact. In addition to the reminder that no party confidences are permitted, the parents are told at the beginning of the interview that no feedback, advice, support, or discussion of known information or sources will occur. These prohibitions prevent the incidental confusion of role boundaries and sustain the practice of equitable time and process (Weissman, 1991).

In reviewing cases regarding ethical violations that arose during forensic parenting evaluations, it appears that the complaining parties feel abandoned and betrayed by the evaluators. An evaluator who creates the impression of objectivity will be less likely to endure the process of defending her- or himself during an ethical violation investigation or malpractice lawsuit (permitted in some jurisdictions). Party feelings of abandonment and betrayal are less likely to emerge if the evaluator adopts the objective stance recommended above.

The varied and complex nature of parenting requires a careful review of factors related to the psychological and practical functioning of each individual in the family. Consistent with the parameters of the "best interests of the child" standard, the evaluation focuses on (a) the instrumental parenting capacity of each potential caretaker (including parents' significant others and grandparents), (b) the psychological and developmental needs of the child, and (c) the resulting fit between the children and the parents. We advocate an assessment of behavioral functioning to produce corroboration of reports by each party and collateral individuals. Behavioral evaluation conducted through clinical interviews also assists with identification of specific behavioral patterns, as well as facilitating a review of parenting weaknesses and strengths (Bray, 1991).

The clinical interview begins with a review of each individual's identifying demographic data, including each party's name, current residential addresses, all telephone numbers, current marital status, and occupation. The interview then transitions into a brief review of the individual's family and personal history. This includes review of childhood family environment and structure, previous and current stability and arrangement of the family of origin for each individual, and a description of the stability of family finances and functioning. Questioning focuses on descriptions of possible situations involving chaotic and entrenched family conflicts, enmeshed or disengaged relationships, and emotionally neglectful or abusive family environments. Data about the family of origin's use of substances, criminality, psychiatric history, and treatment are also useful in understanding possible models for current parental style. As seen in the review of the literature above, parties who are incapable of settling family law matters may have histories replete with such data.

The interview may also include questions that focus on the possibility of specific traumas and stresses for each individual, particularly for the children. Inquiries may focus on historical and current experience with physical, sexual, and emotional abuse; physical neglect; domestic violence; sudden and traumatic loss; parental abandonment; exposure to community violence (e.g., drive-by shootings); traumatic accidents; natural disasters; and immigration trauma.

The evaluation then reviews the educational history of each individual, with specific interest in academic performance and behavior in schools and the history of learning disabilities and special education classes. Following this, the evaluation reviews the individual's employment history, paying particular attention to lapses in employment, difficulty with co-workers, occupational training, and experience. This is followed with a review of social and recreational history, evaluating each individual's relationship skills, social adjustment, evidence of current peer support, presence of social isolation, involvement in delinquent behavior with peers, and possible gang involvement. Also important to review is the individual's approach to resolving interpersonal conflicts and their problem-solving abilities. Emotional expressiveness may be noted.

At this point, psychiatric history and treatment are reviewed to investigate pre-existing and current psychiatric disorders, including past illnesses that required care. Include details about presenting symptoms, extent of incapacity at the time, the type and duration of treatment, efficacy of the treatment, and the names of doctors and hospitals that provided the service. Questions may also focus on the party's interest in seeking counseling for themselves and their children, given the stress of their separation. This set of questions is followed with a review of the individual's medical history to understand the presence of previous and current medical problems. Information is also collected about the individual's prescription or over-the-counter medications, use of vitamins and herbs, the regularity with which they consult with a doctor, the name of their doctor, and frequency of visits. The evaluator also collects information about frequency of smoking and allergies to medications and other stimuli (e.g., mold, cat hair). A previous and current substance use and abuse history is collected, including information about consumption of beer, wine, liquor (type), marijuana, and other drugs.

A mental status examination offers an efficient approach to collecting data about mood and neuropsychological symptoms. This includes information about mood and anxiety disorders, perceptual disturbances, content and process of thought, suicidal and homicidal intent, language, orientation, memory, concentration and attention, abstract thought, fund of knowledge and intelligence, insight, and judgment.

Assessment of parenting capacities investigates the following areas: who carries out functional parenting responsibilities; the adult's awareness of, and attention to, the child's medical and physical needs; and evidence of emotional investment in the child. In addition, the evaluation reviews whether the adult has facilitated the child's social relationships with siblings, peers, and adults. It assesses each party's ability to perceive and accurately read the child's cues and communications about needs, to respond appropriately and consistently to the child, and to cope with stress and to exhibit self-control and stress management skills. Questions also focus on emotional coping skills (e.g., abilities to identify, express, and tolerate negative feelings), the ability to identify the independent needs of the child and appraise the child in a positive manner, and the ability to recognize when the child cannot provide gratification for the parent and to assertively protect and respond to the emotional and developmental needs of the child. Each party's consistency of parenting—establishment of rules, limits, and structure—and their approaches to consequences of misbehavior are assessed.

Parent and child relationships require particular attention about the ways in which parents spend time with their children, the quality of their communication and attention to their children, the quality of their affection, and the encouragement of independence of the child. Evaluation of care-taking routines and conflict between parents and children may also reveal factors that define the quality of the parent and child relationships and attachment (Deutsch, Rotman, & Ward, 2001).

Ethnicity/Cultural Competence

Demonstrating cultural competence is essential in custody evaluations. We advocate the philosophy that no one culture offers the gold standard in child rearing and that evaluators must learn about cultural practices, which necessarily influence family development, within the context of the specific cultural heritage (Roll, 1998). For instance, if inflicting pain and anguish on a child through parental shaming is alleged to be culturally acceptable, the evaluator does not accept at face value the parent's contention. The suspect contention is verified by a cultural consultant.

People from different cultures satisfy basic human needs (e.g., food, shelter, relationships), develop ideas about community (e.g., safety, order, and procreation), and approach parenting (e.g., health, identity, and child rearing) in unique ways (Azar & Benjit, 1994; Azar & Cote, 2002). Evaluators appreciate cultural variations in the practice of child care (e.g., whether children sleep with their parents) and also determine whether these practices follow the best interests of the child. Evaluators should read through the *Guidelines for Providers of Psychological Services to Ethnic and Culturally Diverse Populations* (American Psychological Association, 1990) to increase cultural competency in evaluating families with diverse background.

Beyond reminding evaluators to attend to cultural factors in custody disputes, we note that specific issues arise in parenting evaluations that require specialized attention (Azar & Benjit, 1994; Sue & Sue, 1999). For example, the evaluator may choose to include information in the interview report about language issues, cultural style in complaints, and cultural influence in coping skills and belief systems. A parent who advocates breast-feeding his or her 4-year-old may contradict professional assumptions about appropriate parenting. Evaluators may choose to heighten their sensitivity to avoid making judgments that revert to European American norms, as well as confuse ethnic subgroups as members of the same broad category. Cultural beliefs also influence definitions of health and normal behavior, members of families and communities, and significant events in the family life cycle. Areas of potential misunderstanding include attitudes and strategies in problem-solving, response to mental health professionals, and responsibility delegated to children and the degree to which children should respond to caretakers. Culture also influences the defined roles of parents and children, issues of familial obligation and responsibility in the family, and methods of communication of affection and information.

Religion

Disputes about choice of religion and religious training are on the rise in family litigation. Although this area is given little attention in research, in some cases, religion choice influences lifestyle, medical care, parental attention, child development, and even custody (e.g., in some Muslim faiths, children younger than age 7 stay with their mother and after age 7, with their father). Evaluators will find themselves examining issues related to the religious identities of the children and the parents. Family dynamics in cases that present religion as the only issue of dispute will require the evaluator to distinguish facts from beliefs, as well as religious beliefs from religious practice (e.g., use of corporal punishment). The evaluator guards against his or her own biases and ensures that she or he does not discredit the party with the stronger religious beliefs. The evaluation investigates the rigidity of the person's belief by comparing the contrasting views of the parties and their respective families as those religious beliefs and practices might compromise the child's best interests. While children can be confused by mixed-faith marriages, it is important to look at each parent's ability to remain flexible and support the child's interest in each parent's religious practices (Wah, 1994, 1997).

In addition to culture and religious differences, differences between parties and their family members in life experiences, values, and expectations exist. Low-income and large extended families (e.g., in which a grandmother provides primary parenting) may provide additional complexities to the evaluation. In particular, low-income individuals are usually not familiar with professional practitioners and may be anxious about the professional and the specific procedures. Evaluators should not alter the procedures or descriptions for parties within the same case, unless there is a fundamental language barrier (in which case there should be a translator who is either court appointed or approved by both parties). Careful use of language, avoidance of jargon, and slower pacing in the evaluation may provide sufficient time for individuals to adjust to the assessment procedures. As with all procedures, frequent checks of the party's understanding may be warranted.

Domestic Violence

Between 3.3 million and 10 million children annually witness violence between family members (Appel & Holden, 1998). About 40% of children living in violent families are themselves abused (Appel & Holden, 1998). Evaluations involving allegations of domestic violence are complicated. Mental health professionals are advised to obtain specialized training on the legal guidelines for child visits and custody in divorce cases that involve domestic violence. The best interests of the child standard addresses domestic violence by outlining protections for the health, safety, and welfare of the children. Any history of abuse by one parent against the children or against the other parent requires the court to make findings regarding the abuse on the legal record in most jurisdictions. However, courts are more likely to refer cases for evaluation where allegations of mutual violence exist and the pattern of domestic violence differs from the classic type of case where the male is battering the female.

While conducting evaluations, the evaluator applies knowledge about the mental health consequences of family violence, particularly between separating and divorcing parents. The evaluation discloses the ways that domestic violence manifests among family members, the psychological and behavioral impact of family violence on child and adult development, the psychological reactions to domestic violence, the coping strategies, the factors that increase the risk of violence (e.g., substance use, work stress, social isolation), and the barriers to providing optimal care and protection for children. If a known history of domestic violence exists, it can be documented thoroughly by using the Spousal Assault Risk Assessment Guide (SARA; Kropp, Hart, Webster, & Eaves, 1995, 1998) measure to ascertain the level and frequency of violence. Another actuarial measure that outlines the contours of family violence is the Conflict Tactics Scale, a self-report measure of verbal and physical aggression between adults that captures data from the history of the relationship and for the past year (Straus, Hamby, Boney-McCoy, & Sugarman, 1996).

Evaluators assess the allegations of domestic violence by providing the best information possible, informed by the interviews, records, and collateral contacts to delineate the pattern of violence. Evaluators also look for violence directed at siblings and at pets because such violence often is missed in the context of interparental violence. Questions aim to elucidate more detail about the frequency and duration of aggression; length, nature, and progression or history of aggression; the degree of aggression or violence within the offense, including use of physical force and restraint, weapon, or threat to use a weapon; the degree of coercion use (e.g., bribes, substance use, games, threats); the severity, including the first documented offense; and distinction of the pattern of violence.

Additional data are collected regarding the following aspects of violent behavior: evidence of termination of assault when a victim protested or showed distress, predatory behavior (e.g., stalking, staking out locations to observe a victim or enhance victim vulnerability, roaming in an area where there is high potential of finding a victim), ritualistic violence, and precipitating factors that precede offenses (e.g., dysphoric mood, fights, explosive anger, use of pornographic media, self-esteem failure, shame, fantasies, peer influence, use of substances, and periods of stressful caretaking of the child). Other areas of evaluation include assessing the following: external motivation for treatment (adjudication or court-ordered treatment, someone is insisting on treatment), internal motivation for treatment, amenability to treatment (the perpetrator's understanding about needing help to change vs. resistance to active engagement in treatment), the degree of cooperation with the assessment, the willingness to discuss his or her own behavior, the degree of honesty and self-initiated disclosure, the presence and absence of emphatic skills and thinking errors, the degree of flexibility versus rigidity of the belief system with regard to intimacy, the degree of control for urges and impulses, the current degree of access to children, and availability of nonviolent and nonabusive social supports.

Approach of the Evaluator During the Interview Process

During the interview, the evaluator pays particular attention to remarks made by the party that suggest minimization or denial is occurring. Trite statements, glib or simple responses to complicated questions, and equivocations or answers embedded among emotionally laden words are queried. Evaluators should never assume that they understand a party's vague response, particularly if a party fails to complete the sentence. Evaluators pursue all minimizations by engaging in active listening. Often asking the party to state a concrete example can provide clarity. Repeating the emotionally laden words of the last statement made by the party can lead to clarification and a deeper understanding of the experience of the party. For instance, when a party says that his childhood was like "Ozzie and Harriet's family" except for his brother's drug abuse problem, the evaluator's voice inflection can register frank surprise as she restates "drug abuse prob-

PRACTICE TIP 4
Capturing the Details

The evaluator uses a laptop computer to enter the responses of each party during the interviews. Because this is a semistructured interview, key questions are formulated in advance and displayed on the monitor. As the evaluator enters the answer from a party, the evaluator can ask the next question to maintain the fluidity of the interview. This approach allows for a further impersonalized stance and a detached objectivity. Immediately following the interview, the evaluator word processes the responses and builds the evaluation report. The details of the interview are unlikely to be lost if this discipline is followed.

lems." If the party's story remains illogical, the evaluator can convey confusion and summarize the statement that remains vague: "On the one hand, you said your family had enough money when you were growing up, but you just said that your mother complained about money. Can you tell me more?"

Throughout the interview, the evaluator remains aware of the allegations made by both parties and looks for targets of opportunity (e.g., the firsthand witnessing of the behavior of the other party that would corroborate a particular allegation) to gather more confirming details about the allegations. Possible sources of independent records are noted so that releases can be obtained later. Factual corroboration can occur by obtaining and reviewing these independent records. In particular, inconsistencies between PHS responses and interview answers lead to further inquiry by the evaluator. In many instances, through active listening and the skilled use of silence, the evaluator will obtain further elaboration.

For instance, if a party responds to a question about prior hospitalizations by holding up her hand and showing a scar along her wrist that occurred because her husband allegedly pushed her through a window, the evaluator can seek further elaboration through active listening. Certainly the evaluator obtains the date of the event. At the end of the first interview, the evaluator inquires whether the party has in her possession the hospital record, which will provide a contemporaneous corroboration of the party's version of events. If the party states that she protected her husband at the time by blaming her cut on a broken dish in the sink, the evaluator can ask the party to produce a contemporaneous record that shows the costs for repairing the window. This receipt should approximate the date of the domestic violence and her creation of an inaccurate hospital record to protect her husband.

Based on the interview results, the evaluator can more fully understand each party's level of insight, treatment amenability, and ability to dampen interparty conflict. Also, hypotheses about the allegations will continue to emerge. For each hypothesis, the evaluator attempts to generate multiple measure corroboration. In particular, the evaluator will attempt to identify incidents at which firsthand witnesses were present, contemporaneous reports about the incidents were made to professionals involved with the family, or independent records were created (e.g., the accounting of the broken window as mentioned above).

6. PREPARE THE RELEASE-OF-INFORMATION FORMS

At the end of the interview, the evaluator presents release-of-information forms that have been filled out in advance based on information provided in the PHS. These releases allow the evaluator to access records and speak to third-party individuals who may be able to inform the evaluator about particular aspects of the allegations raised by the parties. This practice will save time for the evaluator and will further reinforce the impression of conducting a thorough evaluation. Additional forms can be filled out based on disclosures made within the interview about firsthand witnesses or professionals who heard contemporaneous reports regarding the allegations. The evaluator strongly suggests that she or he will contact only collaterals who can provide firsthand information about the allegations or about parenting strengths or weaknesses. Often such evidence leads to a party admitting to the allegation on learning about the detail of the findings during the closing interview.

Even though some jurisdictions may not require formal releases of information, evaluators use them so that each party understands who will be contacted during the course of the evaluation. This practice supports the impression of evaluator fairness and objectivity in the minds of the parties, deters party dissimulation, and saves evaluator time.

7. OBTAIN RECORDS FOR LATER REVIEW

Records pertaining to each parent and child are obtained through release-of-information forms. Each party is asked to produce records that became apparent during the first interview. Potentially informative records may include police incident reports, criminal history reports, juvenile court and juvenile court clinic records, mental health records, medical records, school attendance and grade reports, achievement and standardized testing records, and social services agency records. Psychological and educational testing reports are also important to include. Once each adult has offered permission to access records, the party is instructed to ask the agency for the unredacted records to ensure that a complete record is mailed directly to the evaluator. Each party is given two weeks in which to obtain all of the records. If either party delays, both lawyers are informed informally, first. If either party fails to comply, the evaluation is stopped, a declaration

If the party requests that the evaluator interview nonprofessional collaterals, the evaluator insists on those individuals submitting legal declarations first (called *affidavits* in some jurisdictions, hereafter referred to as *legal declarations*). Each jurisdiction has a declaration form that subjects the person to the laws of perjury if facts alleged within the declaration lack veracity. Nonprofessionals are likely to change their stories as an evaluation process unfolds and the parties exert pressure for support. The party is urged to provide only declarations from first-hand witnesses of parenting behavior or behavior that could affect parenting. Any declaration that lacks specificity or relevant evidence can lead the evaluator to decide not to interview the collateral later and save time. Engaging in this process will lessen the risk of an ethical complaint being filed. Many ethical complaints are founded on party allegations that the evaluator is prejudiced because of inaccurately recording nonprofessional collateral interviews. Declarations establish a written record that can be quoted and reduce the risk of such complaints.

of noncompliance is sent out, and evaluation does not resume until the records are returned.

8. FILL OUT AN ALLEGATION FORM AS AN EXAMPLE

A set of allegation forms (see Appendix F) is provided to each party at the end of the interview. The evaluator chooses the allegation raised by the party that appears to be most injurious to the children. The evaluator explains to the party that an allegation form should be completed about each allegation, with the three examples of the worst instances of each allegation being provided. The evaluator also models for the party the degree of specificity required. While the party looks on, holding a copy of the forms, the evaluator completes three forms about the most injurious allegation raised by the party by asking the party to talk through the three worst incidents of the allegation (copies of these completed forms are sent home with the party to serve as models). The evaluator presses hard for detail and specificity. For instance, if the party has alleged emotional abuse of the child by the other parent, the evaluator will learn through the three concrete examples what parenting deficits might exist and how the deficits have produced specific symptoms in the child. The evaluator also may want to take the opportunity to learn about how the complaining party would parent the child differently in the same circumstances.

Although parties have had plenty of opportunity to provide great detail about each allegation when filling out the PHS, many will fail to provide sufficient detail in this latter context. Because of the modeling of thoroughness during the interview, this second round of written inquiry about the allegations will often lead to greater specificity, identification of firsthand witnesses or professionals who heard contemporaneous reports about incidents, and closure about allegations to be evaluated. Typically, several of the allegations will not be founded on any corroborated evidence. Unless a pattern of behavior emerges through this process and other parts of the evaluation, the allegation may be viewed as suspect and the final report will indicate the absence of independently corroborating evidence obtained during all of the evaluations procedures. It also will provide an additional opportunity for cross-validation between written measures and interview data. Each party is given a week in which to return the allegation forms. If either party delays in completing the forms, both lawyers are informed about the delay. If either party fails to comply, the evaluation is stopped, a declaration of noncompliance is sent out, and evaluation does not resume until the forms are returned.

9. END PHASE 2 WITH PARENT–CHILD OBSERVATION

The interview ends with the scheduling of a parent–child observation in the office. The evaluator instructs the parent "to be prepared to play with the children" for about an hour at the next appointment. If there are allegations of an inadequate or unsafe home setting, then the evaluator schedules a home observation instead. If the party has a new life partner involved with the children, then the party is instructed to have the partner into the office on a particular date and time to complete the MMPI–2. The evaluator completes the first clinical interview for both parents before Phase 3 of the evaluation begins.

10. INTEGRATE DATA IMMEDIATELY AFTERWARD

Immediately following the interview, the evaluator writes down the responses of the party and begins to build the evaluation report (see Part III of this book for a model). The details of the interview are unlikely to be lost if this discipline is followed. As the need for additional information becomes apparent, the evaluator embeds within the evaluation report ad-

PRACTICE TIP 6
Scheduling

Evaluators always schedule the next part of the evaluation process before a party leaves the office. This best practice will save time by avoiding telephone calls. In addition, it prepares the party for the next step of the evaluation process and provides an opportunity for the party to raise questions that can avoid the necessity of later telephone responses.

ditional questions to pursue. On receipt of the allegation forms, the evaluator writes out the specifics of each allegation.

Both the psychosocial section and the allegations that the particular party raised about the other parent are sent to that party for review and additions. No further suggestion is necessary to make in the cover letter that accompanies the request for review. This approach enables the evaluator to gain further clarification about the questions that were not answered during the review of the PHS and interview data. In addition, such a review cuts off a later party complaint that the evaluator misrepresented or failed to insert detail that allegedly might have affected the outcome of the evaluation. Not only does this approach help to ensure that both parties will believe that they have been fairly and thoroughly evaluated, but it produces a contemporaneous record of party satisfaction with the results of these sections of the evaluation. Ethical and malpractice risks are reduced accordingly. In a discussion section of the report (see model report in Part III of this book), the evaluator also begins to list the hypotheses that have emerged from the different sources of data. The allegations and hypotheses about the allegations are listed within the discussion section under the substantive standards by which the jurisdiction organizes its evidence to determine the residential schedule of the children and the allocation of the decision-making authority of the parents. As the evaluation unfolds, the evaluator will apply the best practice of not arriving at a finding unless multiple measure corroboration suggests that such a finding is warranted. This method of depending on convergence of multiple measures before arriving at a finding prevents the evaluator from being unduly influenced by any single measure.

Information in a comprehensive parenting evaluation comes from many sources. Research strongly suggests that a perceived inequitable process rather than a perceived inequitable outcome most likely influences party dissatisfaction with the final divorce decree (Sheets & Braver, 1996). Unless the evaluator is perceived to have conducted a broad-based, fair, multiple-measured evaluation of both parties, a party may contend that biased evaluating has affected the reliability of widely used psychometric tests and the valid interpretation of all other evaluation evidence (Weissman, 1991).

6

PHASE 3: OBSERVATIONS OF PARENTS AND CHILDREN

The following procedures are implemented during this phase, as described in detail below:

1. Conducting the scheduled parent–child observations
2. Conducting stepparent–child observations if allegations about a new life partner have arisen
3. Approach to the structured observation process
4. Instructions for parent–child observation
   - Instruct the parent "to do something fun together." First the child directs the activity for 15–20 minutes.
   - Interrupt child-directed play with a knock on the door so that the play shifts to being parent directed for 15–20 minutes.
   - Interrupt parent-directed play within 12–20 minutes by entering the room and handing the parent an Achenbach Child Behavior Checklist to complete for each child.
   - Provide the second signal to start the clean-up process about 50 minutes into the observation.
   - Ask the parent how this observation compares to other play that the parent has experienced with the child.
5. Process of observation for parents and adolescents

6. Expected baseline parenting behaviors
7. Ending of observation process and scheduling of last appointments with parties
8. Home visits
9. Immediate writing after observation and writing of preliminary evaluation report.

1. CONDUCTING THE SCHEDULED
PARENT–CHILD OBSERVATIONS

A parent–child observation occurs 7–14 days after the first interview. The evaluator has established separate one-hour appointments with each parent at the end of the first interview. The time of day and day of the week of the appointments are similar to reduce temporal confounds and so that neither party can later complain that scheduling differences affected the behavior of the children. On occasion, a party will inquire about the instruction "to come prepared to play with your child for an hour." The evaluator simply restates the instruction.

2. CONDUCTING STEPPARENT–CHILD OBSERVATIONS IF
ALLEGATIONS ABOUT A NEW LIFE PARTNER HAVE ARISEN

If allegations have been raised about the stepparenting of a life partner, a life partner–child observation occurs after the parent–child observations of the parties are completed (e.g., observation with step-parent and children together).

3. APPROACH TO THE STRUCTURED
OBSERVATION PROCESS

The videotaped interaction occurs with few toys or aids. Most parents will have understood the instruction about coming to play for the hour. Although it is noteworthy if a parent provides a variety of activities, games, books, materials that are age appropriate, some parents will fail to recognize the import of the instruction. The evaluator assesses whether the materials brought to the observation are age appropriate. If disorganization is an allegation raised by the other party, the evaluator can ask about the parent's perception of the instruction during the closing interview. Lack of organization in this part of the evaluation process may mirror disorganization in several other parts of the process. Depending on the response of the party, such an occurrence may serve as independent evidence about the

The evaluator views the interaction through a one-way mirror or video monitor or through later review of the videotape. It is strongly recommended that the parent–child observation be videotaped because of the wealth of data that arises during the structured process. Later contemporaneous review of both parent–child observation tapes may provide more-telling comparisons of parenting strengths, weaknesses, and bond with the children. The parties will be familiar with being videotaped by the time of the observation session. Sometimes, the evaluator will need to remind them about the disclosure statement they signed that gave expressed permission for the taping (as was discussed earlier, such an approach is designed to meet certain requirements set forth in the ethical standards 3.10 and 4.03 of the APA *Ethical Principles of Psychologists and Code of Conduct*, 2002).

---

disorganization of a party. Occasionally, a parent talks or plays without the use of aids as a matter of individual preference. The quality of the parent–child interactions is not necessarily determined by whether materials are present.

4. INSTRUCTIONS FOR PARENT–CHILD OBSERVATION

If none or not all of the children are adolescents, the evaluator instructs the parent to discuss with the children why they are visiting the clinic. The evaluator then instructs the parent and children "to do something fun together," first with the child directing the activity and then with the parent directing. A clean-up phase follows (when a structured opportunity occurs for all of the belongings of the party and child to be collected and the clinic's toys to be put away). The parent is instructed that he or she should shift to the second or third phase of the observation once he or she hears a knock on the one-way mirror or the door. The evaluator demonstrates at the time these instructions are delivered how the knock will sound so other building noises will not mislead the party. Very simple written directions are provided to the parent about this process. In addition, the party is instructed to stay in the room until the evaluator returns to the room and formally ends the observation. Often during the waiting at the end of the observation, parent–child interactions will provide telling data. For instance, a child might comment during the wait, "Have I been good enough to go get ice cream, Daddy?" indicating that the child had been coached before the session to act in a certain manner. Or a parent will completely ignore the child after the structure of the observation has ended.

The first two phases of the observation continue for 15–20 minutes depending on a natural break point in the activities. The evaluator knocks

PRACTICE TIP 8
Parent–Child Observations

Much of the richest data about the parent–children relationships emerges during "transitions." Transitions provide an opportunity for parents to demonstrate their ability to prepare the child for the next activity, their skills at delivering instructions, and the child's ability to comply with instructions. Often the transition will prompt many questions from the child. The parent's manner and responses to the questions provide further detail about the parenting skills. Therefore, if a party brings board games or playing cards to the observation, the evaluator should validate the parent for being organized and prepared to play but instruct them not to play with these materials during the observation. Board games and cards typically result in too few transitions.

when a period of static play has continued into this 15–20-minute range. However, the parent-directed play is interrupted (within the second 15–20-minute period) by the evaluator entering the room and handing the parent an Achenbach Child Behavior Checklist (Achenbach, 1979, 1991a; Achenbach & Edelbrock, 1979, 1981, or similar instrument to complete for each child that will provide a standardized opportunity to the parent to provide specific information about a child's physical and psychological symptoms that may be of concern). This unexpected interruption provides both surprise and a task that allows assessment of a parent's ability to remain flexible and manage at least two tasks at once. Around 50 minutes into the observation, the second and last knock forces the transition to clean-up.

5. PROCESS OF OBSERVATION FOR PARENTS AND ADOLESCENTS

The evaluator instructs the parent and children to discuss a series of questions. Although the allegations of the case may shape some of the questions, typical instructions include plan for something fun to do together, discuss a typical day within the household of the parent, outline the family rules and daily chores expected of the children, and discuss what happens when someone breaks family rules. Whatever questions are to be discussed are written in advance and handed to the parent. The parent is instructed not to discuss the next question until a knock occurs. As stated above, often during periods of waiting, parent–child interactions will provide telling data.

6. EXPECTED BASELINE PARENTING BEHAVIORS

During the review of the observations, several fundamental parenting behaviors should emerge. The strength of the relative emotional bond between the parent and the children is then assessed on the basis of the observed competence of each parent during the interactions. These observational data deepen the clinical judgments about parental strengths, weaknesses, and bond. Our colleague Molly Reid, at the University of Washington, provided the following operational definitions of expected baseline parenting behaviors:

- *Compliance* occurs when the child obeys instructions within a short period of time (a few seconds).
- *Noncompliance* occurs when the child fails to follow instructions within a short period of time.
- *Inappropriate behavior* occurs when the child whines, sasses, fails to exercise common courtesy, cries, yells, destroys or attempts to destroy an object, hits the parent, or repeatedly asks the same question after it has been answered.
- A *direct instruction* is a clear statement by the parent telling the child to perform some specific behavior. The parent models common courtesy whenever issuing a direct instruction. Direct instructions can also include forced choices ("Please pick up the toys and put them on the shelf" and "Please pick up the blocks or the dinosaurs"). An *indirect instruction* occurs when the parent's direction to the child is vague, ambiguous, or implies that the child has a choice ("Let's clean up" but father actually means, "*You* put the *toys* on the *shelf*"; "Why don't you. ....").
- A *question* is any interrogative statement. Many parents inappropriately use questions when they should use direct instructions ("When will you clean up?" but mother actually means, "Put away the toys in the room now").
- A *descriptive statement* is any parental verbalization to the child that describes what the child or parent is doing. Such statements are important because they offer reinforcing attention to the child regarding specific behaviors. Inappropriate behaviors are not described. Descriptive statements are encouraging and validating to the child ("You are really getting the puzzle put together fast"; "Oh. You're stacking the blocks on each other. I'm stacking my blocks, too").
- *Labeled praise* is a reinforcing statement specifically identifying for the child what child behavior the parent likes ("Well placed, Susan. You stack those blocks wonderfully"; "Thank you for putting all of the blocks away just like I asked").
- *Unlabeled praise* is a reinforcing statement or phrase that is vaguely unspecific ("Good boy!"; "That's nice."; "Okay").

Immediately following the observation, the evaluator asks the parent how the observation compares to other periods of play that the parent has experienced with the child. Almost always parties contend that the observation was similar to other periods of play, because even a parent with parenting deficits generally remains unaware of the deficits. If the parent suggests that the parent–child observation has been compromised by any factor, the evaluator clarifies how the observation was compromised. The explanation may be noteworthy and can provide independent evidence about a particular allegation. At that point, another parent–child observation is scheduled so that the party cannot later contend that insufficient or poor data collected during the observation occurred. The party will view the second observation as serving the interest of fairness.

- *Physical praise* occurs whenever the parent gives the child a hug, a pat on the back, a kiss, or any touching as apparent praise for good behavior.
- *Critical comments* are any negative, apparently punishing, statements to the child ("No!!!"; "You know you are not supposed to do that"; "What's the matter with you?!"; "Can't you do anything I tell you to?!"; "Now look. You've got the whole room in a mess"; "I don't like that").
- *Ignores inappropriate behavior* is noted when the parent makes no verbal or physical response to inappropriate child behavior. Healthy parenting involves finding a balance when helping the child to develop prosocial or effective instrumental behavior. Constant management of the child by the parent is authoritarian and limits independent negative consequences from arising that are unrelated to the parent involvement. Children are less likely to develop self-efficacy as a result. Instead, they are shaped only by the externalized reinforcement of the parent.

7. ENDING OF OBSERVATION PROCESS AND SCHEDULING OF LAST APPOINTMENTS WITH PARTIES

At the end of the observation, the parent receives no feedback about her or his performance. Instead, the evaluator reduces the possibility of later party complaint by asking the party to compare how the play seemed in contrast to play with the child at other times. At the end of the observational session, the evaluator schedules a final clinical interview that typically occurs 2–3 weeks after the last scheduled observation. If the Achenbach Child Behavior Checklist forms are not complete, the evaluator requests their completion before the party departs.

8. HOME VISITS

If there are allegations of an inadequate or unsafe home setting, then the evaluator schedules a home observation rather than an in-office one. Home visits are to be avoided, if at all possible, because they lack standardization that could influence clinical judgment and require more evaluator time than in-office observations. It most cases where allegations of neglect or lack of cleanliness have emerged, the child protective services of the jurisdiction has conducted an onsite inspection. The evaluator can learn from this collateral information whether the allegation is possibly founded. Other measures of the evaluation will help determine whether the party's disorganization is causing the slovenly conditions in a home.

The structure of the observation follows what was outlined above. If a home visit is scheduled for one of the parents, one must also be arranged for the other parent. Parallel conditions of the evaluation must continue throughout the process.

9. IMMEDIATE WRITING AFTER OBSERVATION AND WRITING OF PRELIMINARY EVALUATION REPORT

Evaluators should follow the advice in Practice Tip 3 and write further on the evaluation report immediately following each contact with a party. After completing both parent–child observations, the evaluator writes a draft evaluation report that includes preliminary findings and recommendations based on the test, interview, and observational data taken from both parents. This is accomplished before reviewing the documents provided by opposing counsel or contacting the professional collaterals (e.g., teachers, physicians, counselors) or nonprofessional collaterals (firsthand witnesses of parenting deficits or other behavior that would have a direct impact on parenting).

PRACTICE TIP 10
Report Writing

By the end of the parent–child observation phase of the evaluation, several opportunities will have arisen to corroborate each allegation. Evaluators should use the allegations that the parties have raised to direct the writing of the discussion and recommendations of the report. Fleshing out hypotheses with the data collected so far in the evaluation process will help construct the questions to pose to collateral reporters (other professionals who have been involved in the case before the evaluation; nonprofessionals who have observed firsthand evidence of parenting deficits or other behavior that would have a direct impact on parenting). Allegations that remain uncorroborated by psychological test results, interview data, or parent–child observation findings are less likely to be substantiated during the review of the legal documentation, past professional evaluations or treatment notes, and collateral interviews.

Writing the preliminary report at this juncture lessens the opportunity for an attorney to impugn the evaluator's credibility during cross-examination and negates any inference that the collateral evidence unduly influenced the evaluator and affected the independence of the evaluation. Parties may also view the process as "fairer" if the evaluator draws independent conclusions before incorporating the collateral information.

The preliminary report focuses on the consistency of the data across multiple collection points and emphasizes thorough documentation of information and sources. It notes discrepancies and any limitations of the data (e.g., problems with reliability or validity of testing). It addresses the threshold issues identified by party allegations through providing descriptions of relevant history about the psychological, familial, and individual aspects of the parties. The report outlines the parental strengths and weaknesses in enough detail to give sufficient evidence for a court to rule on arrangements that would serve the best interests of the child (Weissman, 1991; e.g., statutory directives about the factors to consider, Revised Code of Washington 26.09.184). The report also suggests who would best provide for the child's changing needs. Such approaches are designed to meet certain requirements set forth in the ethical standards 9.01 and 9.06 of the APA *Ethical Principles of Psychologists and Code of Conduct* (2002) and APA *Guidelines for Child Custody Evaluation in Divorce Proceedings* (1994), guidelines 3, 11–14.

If concerns about long-term emotional and physical disorders or substance abuse arise, then the evaluator describes in the report any impairment of parental skills. Diagnoses are avoided and instead specific behaviors are operationalized, with attention focused on how these behaviors affect current and future parenting competencies. Such behaviorally descriptive examples help the fact finder understand the complexities of the case and the impact of such behaviors on parenting capabilities. If the data corroborate allegations about impaired parental skills, the report provides recommendations for protecting a child from harmful parental involvement (such an approach is designed to meet the standards set forth in guidelines 3 and 14 of the APA *Guidelines for Child Custody Evaluation in Divorce Proceedings*, 1994). Based on the findings of the evaluation, the recommendations specify a residential placement site, a visitation schedule, the arrangements for future major decisions about the child, a process to resolve future disagreements, and the curricula of interventions that would lead to the remediation of parental weaknesses.

7

PHASE 4: CONTACTING COLLATERALS

In most cases, preparing for and conducting interviews with collateral sources ("collaterals") can be completed during one week. Allegations that either party has raised may be corroborated by evidence from collateral sources that have been involved with the family or the parties before the evaluation. Often the most compelling evidence in custody evaluations is those data that establish a long-term pattern of behavior. For instance, the collateral evidence in a case where a party alleged that the husband engaged in domestic violence included the following data: several declarations from friends who witnessed firsthand incidents of controlling and demeaning behavior that involved the husband being abusive in front of the children; a driving record that showed several infractions, including a "reckless endangerment of others" conviction; collateral interview statements from an ex-spouse that described explicit incidents of controlling behavior that were similar in nature to those reported by the friends (of the party) in their declarations and a description of an explosive outburst that led to the ex-spouse being choked (although she did not report the incident to the police, she provided an emergency room report about bruises on her neck); a work history pattern of many job changes for the husband; and a report from the supervisor of the job he last left stating that the husband had a short temper that often led to customer complaints. Coupled with psychological testing data and parent–child observation findings, sufficient evidence emerged from the evaluation to call for domestic violence treatment and supervised visitation with the children until the treatment produced enough change to warrant less restrictive visitation (see Practice Tip 10). The following procedures occur during this phase of the evaluation and are detailed below:

1. Build hypotheses and questions from the results of earlier measures.
2. Read the documentation and identify additional questions for specific collateral reporters.
3. Interview the collaterals using the specific questions generated.
4. Immediately write the summary of the interview, and send it to the collateral.
5. Insert the corrected collateral summaries into the report.
6. Insert any collateral evidence into the discussion.

1. BUILD HYPOTHESES AND QUESTIONS FROM THE RESULTS OF EARLIER MEASURES

Consistent examples of the allegations will have arisen during all parts of the process by the time the evaluator is ready to write the discussion section of the evaluation report. Reviewing the results of the various measures will assist the evaluator in discerning particular patterns of behavior. As the evidence converges from the various measures, the evaluator draws hypotheses about the allegations. Accurate conceptualizations about the psychological evidence that emerge from the evaluation process are one of the purposes of a well-written discussion section. All of the following sources of data may provide examples of the harmful behaviors of the parties that various collaterals have observed and can be further corroborated by them:

- The Parenting History Survey (PHS) questionnaire has prompted each party in several different ways to raise allegations and describe with some specific examples of the allegations and identify first-hand witnesses to the incidents.
- At the end of the psychosocial interview, each of the allegations raised by the party is identified. Relevant history about the psychological, familial, and individual aspects of the parties is shown to indicate pervasive patterns of behavior that underlie parenting weaknesses and strengths. Additional forms (see Appendix F) are provided to the party to flesh out all of the allegations by prompting both parties to provide

three of the worst examples for each allegation. With the party holding the form, the evaluator has modeled for the party how much specificity is required to assess properly the issues by further prompting the party with open-ended questions about the worst examples of the most alarming allegation. Copies of these samples have been sent home with the party to serve as models. Each party has returned the allegation forms, which should provide greater specificity to those allegations documented by the PHS. Discernible patterns of behavior should connect the testing, interview, and observational data with the data from the allegation forms as the incidents are described about the various allegations. After the psychosocial sections and allegations sections are written, both parties have reviewed, added, and returned additional data about their respective sections of these parts of the evaluation report. The additional data may also be a source for other questions to pose to the collaterals, if inconsistent information emerges.

- The results of the MMPI–2 data will raise further questions about the response sets of the parties and the parties' personality characteristics that may reflect parenting strengths and weaknesses.
- The data from parent–child observations and Achenbach measure testing also may have corroborated allegations or raised further issues that will generate questions to ask collaterals.

As the evaluator writes the allegation sections of the report, each type of allegation listed on the form provides a method for organizing the data that converge (see allegation forms in Appendix F for possible headings). In addition, the evidentiary standards of a particular jurisdiction may also suggest headings under which the evaluator can organize converging data (see the discussion sections of the sample evaluation reports in Part III of this book). To manage this process effectively, the evaluator builds separate documents simultaneously. As the discussion section is written, several other documents are prepared: questions for particular collaterals, questions for an adolescent or a significant other that could provide first-hand evidence, requests for clarifications from each party, and statements about independent evidence that led to particular findings for each party.

As the evaluator writes the rough draft of the discussion section, she or he remains mindful about identifying the following information so that facts can be double-checked during the review of the collateral information and during the collateral interviews: (a) allegations that lack any independent corroborating evidence, (b) the evaluator's hypotheses that have failed to be corroborated by at least two independent measures, (c) the earlier party statements about who would provide firsthand evidence about particular allegations or what professionals have heard, and (d) contemporaneous reports concerning an alleged incident that are not borne out by declarations from nonprofessionals or later collateral documentation or interviews. As discussed in chapter 2, clinical judgment is easily affected by poor evaluation methodology. Remaining skeptical about hypotheses that are generated will lead to more accurate results.

The next task for the evaluator is to build a list of open-ended questions that can be answered during document review and asked of each collateral during the interviews. In addition, the evaluator prepares some questions that will assist in assessing the collateral's objectivity and judgment based on their interactions with the party and relevant past professional experiences. As the evaluator reviews the collateral documentation, additional open-ended questions will become obvious, and the existing questions can be edited. For example, in the D. vs. M. case found in Part III, the following questions were prepared by the evaluator before Ms. C., MSW, was interviewed:

1. How would you characterize your interactions with A.?
2. How would you characterize your interactions with each of her parents?
3. What were your conclusions after evaluating A.?
4. What evidence led you to those conclusions?
5. What information did A. specifically share with you about her parents?
6. What evidence did you have that support the allegation that her father abused A.?
7. Did A. share information about her abuse without any prompting from her mother?
8. What do you recall about the reactions of her mother as A. shared her story?
9. Do you have any reason to believe that A. was told to say what she said?
10. What is your opinion regarding the level of emotional support provided to A. by each of her parents?
11. What do you believe are major issues that A. needs to address in psychotherapy?
12. How many years have you practiced as an MSW?
13. How many hours a week do you work with children from families involved in family law or dependency cases?
14. Do you have any specialized training in working with families that are involved in family law or dependency cases?

2. READ DOCUMENTATION AND IDENTIFY ADDITIONAL QUESTIONS FOR SPECIFIC COLLATERAL REPORTERS

Focusing on the questions for each collateral will save several hours of work for the evaluator as she or he reads through the documentation provided by the parties. The goal is to review the documentation only once and organize the notes so that a particular document can be easily found later. Sticking removable flags to the particular sections works best because they are easily removed if a party wants to copy the document. This prevents the undue attention of the lawyers being focused on particular sections of documents that the evaluator has reviewed.

Corroborated factual details will emerge from this process. Conflicting information also will stand out. The evaluator can design additional questions to ask the relevant collaterals to understand how inconsistencies in the data have emerged between collateral documentation and the evaluation results. An example of this is the information provided on the teacher's report form of the Achenbach measure (1991b). Such attention to these confirming and conflicting details will help ground the evaluator's clinical judgments, in part, on the verifiable observations of independent professionals. Any discrepancies may be the result of limitations in the manner of collecting the data (e.g., the credibility of a collateral because of limited objectivity or experience) or in the interpreting of the data (e.g., evaluator bias).

On occasion, an evaluator may contact nonprofessional collaterals (e.g., family members). They may be in a unique position to witness the behavior in question and can submit declarations about witnessed events related to harmful behavior that was directed at or might have affected the other party or children. Such interviews obtain as much specific detail as possible that can be corroborated by other independent measures. For instance, in domestic violence cases, nonprofessional collaterals may be able to describe the frequency, manner, and severity of the violence similarly to the reports of other collaterals. Such corroboration leads to firmer findings. Which collateral to contact depends on the nature of the allegations. For example, if one party alleges that the other abuses substances, then the evaluator may contact the party's employer, who may have noticed work-related consequences associated with substance abuse. Work-related effects of substance use provide strong evidence that a party has developed a dependency on substances. However, the evaluator should contact non-professionals with great care because of the likely discussions of sensitive information that result (such an approach is designed to meet certain requirements set forth in the ethical standard 4.04 of the APA *Ethical Principles of Psychologists and Code of Conduct*, 2002).

In the *D. vs. M.* case, a declaration from Mr. T., one of Mr. D.'s friends, had indicated that he detected alcohol on Ms. M.'s breath when she was at work. The following questions were prepared and asked of Ms. M.'s ex-supervisor at work:

1. Please describe your impressions of Ms. M. and the type of relationship you had with her.
2. How long did you supervise Ms. M.?
3. Did you have any concerns about Ms. M.?
4. Did her coworkers or customers raise any concerns about Ms. M.?
5. Did Ms. M. have any unexplained absences?
6. Did she ever return late for any of her breaks?
7. Did Ms. M. ever use alcohol while on the job?
8. Did you ever smell alcohol on her breath?
9. Did you ever see Ms. M. intoxicated on any other occasion?
10. Would you take her back as employee if she wanted to work for you again?

3. INTERVIEW THE COLLATERALS USING THE SPECIFIC QUESTIONS GENERATED

The evaluator contacts the collaterals, usually by telephone. The evaluator should leave a succinct message, if they cannot be reached directly. The evaluator identifies that she or he is calling for information about one of the collateral's clients, students, employees, and so forth, who has been ordered by the particular court to be evaluated by the evaluator. The evaluator leaves two or three time blocks during which the collateral or the assistant of the collateral can reach the evaluator directly to discuss the identity of the party and to receive a faxed release form signed by the party (Appendix G). These forms include an explanation of the purpose of the evaluation and a waiver of confidentiality. A 15-minute telephone appointment is left on the voice mail message or arranged during a conversation in the event of reaching someone in person.

On occasion, despite the interested party having signed a release form, a collateral reporter will refuse to be interviewed. If the interested party is unable to persuade the collateral to speak with the evaluator, the lawyers may be asked to intervene if the data likely to be obtained are significant. If the lawyers for the parties cannot persuade the collateral to talk voluntarily, the lawyers can depose the collateral. A copy of the deposition then is forwarded to the evaluator. When faced with the prospect of deposition, the occasional recalcitrant collateral usually agrees to talk with the evaluator without further involvement with the lawyers.

As noted above, the evaluator prepares for the interviews before talking with the collaterals. The evaluator asks open-ended questions of the collaterals while refraining from revealing information or sources of infor-

PRACTICE TIP 11
When to Interview Guardians ad Litem

In the cases in which guardians ad litem (GAL) are involved with the family, they are interviewed after all of the other collaterals because their impressions are likely to be more complete, given their experiences with the entire family. In particular, contradictions in the data are presented to the GAL for clarification. Besides the evaluator, the GAL will have formed the most global, objective impressions of the evidence related to the various allegations. Discrepancies in the findings of a GAL and the evaluator may be the result of limitations in the manner of collecting the data (e.g., the credibility of a collateral because of limited objectivity or experience) or in the interpreting of the data (e.g., bias). The evaluator seeks GAL clarification about any discrepant finding by inquiring about the specific evidence that corroborates the finding.

mation as much as possible. This approach will lead to fewer hard feelings on the part of the parties as they learn from the collaterals what occurred during the interviews. The evaluator should count on the parties contacting the collaterals to determine what transpired between the collaterals and the evaluator.

As the collateral responds to each question, the evaluator uses active listening skills, in particular reflective listening, to continue obtaining as much information about allegations as possible without unduly influencing the collaterals' responses. Such an approach protects from evaluator bias affecting the interview. More accurate clinical judgments are likely to be made about the collateral data as a result. During the interviews, as much as possible, the evaluator asks the collateral to provide examples of specific behavior. Rich conceptualizations about the parties and their relationships with the children become easier to develop as complicated interactions are operationalized.

4. IMMEDIATELY WRITE THE SUMMARY OF THE INTERVIEW AND SEND IT TO THE COLLATERAL

As soon as the interview is completed, the evaluator informs the collateral that a written summary of the interview will be faxed or electronically mailed to the collateral later that day. The collateral is asked to return the summary with any additions as soon as possible.

5. INSERT THE CORRECTED COLLATERAL SUMMARIES INTO THE REPORT

The evaluator inserts into the report the corrected collateral summaries. Although some of the collateral interview will not be reported in

By asking the collateral to review the summary of the interview and supplement the summary with any additions, the evaluator may gain further clarification about the facts that may not have arisen during the interview. In addition, such a review reduces the likelihood of a later party complaint that the evaluator misrepresented or failed to insert a detail that allegedly might have affected the outcome of the evaluation. Not only does this approach help to ensure that both parties will believe that they have been fairly and thoroughly evaluated, it produces a contemporaneous record of collateral satisfaction with the results of the interview. Such a practice minimizes a lawyer exploiting differences that may have arisen because of a nominal miscommunication at the time of the interview. Both ethical and malpractice risks are reduced accordingly.

the summary, the summary adequately reflects the entire interview. The evaluator leaves out any material that does not directly bear on the party allegations, or if reported, would not serve the best interests of the child (such an approach is designed to meet certain requirements set forth in the ethical standard 4.04 of the APA *Ethical Principles of Psychologists and Code of Conduct*, 2002).

6. INSERT ANY COLLATERAL EVIDENCE INTO THE DISCUSSION

Any collateral evidence that either confirms or strongly calls into question any of the hypotheses is incorporated into the discussion section. For instance, turning to the case in Part III, based on the questions described above for the collateral interviews of Ms. C. (the MSW) and Mr. F. (the supervisor of the adult establishment that Ms. M. worked in), the evaluator of the *D. vs. M.* case generated collateral evidence that corroborated two findings of the evaluation. A. and Ms. M. described to Ms. C. welts from a beating that did not differ from the statements they made in a police report a year earlier. In the interview with Mr. F., he reported no use of alcohol by Ms. M. during her employment. The adult entertainment establishment had conducted random urine analyses and breathalyser tests on its barkeeps. Ms. M. never tested positive for any substances, nor did Mr. F. ever observe Ms. M. intoxicated. None of the employees or customers had complained about Ms. M. in any respect. This evidence countered the declaration of Mr. T., Mr. D.'s friend.

The opinions of the professional collaterals and the evaluator sometimes differ. When they do, such as occurred somewhat between Ms. C. (the MSW) and the evaluator in the *D. vs. M.* case, the differences typically arise because of the other professional's limited exposure to the case in contrast to the evaluator's dozens of hours of exposure. Other differences in opinions about parental strengths and weaknesses tend to result from the professional's exposure to only one side of the available information or limited experience with family law and dependency cases. If the opinions of the professional collaterals and the evaluator differ, the evaluator delineates the differences in the final report and the evidence upon which the differing opinions are based. The evaluator remains particularly vigilant about her or his own bias under these circumstances.

8

PHASE 5: CLOSING INTERVIEWS AND DATA INTEGRATION

The final clinical interviews of the parties typically occur within the week following the last of the collateral interviews. After the evaluator integrates the collateral information into the next draft of the entire report, he or she does the following:

1. Identify conflicting details and prepare open-ended questions that would help clarify inconsistencies.
2. Interview any significant collateral immediately before the closing interview with the party most likely to apply pressure.
3. Make decisions about child interviews.
4. Interview the child with care.
5. Identify all of the findings about the party with the facts that support each finding.
6. Interview and report all findings about the party with the facts that support each finding.
   - Ask the party to respond to each statement precisely, without straying from the subject. If the party makes an admission, then ask him or her to provide two concrete examples of the behavior of the concern. Use the allegation forms to document the admissions.
   - Challenge any inconsistencies or discrepancies during this

second part of the closing interview. Box the party in and pierce denial and minimization by presenting the facts in an evenhanded manner.

- Prepare the party for the worst outcomes and provide him or her with the opportunity to express dissatisfaction with the evaluation process and to provide alternative explanations to account for the facts that the evaluation has gathered.
- Provide the parties with an additional week to submit contradictory evidence in declarations with releases so that you may talk to any new declarant that might emerge.

7. Insert admissions or other evidence that corroborates the findings into the final report.

1. IDENTIFY CONFLICTING DETAILS AND PREPARE OPEN-ENDED QUESTIONS THAT WOULD HELP CLARIFY INCONSISTENCIES

The closing interview consists of two discrete parts. The first part clarifies any details that are missing or are inconsistent with the findings of the evaluation. The second part is built around prestructured statements about what particular measures resulted in the evaluator reaching the various findings. During this second part of the interview, the party has an opportunity to examine how each of the findings was formed and comment about the details that led to the finding. This is the part of the process in which the parties learn about the findings about themselves that have emerged from the evaluation process.

As the evaluator integrates the material gleaned from the collateral process, conflicting factual details may still emerge. The evaluator prepares open-ended questions to clarify any inconsistencies that would help to elaborate assumptions or could explain inconsistencies. For example, in the D. v. M. case in Part III of this book, Mr. D. furnished a declaration written and sworn to by Mr. T. that he witnessed Ms. M. working in an adult entertainment establishment and thought he smelled alcohol on her breath at the time. Mr. D. also suspected he smelled alcohol on her breath several times when he arrived at her apartment. The evaluator asked the following questions of Mr. D. in the first part of the closing interview:

1. Please describe your relationship with Mr. T.
2. What type of relationship does he have with Ms. M.?
3. Are you aware of any procedures in the adult entertainment establishment that Ms. M. worked in that would show whether she was using substances?

PRACTICE TIP 13
Back-to-Back Interviews of Third Parties Easily Influenced

Because of the pressure that many parties will apply to an adolescent child or a significant other, interviews with these individuals occur the hour preceding the final interview with the party most likely to engage in such behavior. The evaluator can protect the adolescent or significant other from retribution by shielding the material learned during the interview with the child, if necessary. Rarely will the information from an adolescent or significant other deviate from facts gleaned with other measures. As a result, the party will hear about all of the other data that led to particular findings and will not come away from the final interview blaming the child or significant other for any of the findings.

4. Whom did you talk to about the alcohol on Ms. M.'s breath on the occasions you detected its presence?

Answers to questions of this type could lead to responses contradicting evidence arising from other sources.

In some cases, the evaluator may want to present hypothetical situations to assess parenting knowledge and skills relevant to the specific issues raised during the evaluation. For instance, if one party alleges that the other parent is easily embarrassed by the child in public settings and that this results in the parent responding harshly, the evaluator might ask that parent how he or she would respond to his or her 3-year-old child wanting something delectable in a grocery store and pitching a fit when the parent says "No, you cannot have it." The parent's response may provide more detail about the allegation that can be presented later during the closing interview. Such contemporaneous admissions, and reminders of such admissions, can lead to an easier acceptance of a finding.

2. INTERVIEW ANY SIGNIFICANT COLLATERAL IMMEDIATELY BEFORE THE CLOSING INTERVIEW WITH THE PARTY MOST LIKELY TO APPLY PRESSURE

The evaluator can further clarify contradictions of evidence if an adolescent child or a significant other, a possible first-hand witness of the interaction, is interviewed immediately before a particular party. For instance, some of the data produced for the evaluation in Part III of this book resulted from the evaluator asking Ms. S., Mr. D.'s significant other (who was interviewed before Mr. D.'s closing interview), about her relationship with Mr. T. and his reports to her regarding alcohol on Ms. M.'s breath. The evaluator asked what concerns Mr. D. typically expressed to her. Ms. S. reported that Mr. D. did not express any concerns to her. Later in the interview with Ms. S., after several other questions about her experience of Mr. D.'s parenting and discipline practices, the evaluator asked whether Ms. S. could list the concerns Mr. D. or she had about Ms. M. Ms. S. reported that she thought Ms. M. was a good mother and that the conflict arose between Mr. D. and Ms. M. because she was not a member of any Christian church. When pressed to identify any other concerns, she could not report any. Along with other corroborating evidence from other sources, the evaluator felt more confident that the allegation about Ms. M having an alcohol abuse problem appeared unfounded.

3. MAKE DECISIONS ABOUT CHILD INTERVIEWS

Typically, the evaluator does not interview a pre-adolescent child individually or even ask about their preferences for placement or visitation. This protects them from feeling responsible for any outcome associated with the evaluation (Melton et al., 1987), a developmentally plausible result. It also remains the best practice approach in light of the validity and reliability concerns adequately documented by the literature (Ceci & Bruck, 1993). Children in this type of context are highly suggestible. They are prone to inaccurate reports not only because of parental coaching but also many other factors (Ceci & Crotteau Huffman, 1997).

The evaluators may invite some adolescents, depending on the nature of their parents' allegations, to undergo psychological testing (e.g., the MMPI–A and Achenbach) and individual interviews following the interviews of all other collateral reporters and immediately preceding a closing interview with one of the parties. If sufficient evidence has emerged from all the other evaluation measures, the evaluator may not need to interview the adolescent and run the risk of colluding with the high-conflict process by involving the child as a witness against one or both parents. Quite typically, adolescents are placed in the middle of the conflict by parents, who use them as confidants, messengers, pawns, or warriors. Because of this possible pressure the interview occurs the hour preceding the final interview with the parent most likely to engage in such behavior. The evaluator can protect the adolescent from pressure or retribution by shielding the material learned during the interview with the child. Rarely will the adolescent's information deviate from facts gleaned with other measures. As a result, the parent will hear about all of the other data that led to particular findings and will not come away from the final interview blaming the child for any of the findings.

Interviews may seem necessary because the child was alleged to have observed or endured actual incidents that may provide evidence of parenting deficits, domestic violence, child abuse, or the use of high-conflict tactics. Evaluators should consider carefully whether the information was already divulged to another professional and whether a second interview will substantially improve the information already collected. In addition, focused information can be gathered from the particular child's school about the child's functioning and developmental needs. This is a specialty interview practice, and evaluators should have particular training in evaluating the context and developmental course of the child's behavior (Saywitz & Camparo, 1998).

4. INTERVIEW THE CHILD WITH CARE

Before conducting interviews with the adolescent, the evaluator cautions him or her that he or she is not responsible for any outcome of the evaluation. Using the analogy of a complicated jigsaw puzzle, the evaluator strongly indicates that the interview data to be gained from the adolescent will represent only a few pieces of the puzzle. The evaluator pointedly describes the other measures that will be relied on to form findings for the evaluation. Only children or adolescents with sufficient maturity to understand the caution should be interviewed. Asking the child to reiterate what you have just explained will help you determine whether the child understood the caution. It is also one way of assessing competency of the child to comprehend, process, and express specific, important information. This information may become useful later in determining how and if the child was able to observe and describe specific events that a party contends he or she allegedly witnessed.

The key to conducting child interviews is to maximize the child's level of comfort with the evaluator. Using a warm speaking voice with a smile generates a supportive environment that reduces the child's anxiety. It does not increase the child's suggestibility, and social psychological research suggests that it reduces anxiety, which can produce inaccurate reports. The evaluator gives the child permission to say what he or she wants and, more importantly, to indicate when he or she does not know the answer and that it is okay not to know the answer. The evaluator tells the child not to guess, stating "If I repeat a question, it's because I might have forgotten the answer and not because you gave the wrong answer," and "Correct me if I get it wrong."

Finally, the evaluator should check with the child to ensure that he or she knows the difference between imaginary and real events. The evaluator asks, "Please show me that you know the difference between imaginary and real events. If I told you a story about you and me going to the moon yesterday, would that be a real event or an imaginary one?" And, "If I told you that today you got in your Mom's car and rode here and came in the door over there and then you and I met each other for the first time, would that be a real or imaginary event?" After the child answers, the evaluator asks, "Please focus all of your comments during our interview on real events that you personally have seen or heard." Such an instruction also suggests that the evaluator wants the child to focus only on first-hand information. (Evaluator can modify instructions as appropriate for younger children.)

While meeting with the child, the evaluator may focus on information about the family to see if the child understands the dynamics of his or her family and the family's contribution to the evaluation (see Appendix H for an example of an adolescent interview). As much as possible, the evaluator uses open-ended questions to encourage disclosure that are uncontaminated by the evaluator (e.g., "Tell me about your mom and dad." "What do you like about your mom?" "When you're sick, what happens to you?"). Use close-ended questions when you are trying to narrow in on issues that require detail (e.g., "When you heard your mom cry, were you upstairs or downstairs?"). Leading questions that include the content and the answer in the question are avoided (e.g., "Your mom really told you to say that, didn't she?"). Additional questions for the adolescent may focus on daily routines, care-taking practices, soothing practices, and the person that the child relies on for care and reassurance. The evaluator may also look for subject matter that the older child or adolescent is avoiding.

5. IDENTIFY ALL OF THE FINDINGS ABOUT THE PARTY WITH THE FACTS THAT SUPPORT EACH FINDING

The second part of the closing interview is built around the evaluator reporting each of the corroborated facts about the various findings (such an approach is designed to meet certain requirements set forth in the ethical standard 9.10 of the APA *Ethical Principles of Psychologists and Code of Conduct*, 2002). This is usually the most difficult part of the evaluation process for the evaluator. If performed effectively, these statements about the facts supporting the findings will lead to the party making admissions. The evaluator challenges any inconsistencies or discrepancies during this closing interview. The evaluator does this, in part, to test the parent's judgment and his or her response to factual information that is likely to make them uncomfortable. In effect, the evaluator uses the independent facts about a finding to box in the party and pierce the party's defenses of denial and minimization. This final interview prepares the parties for the worst of outcomes, provides an opportunity for them to offer alternative explanations or facts about the findings, allows them to express their dissatisfaction with the evaluation process, and permits an expression of their feelings. This step appears to lessen the anger of the parties and may be integral in diminishing the likelihood of an ethical complaint. After this step, the parties usually believe they have had a full, fair opportunity to dispute any evidence that emerges from the evaluation process.

In preparing the statements, the evaluator recites only the facts that have emerged from the corroboration of at least two independent measures (such an approach is designed to meet certain requirements set forth in the ethical standards 3.04, 9.01, and 9.06 of the APA *Ethical Principles of Psychologists and Code of Conduct*, 2002 and the guidelines 3, 11, 12, and 13 of the APA *Guidelines for Child Custody Evaluation in Divorce Proceedings*, 1994). The party is asked to respond to each statement precisely, without straying from the subject. After each question or statement that the evaluator makes, the evaluator provides an opportunity for the party to respond. For example, the statements about the facts regarding the allegation in Part III that Mr. D. engaged in domestic violence were prepared as follows:

1. Mr. D. is it true that you engage in domestic violence?
2. You reported to me in our first interview that your temper is "always in control and never flared." I've learned otherwise during this evaluation. Are you sure you did not engage in domestic violence?
3. The results of your psychological testing, specifically the findings of the MMPI, place you squarely in that population of people who harbor chronic, intense anger. Such people appear overcontrolled, but occasions arise when they are unable to inhibit violent outbursts. Isn't this what happened when you, after a period of pressure-cooking in stressful situations, erupted without thinking through the consequences of your actions?
4. Don't you use physical punishment against A. and have struck her several times with a belt?
5. Do you deny that, on occasion, these blows caused welts?
6. Isn't it true that you have acted in a similar manner with her other half-siblings on many other occasions?
7. A.'s consistent answers to the police, CASA interviewer (a volunteer who serves as an investigator for courts in some of the jurisdictions), and her counselor when asked about the marks were that you "whopped her" and caused the welts. Are you saying she's not telling the truth?
8. When the police asked the other children in your household what happened, they reported that you "whopped" them both with the belt and with your hand. Didn't they tell the truth to the police?
9. Though you have never denied to me that you were the one who left the welts and bruises on your daughter, you did deny doing so to the police, CASA interviewer, and A.'s counselor. Weren't you the one who caused those welts and bruises?

10. You know that Ms. M. had to seek medical attention for A.'s welts. Are you saying A.'s report to the medical authorities that you "whopped" her is a lie?
11. Isn't it true that you struck Ms. S. with a baseball bat and pulled her hair such that the investigating detective found a clump of her hair at the site of your battering?
12. As part of this incident, Ms. S. reported that you tried to burn the apartment, an accusation written up by the arresting officer at the time of the battering. Are you saying Ms. S. made this up?
13. At an independent evaluation, a domestic violence evaluator found you a candidate likely to benefit from treatment. Are you saying that this independent evaluation is wrong?

Each of the other findings is detailed in a similar manner so that the evaluator can present the complete evidence to the party to either gain an admission, or at least provide notice as to the outcomes of the parenting evaluation.

6. INTERVIEW AND REPORT ALL FINDINGS ABOUT THE PARTY WITH THE FACTS THAT SUPPORT EACH FINDING

Before beginning the interview, the evaluator provides an oral disclosure about the closing interview process. The evaluator describes the two parts of the process as follows:

> I am going to first ask you questions about issues that need some clarification. After this part of the closing interview, we then will get to the tough part of the process. I will lay out the evidence collected during the entire evaluation about the other party's allegations regarding you. Please respond to each statement and question. Respond precisely to each question. Please try to stay on the subject. We have a lot to cover during this closing interview. If you are not responsive to this question, I will interrupt you, make another statement, and ask another question. Please remember that the evaluation is a parallel process. The other party will go through the same process. I need to ask you about the findings regarding you to ensure that the judge will receive a complete picture.

Using this additional oral disclosure, the evaluator starts with the finding about the most harmful allegation and proceeds to recite the evidence, one statement and question at a time. The evaluator's demeanor remains objective and professional. No matter what the provocation from the party, the evaluator maintains this composure. We recommend that the closing interviews be videotaped, too. Most parties remain under control under these conditions. If necessary, provide a disturbed party with a break before continuing the closing process of discussing the evidence. On his or her return, to help the party understand a finding about emotional liability, the evaluator can replay the tape to show the party the section in which he or she became overwhelmed before continuing the interview. Often the demonstrative evidence will calm the party as she or he admits to the lack of control so evidently captured by the camera.

If the evaluator gains an admission, ask the party to provide two concrete examples of the behavior in concern. Evaluators should use the allegation forms (Appendix F) to document the admissions and praise the party specifically for his or her honesty and forthright admissions. If the party remains in denial about the particular finding, evaluators should wrap up the discussion about the finding by concluding that nothing the party said has changed the finding and immediately move to discussing the statements and questions about the next finding. Sometimes despite many independent facts that corroborate the finding, a party will categorically deny their import and the finding itself. At the end of the closing interview, if a party wants to add evidence, allow the party one week to submit contradictory evidence in declarations, with releases so that the evaluator may talk to a new declarant who might emerge, if necessary.

7. INSERT ADMISSIONS OR OTHER EVIDENCE THAT CORROBORATES THE FINDINGS INTO THE FINAL REPORT

The evaluator keeps up the gentle discipline of working on the evaluation report immediately on completion of each closing interview. The evaluator incorporates into the final evaluation report all of the admissions of the parties and other evidence that corroborates the findings. She or he also has rewritten any parts of the discussion section that lack sufficient support or that have been called into question by party explanations.

9

PHASE 6: PRESENTATION TO COURT

The following procedures occur during this phase of the evaluation:

1. Prepare for case review with the attorneys.
2. Meet with the attorneys of the parties (and the guardian ad litem [GAL], if one has been assigned).
3. Prepare and act as an expert witness during discovery.
4. Prepare and act as an expert witness during trial.
5. Meet with a party that requests more interaction about the findings of the evaluation after a final settlement or court order is issued.

1. PREPARE FOR CASE REVIEW WITH THE ATTORNEYS

The purpose of the review is to encourage the attorneys to reach a settlement based on the substantiated facts of the case and the credibility of the evaluator. An appointment with the attorneys (or, if one or both of the parties are *pro se*, with that party or parties) is arranged by telephone call. Such a meeting is best scheduled in the early morning or late afternoon to avoid scheduling conflicts with trial calendars. Confirmation that the attorney is able to attend the meeting is requested. In addition, the evaluator informs the attorneys that neither of the parties should be present at this meeting unless one of the parties is *pro se*. Settlement negotiations are more likely to occur faster if the attorneys are denied the opportunity to posture because of the presence of one or both of their clients.

If no confirmation occurs, the evaluator faxes, e-mails, or sends by certified mail a request for the meeting to each attorney. If the evaluator is unable to arrange the meeting, he or she mails out the report, a copy of the Agreement to Parenting Evaluation (see Appendix A) that the parties have signed, and the evaluator's curriculum vitae (without the evaluator's social security number or home address to maintain privacy) to both attorneys (and GAL, if one exists). The evaluator sends the Agreement to Parenting Evaluation because it outlines the retainer arrangements that are required to be made if discovery occurs.

If the meeting is to occur, a copy of the evaluator's resume and the final report are made for each attorney or *pro se* participant. In the final report, the evaluator highlights no more than three to four sentences for each finding that describe each measure that produced the particular evidence that led to the finding. In addition, the evaluator organizes the evaluation file by the order in which the various sections of the report are written sequentially. For instance, the notes of the collateral interviews and any additions provided by the collaterals are organized in the same order that the interviews are written in the report. This permits the evaluator to find a particular source document if it becomes necessary to do so during the discussion of the evaluation with the attorneys. Yellow tags can be left in the documents where particular evidence was taken. These tags can be removed, if later the document is requested for copying or examination. Such a process prevents undue attention being placed on a particular section of a document by an attorney if a record is later reviewed. The more organized the evaluator appears to the attorneys, the more the attorneys will view the evaluator as credible. Interested readers are referred to Ziskin and Faust (1995) for additional detail about presenting information to attorneys.

2. MEET WITH THE ATTORNEYS OF THE PARTIES

At the meeting with the attorneys, the evaluator remains uninfluenced by the situational demands that can lead the evaluator into being viewed as simply another advocate. In particular, the evaluator's demeanor should not change, no matter what question is asked. The evaluator best assists the attorneys to understand the psychological evidence that emerges during the evaluation by adhering to an educational role. The evaluator's demeanor remains professional and matter-of-fact throughout the review of the evaluation.

Five tasks occur during this meeting: (a) Credentials are provided, (b) methodology of the evaluation is described sequentially, (c) allegations

PRACTICE TIP 14
Emphasizing Neutrality

If one or both of the attorneys refuse to attend the attorney meeting, under no circumstances should the evaluator have contact with either of them until the case has been settled or discovery and trial are to occur. Out-of-court statements can be used to impeach the evaluator's credibility later. Therefore, the evaluator declines to make any statements unless both attorneys are present or one attorney has retained the evaluator as expert witness. The evaluator is viewed as an expert witness by the authority of the stipulated agreement or by the order appointing the evaluator. One or both of the lawyers can call this status into question at trial.

and findings are briefly discussed, (d) the report is distributed, and (e) attorney (or *pro se* litigant) questions are answered. The first four parts of the review take no longer than 30 minutes to hold the attention of the attorneys and to set an orderly foundation for their questions. The attorneys are asked to hold their questions until this time.

First, the evaluator describes the educational degree(s) and license(s) held; teaching experience; number of lifetime hours conducting evaluations and therapy of children, families, and adults; and the number of hours spent on the case. The curriculum vita is usually distributed without additional comment.

Second, the evaluator outlines the procedures of the evaluation. He or she emphasizes the best-practice standard of arriving at a finding about a particular allegation only after multiple measure corroboration has occurred. Third, the evaluator discusses the allegations and findings. He or she summarizes each allegation and briefly describes what measures led the evaluator to reach the finding. As the evaluator discusses the findings, counsel has an opportunity to view the demeanor of the evaluator and the plausibility of the conclusions.

Fourth, the evaluator distributes the report to the attorneys and asks them to turn to the beginning page of the recommendations. The attorneys are urged to read the recommendations and to begin asking their questions when they are ready. Until a direct question is asked of the evaluator, she or he remains silent. Often, the attorneys will begin to address each other or make statements about the report. To maintain the role of an educator, the evaluator remains detached from this type of attorney interaction.

Finally, an attorney will ask the evaluator a direct question. If applied, the following suggestions will help the evaluator educate the attorneys during responses and avoid raising doubts about the evaluator's credibility or knowledge (Bennett, Bryant, VandenBos, & Greenwood, 1990; Luvera, 1981; Pappas, 1987; Watson, 1978):

- Answer questions directly and concisely without volunteering unsolicited information. If a "yes" or "no" will suffice, say no more, but if an answer requires qualification, you're not compelled to give more than a simple response.

- Respond to understandable questions only: Paraphrasing a confusing question may suggest an entirely different matter unrelated to the attorney's inquiry. Ask that the lawyer state the question differently.

- Draw reasonable inferences between the data of the case and your expert knowledge: This type of opinion evidence is based on reasonable psychological probability and is not subject to the stringent demands of scientific validity or reliability.

- Use plain language: Explain all technical terms, so that a lay, undereducated audience would understand. Also, avoid using extreme adjectives or superlatives.

- Refrain from stating that any single article or text is authoritative, or you will be viewed as having relied explicitly on the article or text to formulate opinions. Opposing counsel may use any part of such an article or text to impeach your credibility then or later during discovery (described below) or at trial.

Attorneys may seek to test the credibility of the evaluator by using any of the following strategies: First, one of the attorneys (usually the attorney who perceives that her or his client has fared worse) may skip from one subject to the next in attempt to keep the evaluator off balance. To handle this, the evaluator keeps the points above in mind as responses are given. The examiner can also slow attorneys down by having them point out the specific area of the report that they are referring to, or provide a broader reiteration of the question. Second, attorneys may summarize the evaluator's finding inaccurately, using connotative words or shading the wording to their advantage (e.g., "So doctor, you say here that the other party *hesitated* to answer some of your questions; what explains that kind of arrogance?"). The evaluator corrects the summary and addresses the question at hand specifically by listing each measure that led to the particular finding being corroborated. Attention to detail and the meaning of words is critical (given that many terms have independent legal significance apparent only to attorneys). Third, an attorney may ask compound questions that assume facts not raised by either party during the pendency of the evaluation. The evaluator separates the unproven assumptions to avoid the taint of speculation and simply states that either party—despite many opportunities to do so—did not raise the issue during the evaluation. Fourth, questions involving a period of time are particularly difficult, and any answer should be labeled as an estimate. For instance, an attorney might ask how long the parties should remain in coparent counseling (see

Part III in the recommendations section of the sample reports), but too many intervening factors would influence the course of coparent counseling to allow anything but an estimate.

At the end of the questions, the evaluator instructs the attorneys to take a copy of the report for review. The evaluator also suggests that if further questions arise after their review and initial settlement negotiations, then they can arrange a conference call that includes both of them (and the GAL, if one has been appointed). Such a call would encourage further settlement discussions by addressing issues that the attorneys have been unable to resolve. Once again, during this telephone call, the evaluator serves as an educator (not as a mediator) and does not talk unless a specific question is asked. Finally, the evaluator reminds the attorneys that if the evaluator were to serve as an expert witness during discovery or trial be-cause the settlement process has failed, the evaluator would require an additional retainer. The evaluator provides the attorneys the Agreement to Parenting Evaluation (see Appendix A) signed by the parties and asks them to notify her or him about what additional process will occur so that the amount of the retainer can be given at that point in time.

Sometimes, neither attorney will ask questions. In this case, the evaluator thanks the attorneys for coming to the meeting and reviews the material mentioned in the last paragraph.

3. PREPARE AND ACT AS AN EXPERT WITNESS DURING DISCOVERY

In some cases, the attorney meeting may precipitate—or fail to avert —a formal discovery process. The evaluator might receive interrogatories (written questions that when answered provide an authenticated set of responses) or appear at a deposition (arranged by a subpoena or informally by agreement among all the parties) where questions are asked before a court reporter. Both approaches to discovery may occur.

Discovery is a preliminary process for eliminating the least pertinent issues of a case to narrow the dispute. Very specific questions are asked of the evaluator for the following reasons: (a) to explore and obtain more information about the evaluation findings, (b) to seek further clarification about how the findings were reached, (c) to assess the credibility of the evaluator by probing for the weaknesses about the evaluation's methodology and findings or about the persona of the evaluator, and (d) to create an authenticated record that can be used during cross-examination to im-peach the evaluator during trial.

Usually, an attorney for one party will send a letter stating that the matter requires adjudication either through a trial or an alternative dispute resolution process (mediation or arbitration) and arranging for discovery.

The evaluator calls the opposing counsel to remind the opposing counsel of the fee arrangements set out in the Agreement for Parenting Evaluation (see Appendix A). No work should occur on the interrogatories unless the retainer is paid. Nor should the evaluator attend the deposition unless the retainer for the preparation of expert witness testimony and a retainer to cover the estimated time to provide testimony at the deposition are paid.

In preparing for discovery, the evaluator talks with the employing lawyer. This is usually the attorney representing the party who would obtain the greatest number of days of residential placement during the year. The evaluator addresses the following: What are the issues the opposing party disagrees with or believes are irresolvable? What information was produced by discovery since the evaluation report was given to the attorneys that raises questions about the evaluation's findings? and What types of issues are likely to arise during the deposition given the settlement discussions that occurred between the two attorneys? In addition, the lawyer can clarify any procedural nuances of the jurisdiction regarding interrogatories or deposition. Discovery questions can often be anticipated based on these points, and the evaluator prepares to provide sufficient testimony by reviewing the evaluation report and the entire evaluation record.

Interrogatories are rarely used in family law cases. This is particularly true after both lawyers have had an opportunity to scrutinize the evaluator during the attorney meeting. Nevertheless, some lawyers will use interrogatories to prepare for a later deposition. Answers to the questions of the interrogatories are written concisely and remain consistent with the evaluation report and the record amassed during the evaluation. The evaluator continues to specifically review the relevant text of the evaluation report or a particular document being relied on to answer each interrogatory question.

Depositions are more likely to occur than interrogatories. However, as an evaluator becomes more known in the community, the attorneys'

PRACTICE TIP 15
Handling a *Subpoena Duces Tecum*

If an attorney sends a *subpoena duces tecum* (an order that demands the evaluator's presence and records at a certain location, date, and time) to the evaluator without arranging for the payment of the retainer, the evaluator sends a declaration to both opposing counsel and the judge in the case specifying that a retainer policy was established by the Agreement to Parenting Evaluation (see Appendix A). The declaration should also state that neither a record review nor a deposition would occur until the retainer is paid as called for by this contract signed by both parties. Such a declaration (see Appendix I) will inform the court as to the existence of contract language that should be considered during a motion to compel that is likely to be brought by the attorney who sent the *subpoena duces tecum*. Judges usually enforce contracts if properly appraised of the facts.

meeting following the evaluation will be viewed as a cost-effective, time-saving method by which to narrow the issues in dispute. This approach will result in the evaluator having to appear at fewer depositions and trials as her or his work becomes known throughout the legal community.

Generally, the people present during the deposition will include the opposing counsel, the employing attorney, and a court reporter. The court reporter is also a notary public who will administer the oath. Sometimes, one or both of the parties may attend. In addition, the opposing counsel may employ an expert witness to be present. This expert would suggest lines of inquiry based on an earlier review of the evaluation, discovery documents, and the evaluator's answers at the deposition. The opposing counsel's expert also may assist in assessing the qualifications, capabilities, and demeanor of the evaluator.

Deposition is a formal process that results in a transcribed record that can be used in an exacting manner described above as the case moves forward. Under the rules in most jurisdictions, the deposition can proceed in any manner and to whatever extent that the opposing attorneys agree on. The rules do not limit the number or length of depositions. The deposition is usually scheduled during business hours in the conference room at the opposing attorney's office or conference room at the courthouse. The evaluator always can request that the place and the time of the deposition be changed. Most attorneys will accommodate the demands of an evaluator's schedule and will provide breaks from the deposition. If the lawyer insists on meeting on a certain day and time that is inconvenient for the evaluator, the evaluator states in a faxed letter, e-mail note, or certified letter to the attorneys the reason why she or he cannot attend on the particular date and offers two or three alternative dates. The letter will show that the evaluator has acted reasonably if a later declaration becomes necessary to send to the court after a motion to compel is filed by opposing counsel.

The evaluator can bring anything that may assist at the deposition, including refreshments. The entire case file should be present so that an evaluator can refer to specific documents and the evaluator's notes. Any pause during the deposition will not be noted on the transcript. The break in the action provides the evaluator an opportunity to reflect on certain questions by looking at the record.

PRACTICE TIP 16
Scheduling Depositions and Trial Appearances

Evaluators should schedule deposition or trial appearances for the afternoon hours. This will lead to the evaluator not having to testify for more than 4 hours for any given appearance on that day. In addition, the evaluator could easily take at least three breaks during a 4-hour appearance. A tired evaluator is likely to make mistakes during testimony.

At the beginning of the deposition, an oath is administered to the evaluator, and the opposing counsel will provide some basic instructions about the process before starting the questioning. Every word uttered becomes part of a record unless both attorneys agree to stop recording the action. As noted above, pauses are not noted unless the opposing attorney notes the length of the pause for the record; most attorneys will not do so.

Along with the suggestions made above about evaluator performance at the attorneys' meeting, the following suggestions will help the evaluator educate the attorneys and avoid colluding with an adversarial process by raising questions about the evaluator's credibility or knowledge (Bennett et al., 1990; Luvera, 1981; Pappas, 1987; Watson, 1978):

- Wait until after consulting with the employing counsel during a break from the deposition if an earlier incomplete or incorrect answer requires greater explanation—the lawyer will know best when to return to the line of questioning, if ever.
- Draw reasonable inferences between the data of the case and expert knowledge—this type of opinion evidence is based on reasonable psychological probability and is not subject to the stringent demands of scientific validity or reliability.
- Answer questions about information within any document or text only after the passage in question is read by the evaluator carefully—a refreshed recollection will provide more accurate answers and avoid the opposing counsel's trap of exposing memory deficits when questioning you about the entire document or text.

Generally the employing attorney will participate very little during the deposition. However, he or she will follow the opposing counsel's questioning and instruct the evaluator not to answer certain questions or object to them. The judge will rule on the objections at a later date.

At depositions and at trials, the attorneys may raise objections about the technicalities of the rules of evidence. The primary reason for objections is to keep the irrelevant or immaterial information from being discussed in front of the judge or fact finders. The verdict must be based solely on the evidence presented at trial. The attorneys will manage the presentation of the evidence, in part, by arguing that certain information should be excluded or included according to their interpretation of the rules of evidence. The evaluator stops talking immediately when the employing attorney interrupts. Argument and contention are left to the attorneys. Later, the attorneys must persuade the judge as to the proper evidentiary ruling. Some of the argument and objections may feel as if they are addressed to the evaluator personally. During the wrangling of the attorneys, the evaluator can use the interruption to think carefully and form an accurate response. If at anytime during the deposition the evaluator wishes to consult with the employing attorney, the rules do not preclude taking a recess. A break will permit the evaluator to regain composure as well as a chance to suggest possible areas in the testimony that could be stated more accurately. The employing attorney may wish to redirect the questioning at the earliest possible occasion after the break so that the responses are included within the record.

At the end of the deposition, the opposing counsel will often attempt to foreclose modifications of the record or additional comment by asking the expert to waive the right to read and vouch for the transcript's accuracy. Retain the right to make changes so that transcription inaccuracies or substantive inaccuracies can later be corrected. In making changes, the evaluator states the reason for the changes, attaches the changes as an appendix, and signs the deposition. A time limit is set by which the expert has to make changes and return them to the court reporter for filing with the court. Make sure to find out about this time limit for the jurisdiction involved. Unless the evaluator returns the transcript within the time period, an unsigned, uncorrected copy of the deposition will be filed with the court. It is best to return the corrections as soon as possible to limit the effects of time on the evaluator's memory and to continue to appear very professional.

4. PREPARE AND ACT AS AN EXPERT WITNESS DURING TRIAL

The evaluator prepares for trial in the same manner recommended above for deposition. It is advisable for the evaluator to reread the entire evaluation report before the afternoon of trial testimony.

Testimony at trial will begin with the employing counsel establishing the qualifications of the evaluator as an expert witness on direct examination. The attorney will ask for a full description of the academic degrees, evidence of specialization, current duties of employment, honors, number and content publications, and previous practical applications of expertise. However, no particular set of criteria exists to establish whether an expert is qualified to provide testimony about family law cases. In general, qualification occurs without difficulty because the expert's credentials were accepted at the onset of the evaluation.

If qualification becomes an issue, the opposing counsel will object that the expert is not qualified and cannot state an opinion. Trial strategy dictates inflicting damage to the credibility of the witness as soon as possible. The opposing counsel will ask the court to conduct a *voir dire* (a preliminary examination to determine the competency of an expert or other witness) with an evaluator before proceeding in an attempt to persuade the judge that the person is not an expert. Even if the judge qualifies the evaluator, the opposing counsel may focus on the supposed inadequacy of the evaluator's credentials or lack of experience conducting family law evaluations to dampen the effect of the evaluator's direct testimony.

Direct examination continues after the evaluator is qualified as an expert. The employing attorney asks open-ended questions to enable the evaluator to convey opinions and the rationale behind them. The employing attorney must not ask leading questions. The evaluator discusses in advance with the employing attorney how the testimony will unfold; the approach used during the attorneys' meeting (see above) can be used again during this part of process.

Parsimonious testimony will help to keep the judge focused on the issues. If the evaluator can establish eye contact with the judge and the judge seems comfortable with such contact, eye contact also may help to keep the attention of the judge. The evaluator testifies in plain language avoiding technical words, assumptions not supported by an earlier foundation, or concepts that assume the judge's knowledge of the evaluation report. All opinions are supported with full descriptions of the data, the gathering techniques, and the inferences drawn from the corroboration of measures. In addition, the evaluator identifies all vulnerable portions of the assessment process or analyses of the results. The testimony remains consistent with the evaluation report, interrogatory responses, or deposition statements.

After direct examination is finished, the opposing counsel will begin cross-examination. The evaluator will often be limited to responding "yes" or "no" to the leading questions of the opposing counsel. In this respect, testifying during cross-examination might appear easier than during direct examination. However, opposing counsel will attempt to discredit the evaluator and the evaluator's findings by using tactics described above. A typical attack on the evaluator's credibility will occur as the opposing counsel asks leading questions about the independence of the evaluator and the thoroughness of the evaluation process. Opposing counsel may allege that financial considerations have biased the evaluator. Procedures described above about billing and collecting retainers prevent this type of attack.

Another typical attempt to question the evaluator's thoroughness occurs when the opposing counsel cites inconsistent testimony. The opposing counsel often presents examples of inconsistent testimony unfairly. If the cross-examiner reads from an interrogatory or deposition transcript to show the inconsistency, the material often is taken out of context. Certainly the evaluator can ask to review the document or deposition transcript before responding to the cross-examination question. If the matter has been taken out of context, the evaluator can so state. Such a remark might lead the employing attorney to make an objection if the opposing attorney attempts to close off any elaboration by insisting that the evaluator simply answer the leading question with a "yes" or "no."

Yet another typical method by which opposing counsel attempts to impeach the expert's credibility is to claim a lack of foundation for the evaluator's opinion. The opposing counsel may challenge the evaluator's thoroughness by questioning whether the evaluator omitted certain facts or relied on the wrong facts to form opinions. The evaluator can remind opposing counsel that her or his party had many opportunities to correct or expand the data, and the party failed to do so during the pendency of the evaluation. The evaluator can remind the court that each party completed the Parenting History Survey, which prompted the party in several different ways to raise allegations and specifically describe examples of the allegations. At the end of the psychosocial interview, each of the allegations raised by the party were itemized and detail was specifically requested again. Afterward, the party reviewed and amended the psychosocial history and allegation sections of the evaluation. The party also said that the parent–child observation reflected accurately the party's behavior with her or his child. The reporters approved all of the collateral interviews that were summarized for the report. During the closing interview, the party had further opportunity to contest each of the findings and provide alternative explanations to counter how multiple measures led to the corroborated findings. Judges uniformly are impressed with such thoroughness and attempts to maintain a fair process.

Leading questions can be irritating because they paint a black-and-white picture while leaving little room for accurate explanations. Often, the opposing counsel intends to increase the frustration level of the evaluator and perhaps even provoke an outburst that would compromise the evaluator's professional demeanor. When the opposing counsel allows the evaluator to provide a fuller explanation about a particular issue, the purpose is to lead the evaluator away from the basic facts of the case and give full rein to the expert's pride and wordiness to possibly place her or him in a bad light. Behaving as an educator and as an objective professional can be difficult when being grilled and set up by a good cross-examiner. The best course is to avoid arguing or appearing as a staunch advocate. Instead the evaluator should remain polite, cooperative, and answer all the questions directly and dispassionately.

At the end of the cross-examination, the employing attorney will conduct a redirect examination. Once again the questions will be open-ended and provide the evaluator an opportunity to explain points raised during the cross-examination that may have been misleading or left an incomplete impression because of the expert's brief and simple responses. Often a recess will occur before redirect examination begins. The employing attorney may have suggestions about what points raised during the earlier cross-examination require clarification or emphasis.

5. MEET WITH A PARTY THAT REQUESTS MORE INTERACTION ABOUT THE FINDINGS OF THE EVALUATION AFTER A FINAL SETTLEMENT OR COURT ORDER IS ISSUED

Sometimes a party will want additional time to meet with the evaluator after the settlement or trial. In fact, the Agreement to Parenting Evaluation (Appendix A) suggests that such a meeting is possible. It is strongly recommended that the evaluator conduct such a meeting for two reasons. First, a party can gain closure about the evaluation process in such a meeting, and this closure reduces the risk of an ethical complaint being filed. Second, the party can gain additional information about the evaluation findings that may help the party to understand how to more effectively coparent with the other party.

In most such meetings, the party will raise concerns about evidence that, in her or his view, the evaluator disregarded. The evaluator matter-of-factly reviews the evaluation process and reminds the party that he or she had several opportunities to correct the record or provide additional evidence. The evaluator continues to discuss the findings as they are presented in the evaluation. Often the party will attempt to introduce new evidence of the misbehavior of the other party. It is best to point out that the issue was not raised during the evaluation and that future conflicts between the parties are to be worked out through the alternative dispute resolution process recommended by the evaluation and ordered by the court.

III

ANNOTATED REPORT OUTLINE AND SAMPLE EVALUATION REPORTS

ANNOTATED REPORT OUTLINE AND SAMPLE EVALUATION REPORTS: INTRODUCTION

The evaluation process, the report as an outcome, and a reflection of the evaluation are driven and shaped by party allegations. Allegations will undoubtedly prompt assessment of (a) each adult's capacity for parenting, (b) the psychological functioning and developmental needs of each child, and (c) the relative ability of each parent to meet the needs of the child. In fact, any unresolved allegation about either party is assessed so that sufficient data are sought during the evaluation to arrive at an understanding as to how the particular allegation may affect the parenting of a particular party (such an approach meets the APA *Guidelines for Child Custody Evaluation in Divorce Proceedings*, 1994, guideline 8). Unevaluated allegations, or an inadequate description about their assessment, will deter settlement.

To avoid this pitfall, the report is structured to serve effectively in the legal context (such an approach meets the guidelines established by the APA *Ethical Principles of Psychologists and Code of Conduct*, 2002, 2.01e, 3.04, 9.01, and 9.06 and APA *Guidelines*, 1994, guidelines 3, 11–14). The format and the structure of the report are designed to highlight the convergent measures that enable the evaluator to demonstrate whether any particular allegation has merit.

In this part of the book, readers can first review the annotated structure of a typical evaluation report. After this review, an actual comprehensive evaluation follows so that readers can view how the details of an evaluation are treated in report form. The evaluation report and the two separate discussion sections are compilations of several evaluations conducted by the trainees of Dr. Benjamin's training program. All identifying data about the families or individuals are changed so that no one can be singled out by readers of this book.

10

ANNOTATED STRUCTURE OF A PARENTING EVALUATION REPORT

PARENTING EVALUATION

Referral Source and Purpose

The evaluator writes this section before starting the first interviews. Writing each section of the report as the evaluation process occurs will increase the accuracy of the report. The evaluator details the information in the stipulated agreement or the court order. The names, ages, and relationship of everyone who is to be evaluated and the purpose of the evaluation are identified. If a reader cannot form a clear picture of the purpose of the evaluation by reading this section, then the stipulated agreement or the court order was insufficiently detailed. The evaluator returns to the attorneys or the court for clarification about the purpose of the evaluation. We recommend that the evaluator begin this process with a clear understanding of the issues and structure of the evaluation: the tasks of the evaluation will become more complicated as it progresses, and careful preparation at the start will serve the evaluator well.

Warning of Nonconfidentiality

The section describes how the informed consent was obtained and the limits of confidentiality.

EVALUATION PROCEDURES

This section outlines all of the evaluator's sources of information, the amount of contact with each, and the sequence of the contact.

INTERVIEWS AND OBSERVATION SESSIONS

List who attended and participated at the interview, the date of the contact, and the amount of time spent.

PSYCHOLOGICAL MEASURES

List the tests, questionnaires, allegation forms, and checklists that were used.

COLLATERAL CONTACTS

List who was contacted and the dates of contact.

DOCUMENTS

List the documents that were reviewed as part of the evaluation.

ALLEGATIONS AND PERCEPTIONS BY EACH PARTY

The allegations that each party has made against the other are recounted in this section. List each allegation separately. Start with the *petitioner's* (the party who first brought the custody case) allegations first, and then list the respondent's (the party who is responding to the petition of the other party) allegations.

The responses of the other party to the allegations, the results of the collateral investigation, and other findings are woven into a later section, the discussion section of the report. Also in the discussion section, the evaluator can describe the reactions and attitudes toward the allegation forms and toward the process of specifying examples of allegations.

SOCIAL HISTORIES

In this section the evaluator combines elements of the Parenting History Survey and the structured clinical interview.

EVALUATION OF PETITIONER [Name the Petitioner]

Mental Status Examination

Describe the following attributes and characteristics of the individual: affect, speech, mood, thought, judgment, insight, attention, concentration, memory, and impulse control. Some of these descriptions are just what the evaluator observes during interactions with the party, and some require specific probing questions to assess.

Family History

Obtain family constellation data, including the members of the household, a brief history of the parental background(s), and the parents' formative experiences as children within the family-of-origin household.

Education History

Describe how the party progressed through school. List any significant formative experiences that are school related.

Work History

List the party's work history, including type of work, frequency of job changes, enjoyment of work, advancement or decline in a career, and any disabilities.

Medical History and Substance Use History

Describe any medical conditions such as accidents, periods of disability, major illnesses, and any ongoing physical condition. Also outline all substance abuse, including alcohol, street drugs, and prescribed drugs.

Mental Health History

List any mental health concerns, any problems that might be mental health related, any treatment for mental health, and the party's current mental health status.

Legal History

Describe any significant legal problems. Detail arrests, types of violations, and remedial progress.

Relationship History

Describe each party's significant romantic relationships fostered by the individual. Inquire about specific dates of relationship onset, relationship patterns, progression of the relationships, and changes in relationship satisfaction and functioning. Provide information about relationship trends (e.g., circumstances of the courtship, premarital intimacy, communication style, intimacy preferences, current strengths and weaknesses in relationship functioning, ways of handling relationship termination, and postrelationship status and functioning).

History of the Current Relationship

Describe the present relationship if this individual has developed a relationship after that which produced the children.

Child-Harming Behaviors

Document and describe harmful behaviors.

EVALUATION OF THE RESPONDENT [Name of Respondent]

Apply the same format used with the petitioner. If any other significant adults are part of this evaluation (e.g., in some cases a third party, such as a grandparent, wants custody of the child), then include their psychosocial evaluation(s) next.

RELATIONSHIP HISTORY OF PETITIONER AND RESPONDENT

Describe the relationship between the petitioner and the respondent from start to finish. Outline what brought them together in the beginning, why they had children, what turmoil existed between them, and why the relationship ended. Delineate their pattern of conflict and problem solving. Include an explanation of the outside forces that affected the relationship, such as extended family, economic problems, injury, and societal factors.

CLINICAL FINDINGS

Present the results of the party–child observation sessions and the psychological testing of each party.

PSYCHOLOGICAL TEST RESULTS

Minnesota Multiphasic Personality Inventory–Second Edition (MMPI–2)

Describe the MMPI–2, its history, and its research here. Contextualize any actuarial or computer-generated interpretive statements and the need to find corroboration from outside sources before such statements are given any weight.

Summarize the statements from the MMPI–2 for the petitioner. Then, summarize the statements for the respondent.

Achenbach Child Behavior Checklist (CBCL)

Describe the CBCL and what it expresses. Next, describe the petitioner's response on the CBCL. Then describe the respondent's response on the CBCL. Highlight the differences between the two parties for only those behavioral dimensions that are clinically significant.

PARENT–CHILD OBSERVATIONS

For the Petitioner

Describe the setting, the context, and your observations of the session. Use specific detail, and delineate the pattern of the interaction. Specify which children were present, and add details regarding their behavior, verbalizations to the parent, responses to the parent's directives, and parent's ability to interact with other children.

Petitioner showed the following strengths during this play session:

1.
2.
Etc.

The observation raised the following concerns about the petitioner's parenting:

1.
2.
Etc.

Summarize the individual's general attitude during the observation session and demonstrated skills in parenting.

For the Respondent

Describe in a similar manner the respondent's performance. Write a separate section for each adult whom the evaluator observes with the children.

COLLATERAL INFORMATION

Name of the first person contacted and how he or she is connected to the situation. Then summarize the information that he or she expressed that relates to the situation, especially to the allegations.

Repeat this process for each collateral contact in the order they were contacted.

DISCUSSION

Discuss the findings in regard to the allegations that each party made against the other party. Remember to use at least two methods of corroborating any allegation before presenting a finding. Integrate and connect the information from each of the measures of the evaluation. Arrange the discussion so that the findings address the legal factors considered by the court (of the jurisdiction) in arriving at its orders about residential placement, visitation, visitation restrictions, decision-making allocation, and so forth. Use the legal factors as headings in the discussion section.

Address each allegation by stating the allegation first, followed by a detailing of the information the evaluator has gathered that confirms, refutes, or acknowledges the uncertainty about the allegation. This section is driven by the allegations. Use language that presents information as neutrally and descriptively as possible.

RECOMMENDATIONS

Outline how the findings might shape a permanent parenting plan that the court orders. Make sure that the plan outlined is supported by the findings presented previously in the report. Recommendations follow from the evidence gathered and corroborated by at least two measures.

Residential Placement and Visitation Schedule

1.
2.

Decision Making

1.
2.

Treatment

1.
2.
Etc.

Communication With the Child and the Other Party

1.
2.
Etc.

Dispute Resolution Process

1.
2.
Etc.

Conclude your report by signing and dating it.

11

SAMPLE A. REPORT OF *MR. D. v.* MS. M., EVALUATION FOR MODIFICATION OF PARENTING PLAN

The following are sample reports that demonstrate the format. The reports are based on composites of cases actually evaluated. The parties evaluated in each of these cases have had their identities masked so that no particular fact pattern would lead to a breach of confidentiality.

PARENTING EVALUATION

Referral Source and Purpose

Judge Z., who ordered this evaluation on September 2, 2000, directed [name of evaluator] to investigate and report on issues related to the legal and physical custody of [name of children], issues of visitation, and decision-making allocation arrangements of a permanent parenting plan that may require modification. The parents in this case, Mr. D. and Ms. M., agreed in 1999 to a permanent parenting plan organized by a court-appointed mediator. When their child, A. (DOB: age 11 years), returned from her weekend visit with Mr. D. on October 10, 1998, Ms. M. observed large red welts on A.'s thighs and buttocks. Ms. M. reported this to the police, prompting A.'s transition from her father's care into her mother's home. Mr. D. maintained regular visits with A. per his compliance with certain conditions. The purpose of this evaluation and report is to evaluate all parties in the matter, directly assess the parenting circumstances for A., and to offer recommendations to the Court for modification of the original parenting plan, if necessary. Mr. D., the petitioner, is represented by Mr. P. The defendant, Ms. M., is *pro se*.

Warning of Nonconfidentiality

All parties to this evaluation were informed that the information gathered from interviews, records, and collateral contacts would be used for this report to the Court. It was understood that nothing that was shared would be kept confidential. The parties were made aware about their right to refuse to answer a question or line of questions. All parties acknowledged that they understood this information and agreed to this evaluation.

EVALUATION PROCEDURES

This evaluation is based on information gathered from written and oral interviews, the administration of psychological assessment tests, direct observations of all family members, documentary evidence, and depositions. Pursuant to the Court's appointment, the following evaluation procedures were completed.

INTERVIEWS AND OBSERVATION SESSIONS

Mr. D. interview	10/19/00	2.00 hours
Ms. M. interview	10/21/00	2.05 hours
Ms. M. and A.	11/25/00	1.00 hour
Mr. D. with A.	11/28/00	1.00 hour
Ms. M. interview	12/13/00	1.00 hour
A. interview	12/15/00	1.00 hour
Ms. S. interview	12/15/00	1.00 hour
Mr. D. interview	12/15/00	1.00 hour

(Ms. S. is Mr. D.'s "covenanted wife.")

PSYCHOLOGICAL MEASURES

Parenting History Survey (PHS)
Allegation forms
Minnesota Multiphasic Personality Inventory–Second Edition (MMPI–2)
Achenbach Child Behavioral Checklist (CBCL)

COLLATERAL CONTACTS

Mr. De, Principal, A.'s school	11/29/00
Mrs. Di, A.'s second-grade teacher	11/29/00
Mrs. R, A.'s day care provider	11/29/00
Ms. Ch, A.'s day care provider	11/29/00
Ms. C, A.'s therapist	11/30/00
Mrs. Sa, A.'s first-grade teacher	11/30/00
Mr. F, Ms. M's employer	11/30/00

DOCUMENTS

A.'s grades from school from fall of 2000. 36 documents provided by legal counsel and previously submitted to the Courts since the permanent parenting plan was entered.

ALLEGATIONS AND PERCEPTIONS BY EACH PARTY

Here the allegations that each parent has made against the other are delineated. Their responses, the results of the collateral interviews, and other findings are incorporated into the discussion section of this report.

Mr. D.'s Perception About Ms. M.

Mr. D. was provided with allegation forms on October 19, 2000, with standard instructions for their completion. Mr. D. was called to remind him to attend to the task on October 24, on October 28, and on November 14, 2000. According to Mr. D., he hand delivered two completed allegation forms to the office in the first week of November of 2000. The office staff was not able to locate these forms. A final request to Mr. D. to return the allegation forms within 4 days was made on November 14, 2000. Mr. D. left a message at the office on November 15, 2000, stating that he was frustrated, that it was not appropriate to give him deadlines after the evaluator had lost his papers, and that he was not about to profane the Lord's Day to get the work done. He concluded, stating, "This evaluation stuff is overwhelming me." Mr. D. brought two completed allegation forms to the parent–child observation on November 28, 2000. The allegations raised in the forms were consistent with the allegations raised earlier in the PHS. They include the following.

Allegation 1

Ms. M. uses alcohol and drugs to excess, potentially creating risks for A. According to Mr. D., between September 1993 and the date of the allegation, he smelled alcohol on Ms. M.'s breath when picking up A. from Ms. M.'s home. He also stated that he observed half-filled bottles of whiskey on her kitchen table.

Allegation 2

Ms. M. created or used conflict in an abusive way to the detriment of the child. On one occasion when Mr. D. asked Ms. M. to return A.'s baby bottles, Ms. M. tried to slam a car door on him, screamed obscenities, and "threw a crate of baby bottles" at him. The crate scraped A.'s leg, prompting first aid. For the remaining afternoon, A. was inconsolable.

Allegation 3

Ms. M. withheld contact and access to A., preventing Mr. D. from meeting A. numerous times for more than a year. On one occasion, Mr. D. showed up for his visit, and Ms. M. refused to transfer A. into his care. On September 1, 1997, when he arrived to pick up A., Ms. M. denied access to A. Mr. D. called the police, who made many attempts to get her to answer the door. Ms. M. finally acquiesced and agreed to accept the visitation schedule and gave A. to Mr. D.

Allegation 4

Ms. M. threatened to neglect or physically mistreat A. Ms. M. has slapped A., on numerous occasions, when A. was noncompliant with homework and house chores.

Allegation 5

Ms. M. emotionally mistreats or neglects A. Their daughter spends most evenings alone in her bedroom because her mother is socializing with her boyfriend. Ms. M. allegedly is cruel by telling A. that she looks overweight in the clothes that Mr. D. bought for her.

Allegation 6

Ms. M. is inadequate or incompetent to care for their daughter. A. reports that her mom's house is so messy she cannot have friends visit. In addition, Ms. M.'s poor parenting is reflected in A.'s presentation during visits. A. typically looks unkempt, with uncombed hair and poorly fitted clothes.

Ms. M.'s Perception About Mr. D.

Ms. M. was given allegation forms on October 21, 2000, with standard instructions for their completion. She returned them within the week period of time requested for completion.

Allegation 1

Mr. D. emotionally mistreated A. on May 19, 1993, after he sought access to A. through her mother, without talking to Ms. M. about his intention to visit. A. was distressed about the unplanned visit. Further, Mr. D. emotionally mistreated A. by using A.'s distress to his advantage. On one occasion, Mr. D. held up A., who was crying loudly, in the grocery store, yelling at Ms. M. for upsetting the child. Further, Mr. D. tells A. that her mother is a failure and does not like being a parent.

Allegation 2

Mr. D. uses a belt to punish A. when she is noncompliant. His beatings leave striking welts and bruises, which have been photographed, on both her back thighs and buttocks. A. seemed to be in pain, and was complaining after one beating that occurred the week ending October 10, 1998.

Allegation 3

Mr. D. has threatened to physically harm or mistreat A. By a documented police report, he is seen to have beaten A. once. He has been reported for being physically harsh with his other children at other times.

Allegation 4

Mr. D. has threatened to physically mistreat or harm Ms. M. Mr. D. was physically abusive on two occasions, both of which have been documented with police reports in X County.

Allegation 5

Mr. D. created conflict in an abusive way that jeopardizes A.'s well-being. Since Mother's Day in 1993, Mr. D. manipulates when and how he has custody of A. in an effort to gain the presumption that it is in A.'s best interest to remain in the residential placement of her father because she has been with her father for so long. His rigid and authoritarian style has prevented reasonable negotiation and increased intimidation. Ms. M. stated, "If I disagreed with him, he intimidated me. Telling me that he knew how to play the courts and that he had the favor of the judge because he cared for A. full-time. He insisted from the beginning on having his way."

SOCIAL HISTORIES

History of Mr. D.

Family History

Mr. D. said that his maternal grandparents, whom he considers his parents and calls "Momma" and "Dad," raised him. His mother, who became pregnant at age 18, lived with her parents. Mr. D. reported a mother–son relationship with his biological mother. He thought of his grandmother as his primary parent. As the firstborn son, he was treated as though he was the only child, as his grandmother gave him more attention than his younger brother and sister. Mr. D. grew up in a traditional home in an East Coast city, in which "life was very positive and meaningful. I owe a lot of my optimism to my family's faith in life." He described his grandmother (mom) as "one of the reasons I am who I am today. She was firm, direct, structured, orderly, and loving … in a sense, her understanding founded the environment." He described his grandfather (dad) as "pretty laid back, orderly and structured also, precise about things, neat … disciplined. He was quiet." Mr. D. said his grandparents have "a great relationship. They're still together after 55 years." Mr. D. further described his family, as "not perfect, but definitely not bad … a caring, loving household" absent drug and alcohol use, physical and sexual abuse.

His dad/grandfather was in the Army for 10 years and then became a plumber, an occupation he maintained until his retirement. His mom/grandmother was a teacher, after which she became a full-time homemaker. Both obtained a high school education, and his grandmother obtained her teacher's certificate from a college. He said that the "family lived in an upper-middle-class environment, in a prestigious neighborhood … if there were financial problems I didn't know about it." He did not think his neighborhood was rough compared to current times.

Education History

Mr. D. graduated from high school during the spring of 1985. He reported a C+ average. He thought people would remember him in high school as "someone who likes to be different and well-rounded, outgoing, clean person in appearance, playing baseball and football." He reported that his high school friends would describe him "as a leader who enjoyed a lot of football games, school parties, and baseball." He had enough friends.

Mr. D. attended X College for 2 years. He tried to transfer to X State, intending to play football there. He said his "parents made too much money for financial aid so I went onto the journey of work." His college grades he reported as Cs. He did not graduate from college.

Work History

Mr. D. first worked in a high school as a janitor and had multiple jobs thereafter (he was unable to give a clear history). One job was working for a security company for 3 years. He also worked with children in several ways: as a counselor in outdoor and wilderness camps during two summers, most likely 1987 and 1988, then as a counselor in church settings providing basic education and enrichment to youth, and later for the military forces just before moving to an East Coast city in October 1990.

Having arrived in the fall of 1992 in an East Coast city, Mr. D. lived with friends before going to work for a community service agency that served delinquent youths. He then worked for a temp agency for the following year. In the fall of 1994, Mr. D. became a counselor for at-risk youth with behavior problems. He decided to leave after 3 years because it was emotionally and physically tough work. He described an incident where a young adolescent bit him during a restraint exercise. [During this description, Mr. D. got up from the desk to demonstrate how the counselors carried an out-of-control child so he could show where the child bit him.] Mr. D. transitioned to construction work, doing general labor for 30 months. He left construction for a position with a community agency that oversees urban alternative treatment programs for at-risk youth. He currently holds that position.

Mr. D. stated that he thought that his supervisors were insightful and intelligent. He described that they socialized together on the weekends and that his coworkers had a good relationship with his children and his family.

Medical History and History of Substance Use

Mr. D. reports excellent physical, mental, and emotional health. Mr. D. reports no previous or current substance abuse. He does not smoke cigarettes.

Relationship History

Mr. D. claimed no significant romantic relationships other than with Ms. M., the mother of his daughter, A. He stated that he dated casually in high school, relationships that he said prepared him for the relationship he presently has with his "covenanted wife" (they are not legally married).

History of the Current Marriage

Mr. D. reported that he initiated a "covenanted" relationship with Ms. S. in the spring of 1994. Together, they have 4 children, including C. (age 7), So. (age 6), Mi. (age 5), and Dc. (age 3). Ms. S. works as an office secretary for a real estate company. Mr. D. described his home environment as "loving, kind, open, lots of energy, proactive. People are astounded that we have such a happy environment. We have our moments. It's not perfect. I am happy to have come from the background that I came from. I have been able to implant some characteristics of where I come from and hers, too. She comes from a very Christian family ... very profound. The house is very structured, very ordered ... order is very much in place. We do a lot of talking. We are having to learn conflict resolution."

In terms of the living situation, Mr. D. stated that his girls have two rooms. A. shares with one of the girls and has her own bed. Lately, however, "A. wants to sleep with me. When I get home from work, she'll be ... in my bed and waiting for me. Ordinarily, I wouldn't let kids sleep with me. But based on watching them ... each kid has their own personality ... they are very, very different in their own characteristics. Certain kids make you give them what they want. A. is so attached and codependent. It's like she idolizes me. She is very attached. In the situation she is in right now I let it slide a little bit. I let her know that I still love her. The situation has changed; she wonders what's going on. Actually she kind of understands and is asking a lot of questions and is thinking about things."

When asked to describe his strengths as a parent, he stated, " I would say my strength is ... you look at a child differently ... it is something you are brought into the world with ... each one of them is different, so I parent them differently. Across the board I am encouraging, loving, understanding. I hold my balance being a parent. They can talk to me." [On reviewing this report, he asked me to include in the above paragraph: that he is very proactive; that he is "caring emotionally and physically"; "I do my best."]

On reflecting on his weaknesses as a parent, he stated, "I can't honestly say there are weaknesses because I stand my ground as a parent based on what I know. I still grow and learn as they grow. If there is a weakness it is trying to learn before they get to a point." [On review, he later added, "I'm not perfect, however I do my best."]

When asked about Ms. M.'s strengths, he said, "I haven't seen her be a parent, full-fledged. I would say there is a contrast, like night and day, the way we see issues and parent. I think I am much more firm than she would be. I can't actually say that I have seen her parent or that her parenting is displayed in A. either. ... Not as far as a strength is concerned. I would say that the foundation she has was put in her [A.] at a very early age by me. My philosophy goes that discipline begins at birth. Your interactions with the baby changes how it learns ... their brain begins to work as soon as they are out of the womb. Babies learn very, very quick."

Again, Mr. D. had additions to the above: "Based on characters [sic] I see in A. when she comes home from Ms. M.'s, I disapprove of events that lead to my daughter being disruptive, agitating, and aggressive toward her peers and siblings." He further added to the text on review: "I believe I am much more firm in a sense of structure than she is." He characterized

Ms. M.'s weaknesses as a parent as being "casual in the sense of 'Oh, I'll let you make that choice' when sometimes it is not up to the kid to make that choice; at some point parents need to step in and make choices for children ... just living style in regard to cleanliness in the environment, environment structure, just kind of maintaining a standard of discipline." Mr. D. also asked that the following be added: "Her overall lifestyle lacks direction in order, discipline, structure, cleanliness, and the ability to administer the proper kind of love, care, and attention to herself and anyone's child. This comment is based solely on intuitive and personal observations that I have witnessed."

Child-Harming Behaviors

When asked to identify two child-harming behaviors in which Ms. M. had engaged, Mr. D. responded that while he had heard A. allege such behaviors, he had never witnessed them firsthand, because he never entered the home himself.

History of Ms. M

Family History

Ms. M. was born in a West Coast city and raised in East Coast city. Her family consisted of her mother, her father, and an older brother. Her family was "normal for a working-class family. My parents kept us busy with different activities, particularly in the summer. Dad worked overnight, so I usually saw him at breakfast and before dinner." Ms. M. described her mother as "hard working, always busy with something; working in the kitchen, cooking dinner. We would be doing homework and she would be with Daddy and then it would be time for bed. That was pretty much our weekly schedule. She was pretty much our chauffeur for soccer games and volleyball games and drama class." She described her father as "a hard worker, yet the one who was the funniest." Asked about her parents' relationship, she reported, "Actually it was pretty good. They were very open with each other as far as we knew. Parent stuff ... they weren't going to tell us. But if it affected us they would call us in and have a family conference." I asked if there were difficulties while growing up in the family. "Yes. I was a freshman in high school. I had opened up in class. We had this quality time, 'Circle,' in class. This one girl was telling about how she was uncomfortable about something with her father ... I got up and confessed that my father drank a lot and sometimes beat me. The teacher had to report that to the police. We had to go to court. That was like the biggest problem. My father went through a lot of court appearances. They had him go to AA meetings because he was drinking quite a bit. We all did counseling. We weren't ever separated (although my father had to get his own place for a while)."

"The next big problem was me getting pregnant at the age I did. I was just turning 17, a junior in high school. Neither of my parents liked Mr. D. They thought he was too arrogant, and the age difference was a factor." She explained she was so young, and he was 8 years or so older than she. "My dad told me to think seriously about what I was going to do and then follow through on the decision 100% ... and so long as I stayed in school and got good grades they would help me as much as possible. My mother was more angry about it. My brother talked to me about it ... which was strange because we were not very close ... but he played the big brother role and told me about the same that my father did. It wasn't until after A.'s birth that there was a really big problem. Then there was a lot more fights. I don't mean physically, but arguments breaking out.... It was ... like little kids fighting over the toy, mainly between my father and Mr. D."

In describing her father's drinking and the physical abuse, Ms. M stated, "There was drinking on a daily basis, no question ... my father. Not my mother, although she might drink on holidays maybe. There was no drug use that I was aware of ... no physical abuse of my mother."

"At first it was really rocky. My mother blamed me, said I was lying even though my father admitted it and apologized. I think I admired my father more the way he handled it. He came to me reassuring me that it wasn't me that it was his problem and, unfortunately, I was a part of that. But toward the end it was really good. We were a lot more open with everyone about things, which I really didn't do before. I was really a quiet kid, kept things to myself."

She described her parents' employment backgrounds as follows: "My Mom has been ... a nurse's aide since I can remember. We moved from [one city] to [where they live now] just before I turned 3, and she started working for her school then.... My father was ... an officer for a union when he was killed. He was a shop steward before that and a salesman before that ... at his company. That was the only place he worked before working for the union."

"My father was shot by the police. He was drinking at a park, which was strange because as far as we knew he didn't have alcohol later in his life. But someone walked by and saw a gun and reported it. The police came to the park and found him lying on the ground, and they didn't know if he had shot himself or had passed-out drunk. One police officer thought he heard a gun go off, and they shot him.... It was very hard on me: It was 10 days before my high school graduation; Mr. D. had decided to keep A., we were moving, I was trying to get into college. It was a very rough year."

Regarding family finances, "There was always a struggle there, but we never did without. [We had] cool clothes, and I were [sic] always in drama and gymnastics and my brother in soccer. My parents owned their own home and vehicles."

Education History

Ms. M. received a high school diploma. The significant events of her high school years are detailed above: notifying the teacher of the physical abuse, losing her father, the pregnancy, and losing her child. She said before the pregnancy she had been a slacker in school, although she never failed or was held back. She had to do some night and summer school. After she became pregnant, she said her "lowest GPA was 3.8" and that she finally became a "4.0 student" in her senior year.

In reporting how her peers would view her, she stated, "I have no idea what people (from high school) would remember about me. I was voted most memorable ... maybe because I was walking around as a pregnant senior ... or because I socialized with everybody and didn't stick around just one clique. People would say about me that I was always honest. Back then I didn't use as much tact as I do now. That was something I had to learn ... I was always a good ear in high school and middle school. I was a peer counselor in middle school and sometimes in high school. Even after high school I went back to give an ear to kids ... teachers inviting me to come back and talk to their classes."

Ms. M. said she had enough friends and thought that was because she could mix and mingle with all cliques in the school. She remembered doing drama and gymnastics for a while, playing volleyball for quite a few years, playing basketball for a couple years, as well as playing soccer ... and martial arts. She didn't work during high school.

She described disciplinary problems during high school: "Yeah ... I got in trouble for sneaking out of the house at night to go see Mr. D. ... and because I went to football games and came home 2 to 3 hours after I was supposed to. I was grounded for like 2 months over that one. And otherwise it was the basics of grades not being what they could be and not cleaning my room ... life-threatening stuff for a teenager [said sarcastically]." She graduated in 1993 and took some college courses at the local community college.

Work History

Ms. M. said that after high school she found herself "hunting down attorneys for legal advice." Her work, which she had intended to support her through training to become a dental hygienist, became focused on earning enough to deal with legal-related bills. She worked as a dental aide for a year and a half and then went to work as a receptionist, changing jobs each time she got a better offer. When she became 21 years old, she began bartending. She had hoped this would see her through school, but she reported that the money "was diverted to legal fees," a situation she endured until she could get beyond the courts and back in school. Her clear goal remains to become a dental hygienist. Ms. M. states that she has always enjoyed her work and could not see herself remaining in work she did not relish. She sees her present job as a constant reminder that her career is in her future training. She said she has always had good work relationships; bosses have praised and, in fact, recruited her. Her present boss, she said, "says he is thinking of putting me in management." Her regret about work is that she takes criticism about not being a good mother because she works as a bartender in an adult entertainment establishment. "My daughter has no clue what goes on there ... I've never told her. My family knows, but they don't tell her.... I don't take my work home with me." She stressed that she is "just a bartender" and that she does not take her clothes off at work.

Medical History

Ms. M. claimed good physical health. She said she is prone to getting "strep." She had court-ordered psychotherapy at the time of the discovery of the physical abuse by her father. "I can't say for sure how many times ... more than 3 sessions, somewhere between 5 and 10 times.... It made me feel really uncomfortable to discuss the most intimate parts of my life with a complete stranger. It was easier for me to discuss it with Dad and Mom."

Relationship History

Ms. M. had a dating relationship with a senior when she was a freshman in high school. "We dated about a year and a half, and then he went off to college. It was puppy love." The breakup was hard. "After a weekend I was up and running ... I didn't feel sorry for myself as long as I could have." She had no other relationship before she met Mr. D.

She described her home environment as a two-bedroom townhouse where her daughter has her own room "that she trashes all the time." Ms. M. maintains that it contains A.'s own bed, a cat, a computer, and a TV. "I've been trying to get her into dance, but it's hard because most of the classes are on the weekends. She also spends a lot of time with my mother in my mother's home because of the schedule. My mother watches her for an hour and a half Monday through Thursday. Her day care closes at 6 o'clock, and I don't get off work 'til 7. My mother has a big, three-bedroom home, fenced in with a dog and a little niece to play with.... She [A.] has an awesome day care. We've known them for years. She does really well in school."

In describing her strengths as a parent, she stated, "I am open and honest. I hope that she is that way in return. I stress that no matter what, I want the truth. She is pretty good about it. She might hmmm and haw and give me that look ... but she is pretty good about it. I would like to think I am pretty understanding. I give her guidelines, like cleaning her room ... and she is real honest. ..."

She described her parenting weaknesses as follows: "I am overprotective at times. I ... worry about her constantly, mostly when she is with her dad. ... I don't sleep well. I catch myself spoiling her more than I should, if that is a weakness ... for her it's a strength I'm sure, but. ... I missed a lot of time of her growing up, so I try to suck up all that time I can now. I try not to be overbearing."

She described Mr. D.'s strengths as a parent as follows: "I do believe he wants his kids to be successful, and he encourages them to do things that would benefit them. It's hard to say. I've never really seen him with his kids. I don't get to see the good side. I see him when I drop off A. and when he drops off A., and that's pretty much it. We don't exactly socialize in between."

Regarding Mr. D.'s parenting weaknesses, Ms. M. said, "I don't agree with his using physical discipline, I don't think anyone should ... especially with my daughter ... she is very intelligent and she would understand your words a lot more than your hand. I think he is too selfish. He is more concerned with how it looks than how it is for the kids."

Current Relationship

"He's a guy I have known about 2 1/2 years now. We've been dating about 8 months. We are pretty involved. We share the same views that if we don't see an actual future ... down the road ... we are not exactly talking marriage. It's only been 8 months. But we do share the same views that we do eventually want to get married and have kids with the house." In the closing interview, she reported that he had asked to become engaged. However, because of his ultimate refusal to join her for closing interviews and to sit for an MMPI–2, she told him she is rethinking the future of their relationship.

"We are together in the evenings. He picks me up from work. We share time together and with A. before we go to bed. ... Yes we do live together ... and ... we spend Friday night and Saturday as ... our together-weekend. With A. I am surprised ... because I never saw him with kids or getting along with kids. But I am surprised. ... I always saw him as a big kid himself. But that is an asset for him when he is with A. They get along well. Oh, they butt heads, like when they argue over who gets to play with the radio control car, but that's about the extent of it."

Child-Harming Behaviors

Ms. M. related the incident when she discovered the welt marks on A. "The one I mention is the physical discipline. I know he denies it, but he has done it in the past ... and he is known for not being fully honest. It is very harmful: when I picked her up ... I could see the (very) holes of the belt marks, (she had) been hit so hard. Still, to this day, ... she'll bring it up ... 'when Daddy did this' and that ... that is definitely dangerous. I saw it (the welt marks), my brother did, my mother, the police officer, the caseworker, the photographer for the police department, all saw it firsthand. Then my attorney, a judge, and I am assuming Mr. D. and his attorney saw the pictures." The negative consequences? "We were having a discussion about her room ... like an argument, and we were getting in for the evening. I was relaxing, letting down my hair and reaching for the brush, and she flinched ... she jumped a good 6 or 8 inches away from me. I asked her, 'Do you think I'm going to hit you?' She said, 'No.' I said why would you jump? She just shrugged her shoulders. It is that reaction that frustrates me. She is scared when there is no reason to be scared ... it's that automatic fear." In another example of violence that she suspects has affected her daughter, she described an incident that was reported in court documents: "According to the Court, Mr. D. had beaten his girlfriend ... then proceeded to try to light the house on fire ... douse gasoline and all the babies were upstairs ... my daughter remembers stuff like ... I'm not sure she remembers all the details, but she does remember the fight. That was October, 2 years ago."

"A second one that really concerns me ... they play mind games with A. When ... we first ... had the supervised visits, I would go get her, and I would be walking away with her, and the other kids would be crying because they don't understand why she is walking away, and he started screaming right there in front of a few people at a gas station: 'This is what you're doing; you've done this, it's all your fault,' and he would hold up a baby that is crying and screaming just to show me that it was because I did this. It's the little things like A. coming back and telling me that her dad said that she is definitely going to live with him and she should enjoy her time (with her mom) because it is not going to be for long. ... That had to be a year and a half ago. I don't know about witnesses ... a bunch of strangers at a gas station."

The effect? "A. wouldn't talk to me at all. She absolutely clammed up ... she just went to her bed and cried herself to sleep. ... I let her be ... she slept for an hour ... and a half and came downstairs and cuddled up and asked me why I was trying to take her away from her daddy. I told her that's not what I am trying to do. I am just trying to make sure she is safe. I keep trying to explain it without fully explaining it ... because I am really not supposed to. I am trying to cover all my bases ... and call my attorney and say is this OK (to say); I'm trying not to get in trouble. At the same time I am trying to let her know ... with some shielding."

An additional concern is "Ms. S. has admitted using a belt and a wooden spoon on all the kids. My concern is that this is a woman who has raised a hand to my child ... and I don't do that. Someone who is a stranger to me has the audacity to raise a hand to my child. It concerns me a great deal that if Mr. D. is beating the kids ... because what I hear from A. is that she is the one who takes care of her more than Mr. D., then what kind of a role model is that ... that it is OK to have someone beat on you. That is a really big concern of mine."

"We went to trial, it was brought up in court that they used the belt. And that judge said you don't use the belt ... and this was the final trial, and he was granted custody ... 2 years later when I picked her up, and she had belt marks. That is why I was just galled ... it was the third or fourth time I had to report him for abuse, and nobody did anything ... until now.... Now it is sad ... she will come back and say 'I was really good, I didn't get spanked at all' ... She knows from the case worker that she is not supposed to get spanked ... and if she does she is supposed to ... tell someone."

I asked her about her statement that she might be accused of doing drugs. She explained that she had dated a guy who had been using and ostensibly wasn't when they were dating. She found that he was using and she "kicked him out that very night."

RELATIONSHIP HISTORY OF MR. D. AND MS. M.

Both Mr. D. and Ms. M. described their relationship as troubled from the beginning. He described it as "spotty and troubled." She said "it fell apart from the beginning, when I was going to tell my parents that I was pregnant." They have different versions of how they met. He remembered meeting her in a mall at an ice-skating rink. She remembered meeting him at her school when she was waiting for night school to start and picking up a friend's child from basketball practice. He was attracted because she was "different, cute." She said he "seemed pleasant, nice, open, clean-cut; he talked a good game."

Mr. D. said there were a lot of issues from the beginning: Her parents disapproved. He said she had told him she was older, 19 or so. He said he was 23. The age issue proved to be a problem. They both agreed that they got sexually involved too soon. Although at first Mr. D. visited at Ms. M.'s home, that was short-lived. Ms. M.'s mother drove her to Mr. D.'s apartment for her to visit him a few times. After a short while, the parents forbade Ms. M. to see him. "That's when the sneaking around began," said Ms. M. Her parents did not know that Ms. M. was already pregnant.

The pregnancy seemed to be the beginning of the end. Ms. M. was ready to tell her parents; she had been entertaining the possibility of moving to an East Coast city with Mr. D. But when she insisted on telling her parents, Mr. D. suggested that she not call him anymore. She did tell her parents, and Ms. M.'s mother reported him to the police because she thought there might be a possible charge of sexual molestation.

Ms. M. chose to keep the baby early in the pregnancy. She said she told Mr. D. that it was his choice if he wanted to be involved. She said she knew that she could provide a good home for the baby with or without help. Mr. D. said that he was nervous and excited, knowing that this was his first child. Clearly the couple was at odds by the time of this revelation. He remembered Ms. M. wishing to finish school and thinking that it was best for him to care for the child. He said this is what happened immediately after A.'s birth, at least for the first 2 months: He said he was the primary caretaker. He also said Ms. M. and he were clear by then that they did not want a relationship with each other.

Ms. M. complained that Mr. D. acted as though he believed the pregnancy gave him certain rights to direct Ms. M.'s behavior and tell her what to do. "He told me not to date. He was trying to dictate whom I would talk to, what I would wear . . . like a hand puppet."

After A.'s birth, according to Mr. D., Ms. M. was working or going to school, and he was working. He said he provided child care for the infant through the church. "She was doing her own thing, and I was doing my own thing. We just sort of sat around and had a baby to take care of."

Ms. M. remembered this somewhat differently: She said, "Mr. D. was claiming he and I were going to get back together. . . . He bought me a ring, that kind of thing. I kept saying we could take our time."

Ms. M. said she found out that Mr. D. was expecting a baby with a woman in East Coast city, news she got about the same time A. was born. She said she didn't want to deprive her daughter of her father, so she arranged for him to visit A. at a friend's house or in a park for a short while. It was, according to her, during one of these visits that he took A. from the West Coast city to East Coast city and informed Ms. M. that she would have to go through the courts if she wanted to get A. back. While Mr. D. openly admitted he had become involved with a woman in an East Coast city through his church activities there, he was quick to emphasize that Ms. M. and he were not in a relationship at the time. He did, however, have a different version of how things went after A.'s birth: He said he took her to East Coast city to show his parents. He "proved them [Ms. M. and her mother] wrong" about thinking that he wouldn't bring her back. He said he was gone about a week, and that when he came back he then moved to another West Coast city and moved A. with him. He said he brought her to visit her mother every weekend for 6 months.

During one such weekend, there was [an encounter] between Mr. D.

and Ms. M. and her mother. The upshot of the event was that they didn't think A. should be with him. [They were trying to take her away, take me out of the picture.] He continued to say he wasn't about to let that happen; rather he decided to get Ms. M. to show initiative and be a responsible parent by having to come to a different West Coast city to visit the child. He said she didn't do that until about 4 months had passed.

Ms. M. said that after Mr. D. had taken A. to a different West Coast city on Mother's Day of 1993, she did not see her child for 3 or 4 months. After that time, a visitation was arranged, and "I was allowed to drive up to [West Coast city] Friday mornings and pick her up and drive back [to the West Coast city] on Sunday evenings, every other weekend. On opposite weekends it was mandated that I had to stay in West Coast city." By the time A. was a year old, a visitation schedule had been established. It wasn't until she was nearly 3 1/2 that Mr. D. was finally granted custody.

Both found fault with the other in behavior and parenting, but the visitations, according to both Mr. D. and Ms. M., happened almost routinely. Ms. M. filed an assault charge against Mr. D. at one time. According to Mr. D.'s report, the case went to court and was finally dismissed.

In October of 1998, while A. was visiting her mother, Ms. M. discovered welts and bruises and the imprint of a belt on A.'s buttocks and thighs. She called child protective services, and the police and medical professionals examined A. As a result, Ms. M. then attained custody.

Mr. D. asserted that on that Friday when she left, A. had no bruises and was in good spirits. He said that he was ordered to undergo a batterer's assessment and follow whatever recommendations might come from that. He reported confusion in the steps to attain the assessment, explained that it was exorbitantly expensive, and stated that the county didn't do such assessments. At a second visit in court, according to his report, the judge was irate that he was not in a program. Consequently, he did undergo two different assessments and was accepted into a treatment program. He said on reflection it seemed unfair, and because it was clear that this case was going to trial, he decided he would forestall attending the program, go through this evaluation process, and "take my chances."

In telling her part of this story, Ms. M. remembered the judge telling Mr. D. and his partner, Ms. S., that they were not to hit the children—not only A., but the other three in the home—and that the use of the belt, which she said Mr. D. had brought to court to show the judge, was considered abuse.

CLINICAL FINDINGS

The psychological test results and the results of the parent–child observation sessions are presented in this section.

PSYCHOLOGICAL TEST RESULTS

Minnesota Multiphasic Personality Inventory–Second Edition

The MMPI–2 is a widely used personality measure that is computer administered and scored. The following statements are based on the characteristics of other persons in a large-scale validation study who provided similar test results. MMPI interpretations are useful in defining general trends, and limited weight should be given to specific statements without corroboration from the other measures of the evaluation. Its results should not be used in isolation from the other findings contained in the evaluation. In the integration and presentation of the test data, I use my conservative clinical judgment to select the most likely hypotheses for presentation. I ask the reader to keep in mind the information available regarding these parties and use that to test whether these hypotheses are confirmed or disconfirmed.

Mr. D.'s test-taking approach suggested that he understood the instructions, but he responded very defensively by casting himself in an overly positive light and minimizing endorsement of any psychological difficulties. As a result, the clinical scales probably underestimate his actual experience. Despite this defensiveness, two of the clinical scales were significantly elevated. The most salient characteristic of persons with such a profile is chronic, intense anger. People who respond in this way often appear mistrustful, argumentative, rigid, and moralistic. They tend to make excessive use of denial and projection. These persons appear constricted and overcontrolled and lack insight into their behavior. Typically others view them as angry, argumentative, hostile individuals who harbor grudges. They do not tend to express these feelings directly, and much of the time they may not even recognize them. When they do become aware of their anger, they try to justify it in terms of the behavior of others. They tend to experience unmet needs for affection that may result in unrealistic demands on their loved ones and limit their ability to remain child centered. They can be overly sensitive and responsive to the opinions of others. They usually are able to control the acting out of the hostility when their needs are not met but, on occasion, may not be able to inhibit violent outbursts. After a period of pressure-cooking, this problem with impulse control may arise in stressful contexts when they will act without thinking through the consequences of their behavior. Difficulties in their lives tend to be rationalized or blamed on others. In general such individuals are defiant, uncooperative, and difficult to live with unless their point of view is accepted and followed. Such a profile suggests that such persons are relatively uninterested and unresponsive to psychological treatment.

Ms. M. produced a validity scale configuration that was very defensive by casting herself in an overly positive light and minimizing endorsement of any psychological difficulties. Such a profile suggests she has little insight into the motivations for her behavior or the consequences of her behavior on others. The responses probably underestimated her actual experience. As a result of this defensiveness, no clinical scale elevations occurred, and the following interpretations are based on supplementary scale data. Individuals who produce this type of clinical profile tend to feel tense, agitated, and worried. Often they may experience difficulties starting and following through on projects. Decreased physical activity is likely, and fatigue may be a prominent state. These persons affirm moral virtue, remain excessively generous about the motives of others, and deny distrust and hostility. They seem confident in social situations and deny any sensitivity. However, they resent societal demands and conventions, particularly parental standards. Such attitudes tend to emerge from disturbed family relations.

Achenbach Child Behavior Checklist

This measure directs the parent to respond to open-ended questions about positive characteristics and concerns regarding the child and lists descriptors of a child's daily behavior for the parent to evaluate as no problem, mild problem, or serious problem. It thus provides an opportunity to compare the perspectives of each parent as each responds to the same measure.

Mr. D. and Ms. M. describe their daughter in similar terms when listing her sports, hobbies, activities, chores, number of friends, and level of school performance. They independently report agreement on the best things about their daughter as her being an outgoing, loving, free-spirited, smart girl. Neither parent's responses resulted in any clinically significant elevations.

PARENT–CHILD OBSERVATIONS

Mr. D.

At the end of the first interview, Mr. D. was scheduled to come with his daughter for the parent–child observation. He was told, "Come prepared to play with your child for about an hour." When confirming the appointment with him on the telephone, he was instructed in a similar manner a second time with the same words.

Mr. D. arrived with his daughter, A., on the hour. He brought with him no toys, books, or snacks. On arriving in the observation room, he was instructed about the sequence of events during the observation both verbally and with written instructions for his later review.

After the instructions, Mr. D. immediately began to direct the activity. With the invitation, "Let's move this table out of the way," he moved the table to the side of the room while he scoured the room for supplies. He remarked that there weren't many toys, and told A. that they should have brought a book. He found and then puzzled over a roll of paper that he picked off a toy cupboard in the room. He then directed A. to hold still as he began to wrap the paper (approximately 6 inches wide) around her body several times. He used the paper's self-stick so that it would adhere to her clothing. He then made some marks or letters on the paper with colored markers available in the room. She was startled and then flinched when he began to glue the paper on her nose.

A. took such direction with a smile and a little fuss. She did not resist, but it appeared that she did not understand the game. After about 10 minutes of this, with both father and daughter sitting on the floor with the paper and markers, Mr. D. turned to look at me through the slight opening in the doorway and asked, "Do you have any more toys?" When I responded, "Just what's there," he responded with, "Wow."

For the balance of the hour, Mr. D. would seek some materials, initiate some sort of activity with them, question in a pleasant manner what A. was doing with her part and then converse light-heartedly. The conversation seldom addressed the play or involved A. directly but focused on other interests such as, "Guess where we are going after this. . . . Is that a blister? . . . What do you want to do today? . . . Everybody's going to the beach. . . . I'm moving the furniture out of the garage. . . . We are going to make an office . . . and a playroom."

When Mr. D. directed conversation to the play, it was either directing his daughter or questioning aloud what he might do with some of the (sparse supply of) materials available to him. "You've got to make it [the paper] extend. . . . All right, now what do you want. . . . Any ideas? . . . Lots of little kids' stuff here. . . . Should have brought a book. . . ."

There was a play interaction when both were sitting on the floor playing with the Lincoln Logs, which A. had retrieved and presented for play. Mr. D. asked, "What is that?" To which she answered, "I don't know." And he said, "You're making a window now. Use these before you use those . . . this is a double level." This was the single example of Mr. D. labeling any of the play during the session. He did not offer labeled praise for A.'s initiative and creativity throughout the session.

I did not observe a change when I signaled the end of child-directed play to mark the beginning of parent-directed play. After about 25 minutes, Mr. D. lay on his back on the floor and playfully directed A. to sit on his stomach. She bounced a bit, bracing herself so as not to hurt her father's stomach, and then accepted an invitation to play a sort of patty-cake game from that position. Then silence. Perhaps a minute later, with A. still on her father's stomach, Mr. D. asked A. to "sing for the cameras." She demurely declined. He urged her, with a bribe of ice cream. She still refused.

He offered to sing with her. It was still, "No." This "game" ended with Mr. D. ever so briefly tickling A. under her arms, halfway down her chest. During her giggles she slid off her father's stomach and sat on the floor.

For some time, A. entertained herself in silence. Finally, her father asked her if she were bored, to which she said yes. Then she announced that she had a new book, *The Cat in the Hat*. Mr. D. wondered aloud why she didn't bring it. "Because," she said, "Mom would be mad." She then explained it would have been all right had she brought school books.

Father and child had reverted to placing the self-adhesive papers on one another when he was interrupted and asked to fill out the Achenbach questionnaire. He took it, went for his glasses, and asked A. if she wanted to help. She told him she was going to watch. She only read one of the questions to her father. He, in turn, read some of the questions to her. When he saw that she listened to the questions and feigned to give guidance, he said, "You're more interested in this than you were in me ... when I tried to get you to play."

A. then continued to entertain herself while her father addressed his task. When she lay on the floor next to her father for part of this segment, she whispered to him. He responded by directing her to talk aloud because it was rude to whisper. "You talk aloud, assertively, so people can hear." She accepted with a smile and rose to engage in solitary play with markers and paper.

As the clean-up time was indicated, A. attacked the task at once. Her father said he wanted to help. She said, "No, I can do it." "You're sure?" "Yes!" And she was. She accomplished the job quickly and thoroughly, with a sharp focus. When Mr. D. noticed she had finished, he said, "Thank you." There followed about 10 minutes of silence while he finished the questionnaire and she played with paper and a few markers she could easily store at the end of the session.

The session ended with Mr. D. rising off the floor saying, "Okay, I think I am done. Want to check it?" A. smiled at the remark, put the rest of the markers away, and they left the room. When queried about how the play during the session compared with play that they engage in at home, Mr. D. replied that it was "about the same." A. remained quiet.

Mr. D. showed the following parenting strengths during this play session:

1. He appeared quite comfortable in all interactions with his daughter.
2. He was confident in his ability to engage with his daughter.
3. He was creative in using materials to fashion some play with his daughter.
4. He seemed to have a close and affectionate bond with his daughter.

The observation raised the following concerns about Mr. D.'s parenting:

1. He failed to plan appropriately for an hour's interaction with her.
2. He failed to demonstrate that he could allow his daughter to lead in playtime.
3. He treated her as a consultant to his adult tasks in an age-inappropriate manner.
4. He directed and tried to control almost all of the interaction rather than inviting her initiative.
5. There was more conversation-like behavior than play.
6. It appeared that Mr. D. and A. typically engage in only roughhousing when in play at other times. Except for the roughhousing during the observation, all other play seemed novel and foreign to them.
7. He failed to match the tone and energy level of his daughter. He seemed much more present in the room, eclipsing his daughter.
8. He failed to provide any labeled praise and on rare occasions provided unlabeled praise.
9. She seemed unusually compliant, which suggests that her father and his directions must come first or be obeyed.
10. He was unable to attend to his daughter while involved in the task of filling out the form. This suggests an inability to multitask and maintain focus on the child.

In summary, Mr. D. was comfortable in the one-on-one situation with his daughter and she with him. His style was more to direct activity and conversation than to engage in play. No opportunities arose that would demand limit setting or other kinds of parent direction. A. appeared somewhat younger than a just-turned 11-year-old in handling interactions with her father. She remained very vigilant and quite compliant throughout the session.

Ms. M.

When finished with the initial meeting of the evaluation, Ms. M. was given the instruction, "Come prepared to play with your child for about an hour." She called that evening and left the message that Mr. D. had told her she would not be able to have A. for the scheduled observation time. Both lawyers were called and asked to remind Mr. D. he was to be instructed to allow her access to the child for the observation session. Ms. M. arrived with A. perhaps 7 minutes late. Ms. M. was armed with a new Dr. Seuss book, some game or toy (which I could not make out), and juice.

I told her as we entered the room the structure for the session, that A. would direct play first, then, at my signal, the mother would direct the play and, at my final signal, clean-up time would begin. When she asked, "What do you mean, 'direct the play'?" I told her that it was for her to interpret.

A. asked what her mother wanted to do, and Ms. M. told her that it was up to her to decide what she wanted to do. She then assisted her daughter in exploration of the toy cupboard and laid aside the supplies she brought. A. selected the Legos and initiated the play. She opened the box and presented them to her mother. Ms. M. responded, "Cool," when she examined the contents. The play ensued with A. beginning a design or structure and inviting her mother's participation. Ms. M. followed, asking play-related questions: "What are these? Where do these go? How do they get up the stairs to go down?" She added suggestions: "Perhaps these go together. We have a problem with that one. Let me try to unstick those for you."

A. repeatedly completed a design and presented it. Ms. M.'s response was consistently, "Very good," or "Cool," with no false enthusiasm.

Some parallel play ensued, with A. re-engaging her mother after a brief period of such play accompanied by silence. Then Ms. M. questioned A. on her own satisfaction with her progress and accomplishments. Whatever the response, her mother subtly showed her approval, using a word, "Cool," a smile, a touch on her daughter's hand.

When A. accidentally dropped a Lego design on the floor, A. giggled as she got out of the chair and stooped to retrieve it. Her mother asked, "Are you doing okay?" After that, they both began work on the same structure, without revealing to each other what each had in mind for the final product. They both giggled. During this play A. tidied up and put away those materials they were not using at the time. Her mother responded with "all right!"

Twenty minutes passed during this play, and A. began looking for other toys while they carefully preserved the final Lego structure. She discovered Lincoln Logs just as I knocked on the door to signal time for parent-directed play. Ms. M. immediately began asking A. questions about the Lincoln Logs, told her those were a toy she had as a little girl, and pointed out some letters that they might use for play.

Recognizing the choices, A. chose to play with the letters. Her mother pointed to a word already formed and encouraged her daughter to sound it out. She continued to encourage A., uttering mild approval as she got close, redirecting her to the task when she tried to hurry to another word and providing directions and hints to uncover the pronunciation of the word. "Look at the word. You are playing with the other words and not looking at this one. You got the last part right. Helloooo! Break it down. What does this sound like?" When A. asked what a "y" sounded like, she quickly told her. Finally, A. pronounced xylophone and her mother simply said, "Very good." They played a few more such contests.

Ms. M. continued to offer new opportunities for play and exploration to A., a bit more with the Legos, then the Lincoln Logs. A. discovered a plastic turtle, dinosaurs, an octopus, and a shark. Her mother responded: "Cool." Finally Ms. M. suggested using the box of paper and directed A. to the markers. Together they puzzled about special properties of the markers (they would change colors under specific conditions) and experimented. They played this way together for a long period of time, marked by times of comfortable silence. One time they discovered together the magic of a particularly unusual magic marker. After the discovery they giggled together and smiled at each other. This occurred without conversation.

They were still busy with the markers and paper when I introduced the checklist to Ms. M. She continued to interact with A. while she began marking the form. She narrowed to the adult task for several minutes while A. continued her play. Then A. announced (perhaps proclaimed), "I left my homework at Daddy's." She said it with a smile directed at her mother. Ms. M. reminded her that it was her responsibility to attend to her homework over the weekend when she is at her father's. Her mother's chiding was direct, gentle, and clear. She expressed concern about a solution, engaged A. to help decide on the solution, and resolved what they would do. When A. expressed what seemed to be a shy giggle, her mother reminded her with words firm and gentle: "A., it's not funny. You are supposed to be responsible for that."

A. dropped to the floor and began using markers on an available white board. Ms. M. admonished her that those were not the appropriate markers for the white board. A. continued to use them momentarily while her mother explained that they wouldn't easily erase. "Are you listening?" "Yes." She tried to erase her work. "Oh really?" Afterward, she sought the correct markers to use on the board after hearing her mother's suggestion. That challenge with her mother setting some limits was about a 30-second interchange.

Following this, A. picked up a young child's shape toy and started to play with it. She called out, "I can't get these out, Mommy." This was the first time she had called her mother mommy. She was playing at being younger than her age. Her mother recognized the game as she looked up from her checklist and smiled, responding in the mode when A. asked for a solution.

Following some silence, I gave the clean-up signal. A. asked what that meant with a smile that said she knew full well it was time. Her mother smiled without a word, A. began to put the supplies away, and Ms. M. rose to join her. Ms. M couldn't pass up the opportunity to state, "How come you don't do your room that quickly?" No labeled praise was given to A. for her thorough and efficient work.

They finished cleaning, and A. kept some markers and paper to use while her mother finished her checklist. When she finished, the two engaged in some giggle-play using the markers to make flesh tattoos. It was only then that both focused attention outside the playroom. Both were hungry, and they planned what they were going to do for lunch. At the end of the observation when queried about how the play during the session compared with play that they engage in at home, Ms. M. replied that it seemed "quieter." A. said that she liked the markers.

Ms. M. showed the following parenting strengths during this play session:

1. She appeared comfortable in all her interactions with her daughter.
2. She clearly directed activities when instructed to do so.
3. She was willing and able to have her daughter direct activities.
4. She filled the role of adult at all times and was able to set appropriate boundaries and remain available to her daughter while multitasking as she filled out forms.
5. She set appropriate limits.
6. She used the play-frame as an opportunity to teach and coach and genuinely enjoyed the play for itself.
7. She focused on the present, making the best use of the time.
8. She matched the tone and energy level of her daughter well and demonstrated a very close, affectionate bond.
9. She provided both labeled and unlabeled praise that set a tone of encouragement of her daughter's initiative throughout the session.

The observation suggested the following areas of possible concern about Ms. M.'s parenting:

There may be the tendency for Ms. M. to develop a relationship of companionship too early in A.'s life. On occasion, it seemed that Ms. M. responded to her daughter as a peer rather than as a mother.

In summary, Ms. M. showed herself to be a parent who took direction and flexibly changed her plans. She also was able to direct the play, focus on the present and the play frame with her daughter as the center of the exercise. She set limits, corrected as she saw the need, used descriptors of behavior, and provided clear communication to bring about change. She was appropriately affectionate and physical with her daughter and truly enjoyed her daughter's presence. The play session also demonstrated that she could enhance her daughter's development in a formal manner. Examples of this type of parenting arose while she helped A. sound out words and read from the book.

COLLATERAL INFORMATION

Mrs. Di.

A.'s second grade teacher, Mrs. Di., views Ms. M.'s parenting as active and based on sound judgment. Regarding Ms. M.'s parenting, Mrs. Di. stated that Ms. M. seemed to be constantly interested in her daughter's school progress and behavior. She seeks advice from A.'s teachers, sits with A., and models appropriate responses. It was apparent to Mrs. Di. that Ms. M. lingers when she drops the child at school to ensure A.'s comfort, she maintains notes about school and home behavior as the school requested. In addition, she follows through on her commitments regarding tutoring for A.; she has met with counselors for A.

Regarding A.'s current behavior in school, Mrs. Di. stated that A. gets angry frequently, has hit another child, and yells or complains. She says A. is just now developing skills to handle interactions that do not go her way. She has seen great improvement in her behavior the past few weeks. She said that A. and her mother have a good relationship; she sees them laugh together and kid around together. She reported that she does not know anything about Mr. D., his parenting or judgment, or his relationship with A.

Ms. Sa.

Ms. Sa. was A.'s first grade teacher, during the 1999–2000 school year. She reported that Ms. M. seemed like a young parent who tries very hard and would always follow Ms. Sa.'s suggestions. For example, she kept notes on A.'s behavior and progress from early in the year. Ms. M. brought A. into the classroom each morning and would check in with her; she would help her settle. When A. was in tears, she would take her to the hallway and talk with her, help her learn to use words to deal with her emotions, plan a way to get through the day. Ms. Sa. thought that Ms. M. showed good judgment as a parent because she sought counseling, found help for both of them, worked with the school to help A.'s adjustment, used time-outs and natural consequences for discipline, and avoided the use of any physical punishment. She was also open and honest about A.'s problems, without trying to hide them as parents often do. She saw their relationship as positive and often witnessed them seeming to be physically close. They openly hug each other, and A. seemed to want to please her mother.

Ms. Sa. met Mr. D. when he came into class one day. She remembers very little interaction between him and A. She does remember he stayed on the stool for his whole visit, unlike other parents who would go to the child's desk to review the child's work. She did allow that this was a first time for him and that shyness might have kept him from exploring. At that time, she was unaware of Mr. D.'s relationship with his daughter, parenting abilities, or work background. She did find it strange, she said, that when A. was removed from her father's home "she didn't talk about Dad or what she did with him but rather about grandma and sisters and what she did with them."

Ms. Sa. saw A. as having emotional–behavior problems and stated that academically she was very bright and capable. She remembered that A. always came to school well rested, well groomed, well cared for, with her homework done. She said it was clear to her, however, that A. had been abused, as was manifest in her hyperreactivity and anger outbursts with other students. As she settled into her classroom, fewer outbursts occurred.

Mr. De.

Mr. De. is the principal at A.'s current school. He said he has known A. since her kindergarten year. He described Ms. M. as a very involved and caring mother who is very responsive and communicates well with the school. He saw Ms. M. as showing great patience in mothering A., and good judgment by being very levelheaded in dealing with her. He said he knew nothing of Mr. D. He said that A. has had problems dealing with conflict, disappointment, and responding appropriately when she is angry with someone. He said she had made great progress this school year and has adjusted well, showing great improvement.

Ms. R.

Ms. R. is the day care provider who has known A. in her child care position since A. was about 4 years old. She remembers watching her mother, Ms. M., grow up while she provided care for her older brother and sister. About Ms. M.'s parenting, she said she always brought A. on time and had appropriate backup if she herself couldn't be available for A. She said Ms. M. always has A. well groomed. When A. needs correction, Ms. M. outlines her expectations and reasons for the behavior. If A. is nonresponsive, A. is placed in time-out to encourage reflection and behavior change. "M. doesn't believe in spanking." Ms. R. praised Ms. M.'s judgment as a parent: "When she is not sure of something, she will ask help from people who know so she can stay on the right track." She said Ms. M. and A. have a great relationship. Regarding A.'s present adjustment, Ms. R. said she sees her as active and energetic, a pretty well-rounded child. She said that recently she had problems "smarting off to the teacher, but that subsided pretty quickly." Ms. R. said that A.'s mother does not talk about the father, except for the time recently when she complained about him having A.'s hair cut without telling her. She said that A. "thinks Daddy can give her everything," including things Mom can't or won't. "She enjoys her visits with him and ... has to come back down to reality when she comes back." She said A. will put on that she is "more special" than other children when she first comes back, but that after a reminder she returns to her normal, friendly self.

Ms. C., MSW

Ms. C., MSW, wanted to make clear that her role was to evaluate children for an appropriate diagnosis and treatment when a child exhibits behavioral or emotional problems. She graduated from social work school 2 years ago and found employment at ABC Family Services 6 months ago. This is the first job in which she has evaluated and treated children involved in family law or dependency cases (she typically works 4 hours a week on such cases). It was in that capacity, she was careful to say, she knew A. as a client, Ms. M. as her mother, and Mr. D. as her father. She said she knew nothing about the parenting of either of them.

Ms. C. first saw A. and met her mother on December 2, 1999, when A. was first brought in for evaluation. She saw A. for a total of 6 sessions. She met with both the father and the mother for a joint session, each with A. The final session was June 16, 2000, with Ms. M. Ms. C. initially diagnosed A. as having adjustment disorder with anxiety and then later refined it to adjustment disorder with mixed disturbance because of the report of behavioral problems with the anxiety. The diagnosis was made from her clinical judgment formed during interviews and observations of A. and her parents.

She had concluded that A.'s disturbance had arisen from several possibilities, including the trauma of the severe punishment and physical discipline of the father and the trauma of changing custody. She noted that the father denied using corporal punishment. Both A. and her mother described to her the welts from a beating of A.'s father. It did not appear that her mother prompted A., she noted. However, A. provided very little detail other than mentioning that her father "beat her," and the beating had caused "welts on this part of my body." Ms. C. concluded that it would be hard to make a conclusive statement about these and other issues in the child's life because of A. providing so little detail. Many children, she insisted, have the same symptoms with differing causes.

Ms. C. said A. appeared to like both her mother and her father. She seemed to have an "easygoing relationship" with both of them and showed no signs of fear or intimidation. She said that Mr. D. had made a statement to her that he wanted in the record. She quoted him saying that he had concerns about whether the mother's home was safe and appropriately structured for A.; he believed that his and Ms. M.'s parenting approaches were very different and thought that was not good for the child. Ms. C. did not have any impression as to why Mr. D. would make such a statement. On inquiry from her, he provided no additional comments.

Ms. C. said she saw progress throughout the time of the therapy sessions with A., with a particularly notable improvement from April through June of 2000. She noted that the scary dreams that A. had reported had abated and that the acting out in school had substantially subsided according to the mother's report. Regarding interventions that she might have suggested if similar symptoms continued, she said that the mother had already initiated many: The mother had already begun a program working with the teacher and the school counselor to reinforce the desired behaviors at home and school; they had programmed a way for the child to gain more rewards for consecutive days of attaining behavioral goals; the mother was using grounding and loss of privileges for unacceptable behavior; and whenever A. required discipline, the mother and father were told not to use corporal punishment. "Those things I might have recommended, but the mother had already initiated them. The mother showed concern and good judgment bringing her in to address the problems."

Ms. Ch.

Ms. Ch. was the director of the day care center A. attended the first five years of her life. She insisted that she was not reflecting on Ms. M.'s parenting skills negatively when she said she remembered that Ms. M. did not comply with the law and at times didn't bring the child to care when expected or on time. She surmised that Ms. M. was doing what she thought was in the best interest of the child. She saw as problematic that she did not communicate well or cooperate with A.'s father. She felt strongly that a child ought to have a mother and a father raising a child in cooperation for her best development.

Of Mr. D., Ms. Ch. said he was a parent she would like to see more of in the community. She saw him as very involved in the school, there for A. and for the other children. She said Ms. S. and he were very nurturing for A.'s development, physically and emotionally, and that A. was always clean. She remembered Mr. D. being there for the parent dinner, showing desire, love for the children, and teamwork. She said Mr. D. and Ms. S. treated A. just as they did their other children.

Her concerns about A. included A.'s confusion about parental visits. Ms. Ch. said she could see a difference in A., "vaguely, in her behavior" when she would come back from a visit with her mom. "But she soon adjusted to the program." Regarding her relationship with her mother, Ms. Ch. said "she seemed like she was always happy when she picked her up." And about her relationship with her father, she said, "she seemed always happy to be with her dad as she was with her mom. The dad seemed like he had real good control, but with her mother it was different."

Mr. F.

Mr. F. has employed Ms. M. since her beginning work as a bartender in the adult entertainment establishment. He has relied on Ms. M. as an employee in many ways. She was an honest employee, liked by the customers and fellow employees, and well-respected for her commitment and flexibility to provide overtime coverage. She was prompt for work, readily resumed work after breaks, and handled stressful situations with ease. He stated, "I have never seen someone who is better controlled than Ms. M." No provocation seemed to upset her, according to Mr. F. He reported no use of alcohol by Ms. M. during her employment. The adult entertainment establishment regularly conducts random urine analyses and breathalyzer tests on its barkeeps. Ms. M. never tested positive for any substances or was observed intoxicated or hung-over. None of the employees or customers complained about Ms. M.

All of the above collateral reporters read the narratives about their interviews and made no substantive changes.

DISCUSSION

Each parent has made allegations against the other. Each of these allegations, and other relevant issues, will be discussed in the context of the Washington State Parenting Act and the criteria for modification of a permanent parenting plan RCW 26.09.260:

> (1) Except as otherwise provided in subsections (4), (5), (7), and (9), the court shall not modify a prior custody decree or a parenting plan unless it finds, upon the basis of facts that have arisen since the prior decree or plan or that were unknown to the court at the time of the prior decree or plan, that a substantial change has occurred in the circumstances of the child or the nonmoving party and that the modification is in the best interest of the child and is necessary to serve the best interests of the child.
>
> (2) In applying these standards, the court shall retain the residential schedule established by the decree or parenting plan unless:
>
> . . . (c) The child's present environment is detrimental to the child's physical, mental, or emotional health and the harm likely to be caused by a change of environment is outweighed by the advantage of a change to the child.

Readers of this book, please note that the statutory criteria are set out in italics below so that the lawyers and Judge can easily find how the evaluation evidence leads to the recommendations.

In this section, the findings in regard to the parents' allegations are discussed as to whether, on the basis of facts that have arisen since the prior decree or plan or that were unknown to the court at the time of the prior decree or plan, these findings comprise a substantial change in the circumstances for the child or the nonmoving party (the parent who is defending against the modification action) that cause the modification to be necessary for the best interest of the child.

In May of 1996, the Superior Court ordered a permanent parenting plan that designated the father the custodian of the child and provided the mother liberal visitation. Subsequently, following a history of rancor and disagreement between the parents and the allegation that the father had assaulted the child, the Superior Court issued another order on October 12, 1999, placing the child in the custody of the mother and allowing paternal visitation under the supervision of a [children's agency]. (No such visitations occurred because of ensuing complications.)

PARENTAL ALLEGATIONS

1. **The allegations that Mr. D. used physical punishment in an abusive manner against A. when he struck her several times with a belt, and has acted in a similar fashion prior to this incident; that he is a threat to physically mistreat the child; that he is a threat to physically mistreat Ms. M.:**
   Although he had previously denied that he was the one who left the welts and bruises on his daughter, he has never admitted that he did it to anyone in this ongoing matter; not to the police, not to me, nor to the other professionals involved in this case. He did, however, in the closing interview, deny having made the marks on her. Yet A.'s consistent answers when asked about the marks have been that her father "whupped me." The other children in his household have reported, when asked, that their father, on occasion, has "whupped" them. Indeed, the eldest reported that his father had "whupped" A., as he heard the story, and that his father used the belt sometimes and sometimes his hand to whip the children.
   As reported in the Children's Services report of June 15, 1999, Ms. S. had left a voice mail message for a detective saying that she had hit the child, a statement which, however intended, belied the direct statement of the child and added to the obfuscation. Still further, Mr. D.'s defense coun-

sel in his pleadings for Mr. D. made the argument that the marks resultant of a beating did not cause her caretaker, the mother in this case, to seek medical attention. Because no medical attention was required, he argued, the marks are not the result of child abuse. The point to focus on is not the savagery nor barbarism of the archaic practice of corporal punishment of children, nor its legality. Rather, a pattern of reinforcing Mr. D.'s denial and avoidance of responsibility has arisen, and this pattern permits his anger to mount and result inevitably in the eruption of violence.

In December of 1993, Mr. D. was involved in physical acting out in a confrontation with Ms. M. Although the assault charges were dismissed, the physical striking, shoving, and pushing are on record as admitted to by Mr. D., although he minimized the extent of the violence. Ms. M. gave a detailed account in which she described him grabbing her by the back of her hair and trying to bash her face into the hood of the car. Further, legal declarations attested to by two witnesses corroborated that the violence as described by Ms. M. occurred.

On another occasion, Mr. D. struck his domestic partner, Ms. S., with a baseball bat and pulled her hair such that the investigating detective found a clump of her hair. As part of this incident, Ms. S. reported that Mr. D. tried to burn the apartment, an accusation charged to him by the arresting officer. Demonstrating the pervasive pattern of household denial, Ms. S. later wrote a letter in which she attempted to justify the presence of a gasoline smell. She took responsibility for Mr. D.'s eruption, suggesting she stirred up the fight (out of jealousy about a current issue) and that Mr. D. was acting in self-defense. The other evidence suggested attempted arson by Mr. D. At the time of the police investigation, she admitted to calling attention to the smell in a way to arouse the suspicions of the police and fire department. Again, the charges were dropped. But the bruises and marks on Ms. S. were real, and Mr. D. clearly caused them, as indicated in the police reports in which Mr. D. admitted to striking Ms. S. but explained that the bruises occurred because she bruised easily.

The batterer's assessment found him a candidate likely to benefit from treatment. In response to the assessment, Mr. D. has denied his need for treatment.

During the pendency of this evaluation, Mr. D. was easily frustrated. For instance, he appeared to stifle his frustration with sarcasm when he found himself unprepared for an observed play session with his daughter. Although he did not erupt, he was visibly shaken by the dearth of toys and other materials to occupy his hour with his daughter. During the closing interview, he denied hearing the instruction to come prepared to play for an hour. When the videotape was replayed to show the instruction was given at that time, he commented that the instruction was given in "too quiet a manner."

The results of Mr. D.'s psychological assessment, and specifically the findings of the MMPI–2, appear to place Mr. D. squarely in that population of people who harbor chronic, intense anger. While such people appear overcontrolled, occasions arise when they are unable to inhibit violent outbursts. This is what happened when Mr. D., after a period of pressure-cooking in the stressful situations mentioned, erupted without thinking through the consequences of his actions. He acted out violently, purposefully causing physical pain and harm. Subsequently to the violent acts, he either denied or minimized his culpability in the events.

Deepening the level of concern aroused by Mr. D.'s constant denial is the degree to which he lacks psychological insight. He truly believes his statement that he was not the cause of A.'s injuries (nor of Ms. M.'s, nor Ms. S.'s). He believes that his temper is always in control and never flares. He insisted on this stance, repeatedly, in the closing interview. Such denial when faced with such overwhelming evidence to the contrary makes his tendency toward violent eruptions even more egregious. He often doesn't even know that he has been out of control or remember when he has lost control.

Based on Mr. D.'s past behaviors, psychological test results, and present denial, a grave concern exists that Mr. D. will continue to erupt in violence given stressful circumstances. This was unknown when the original, permanent parenting plan was finalized.

2. **The allegations that Mr. D. emotionally mistreated A. by unilaterally deciding to take her to his home as her primary residence; blaming Ms. M. for his children's unhappiness at A.'s transfer to visit her mother; discussing the likely outcome of this examination with A.; and his use of conflict in an abusive way:**

Although their stories about A.'s move to an East Coast city do not overlap, both Ms. M. and Mr. D. have said that it was a decision Mr. D. took on himself, alone, as the one with the authority to make that decision. In his social history narrative, Mr. D. fondly described his grandmother as "very firm, direct, structured, orderly, loving." His grandfather, too, was "orderly and structured ... disciplined."

Speaking of his current covenanted relationship, he remarked about the order and structure in his family. In the questionnaire screening for battering, he checked that he was the one who made final decisions in the household. (It was a religious conviction.) He complained about Ms. M.'s parenting lacking environmental structure and a standard of discipline.

In play, Mr. D., although asked to first let the child direct the play, directed the play from the beginning and did not cede that role to his daughter at any time. He began that session by rearranging the furniture in the playroom while he fretted over the lack of materials to suit him. Throughout the remainder of the observation he remained in absolute control.

In another instance of rigidity, Mr. D. failed to follow the standard instructions of the evaluation process given at the beginning to all participants. He was to provide copies of pertinent legal documents. Only after several prompts, including calls to his attorney, did Mr. D. bring the legal documents with a note attached asking my staff to make copies of the originals that he brought. He failed to provide copies of the legal documents in a timely manner as instructed repeatedly.

Several times Mr. D. was asked to make copies of allegation forms provided to him. He was instructed to use a separate sheet for each allegation. As chronicled above, he was afforded repeated opportunities to complete this task. On finally receiving the completed work, he had included four allegations on each of two sheets originally provided him rather than making copies of the sheets for one allegation per each sheet as instructed.

In the closing interview, after hearing about the findings related to his behavior, Mr. D. was told that he had 72 hours to present any additional evidence. It took until the end of the week for Mr. D. to obtain police records, which he left under the door of the evaluation offices. He made an unannounced visit to A.'s school, arousing consternation in the school officials about how to accept his visit.

In a letter on his behalf, his supervisor at his current job site praised his effectiveness with children but described his style as authoritarian. Ms. S. concurred with this view. In my closing interview with her she acknowledged that Mr. D. is rigid and authoritarian. She described him as wishing to appear aloof and complex, acknowledging that he often inspires fear by his silent demeanor. She said he often walks away when she is confronting him. This behavior is another indicator of his controlling behavior and inability to engage in reasonable conflict resolution on many occasions.

Ms. S. raised further alarm when she described Mr. D.'s plan for raising A. from infancy (as well as his other children). She said he saw the children as an experiment, trainable to become "his ideal women." He sees himself as training the children with perfect discipline. She said he can say something "one time" and then (she snapped her fingers) he gets an instant response. In developing this description, she said of him that he is a strict, stern parent. He has convinced Ms. S. that adults cannot play that much with children; they have to remain adults and keep the distance.

Concerns about his controlling parenting grew even stronger after witnessing the three children Mr. D. and Ms. S. brought to the closing interview. Although Ms. S. had suggested to him at home earlier that day that it might not be appropriate to bring the children, he insisted, hungry though they were (by Ms. S.'s report). The children, ranging from ages 2 to 9, lined up, beautiful and immaculate, with Ms. S. on one side, Mr. D. on the other. Not a peep. No giggling, no looks toward one another, no jostling, pinching, or whispering. In a word, the children were drastically subdued. They remained this way throughout the 2 hours they were present at my office until they left with their parents at 9 p.m.

Mr. D. has shown himself incapable of the level of reciprocity required by parenting. By both his and Ms. S.'s descriptions of parenting goals and methods to strive for them, the children repeatedly serve as his chattel. The matter he constantly referred to throughout the evaluation is how his parenting appeared, how the children's demeanor and behavior redounded to his glory. This focused gaze on oneself depicts a sense of ownership and of the children being in his life to meet his needs; he does not focus on the development of autonomy of his children in a child-centered approach to parenting.

These examples support and flesh out the MMPI–2 findings that describe him as defensive, argumentative, rigid, moralistic, and authoritarian. It appears from the evidence of this evaluation that he has developed a controlling approach to others in his current life. Coupled with his documented tendencies to erupt violently, this behavior suggests another facet about him not known at the time of the original parenting plan. His need for control and to control is an aspect that furthers opportunities for him to erupt.

3. **Allegations that Ms. M. created or used conflict in an abusive way; that she withheld access to A. from the father:**

    The records of both parties describe the same incidents, albeit with differing flavors. Ms. M. was party to raising a ruckus over the baby bottle incident. Several times Ms. M. did not comply with the court-ordered visitations after the alleged child abuse by Mr. D. Before that, she caused Mr. D. to have to call the police so that he could pick up A. from her home and hand her the official copy of the new visitation schedule. The documentary evidence shows that Ms. M. did not, in fact, know that Mr. D. was arriving, nor did she know that he wanted to give her an official visitation schedule.

4. **Allegations that Ms. M. threatened to neglect or physically mistreat A.; that she has physically mistreated her:**

    Mr. D. asserted and Ms. M. denied that she has struck A. or threatened to do so. The question had been raised and not answered whether Ms. M.'s mother spanked A. one time. Ms. M. denies that her mother has ever spanked a child. She said that physical punishment was a method her parents strenuously objected to. Ms. M. denied using physical punishment, and the testimony of the collaterals, including the therapist, Ms. C.; the day care provider, Ms. R.; and the teachers, Ms. D. and Ms. Sa., have corroborated that Ms. M. does not use hitting or spanking as a means of discipline.

5. **Allegations that Ms. M. emotionally mistreats or neglects A. and that she is inadequate or incompetent to care for her:**

    Mr. D. has complained that A. spends much of her time at her mother's house in her room, while her mother entertains her boyfriend. He further asserted that Ms. M. does not routinely allow her daughter to wear the nicer, new clothes he bought for her. He also said that A. often arrives dirty and unkempt at his house for weekend visits. Further, he said that her apartment is messy and dirty and for this reason the mother seldom allows A. to bring playmates into the home.

    No corroborating evidence exists for any of these allegations. In fact, those who made planned home visits to Ms.

M.'s apartment described it as neat and clean. The collateral witnesses, to a person, commented on A.'s neatness and grooming. Nor is such behavior consonant with what Ms. M. demonstrated during the evaluation. Ms. M. always had A. with her when she arrived at the office. Both A. and she were well groomed. Her psychological profile suggests that she may likely find it difficult starting and following through on tasks, is likely to feel inertia, particularly when stressful conditions have made her tense and worried. However, this isolated test result is not corroborated by any other piece of independent evidence that emerged during the evaluation.

6. **Allegations that Ms. M. uses alcohol and drugs to excess:**

   Mr. D. furnished a declaration sworn by Mr. T. (a friend of Mr. D.'s) that he witnessed Ms. M. working in an adult entertainment establishment and thought he smelled alcohol on her breath at the time. Mr. D. suspected he smelled alcohol on her breath several times when he arrived at her apartment. However, Ms. M. never tested positive for any substances as a barkeep, nor did Mr. F. ever observe Ms. M. intoxicated. None of the employees or customers had complained about Ms. M. in any respect.

   Ms. M. admitted to occasional use of alcohol but denied using alcohol to excess or other illegal drugs. At the same time, Ms. M. admitted that for a time, she was dating and cohabitating with a Mr. R., who had a record of using and selling drugs and who was on probation. She said she kicked him out of the house the very moment she heard from the police that he had drugs in his possession or was using drugs at the time.

7. **Concerns about Ms. M. exercising poor judgment:**

   During the closing interview, Ms. M.'s judgment was questioned: in choosing to have a relationship with a man with a drug history; in selecting and working a job in the adult entertainment industry; and in ignoring court-ordered visitation times (for which she was cited for contempt on one occasion). Ms. M. responded in her defense, that she was unaware of her ex-boyfriend's past and current drug-related behaviors; she worked the bartending job because she could not find work that would pay the money she needed for legal fees; and she was unaware of the schedule and she unwittingly broke it. However, of greater concern is that Ms. M.'s current fiancé refused to accompany her to the closing interview, although I urged her to ask him, and she did, vehemently. This refusal raises still further concerns about Ms.

M's judgment, given her pursuit of a relationship with a partner who fails to help her in such important matters.

Ms. M. also has a troubled driving record: Although never
stopped for driving under the influence, she has been stopped
for speeding, cited for not having insurance, and has had her
license suspended. Again, each of these examples of poor
judgment is of concern.

*Does this evidence of poor judgment provide knowledge that
was not known at the time of the original parenting plan or give
cause to worry about the child's present environment with the
mother?* Everything seems to point to Ms. M. as young, unworldly, and naïve in her pregnancy, birth, and early months
with A. and her interacting with the father. Every collateral
recently interviewed spoke of her in terms of her making
great efforts, listening and learning from guidance, seeking
that guidance and feedback on the changes she was making
in parenting A., and being open to hearing about weaknesses
she might address. There is no doubt about her growing and
developing as an open-minded mother. It appears that her
poor judgment is changing with maturity and that she has
made significant progress in this respect.

THE CHILD'S ENVIRONMENT

*The second issue is a two-part question: Is the child's present environment
with the mother detrimental to the child's physical, mental, and emotional health?
And if so, would the harm associated with the change in home environment
outweigh the advantages of the change?*

Based on the evidence presented above, the present environment
with the mother is not detrimental to A. In fact, in light of all of the
evidence, it appears reasonable to conclude that A. will likely be harmed
if she is returned to the custodial care of her father.

One issue remains that commands attention. By all reports, A. enjoys
good relationships with her siblings and a particularly close bond with a
sister about 6 months her junior. Every effort must be made to assure her
continuing relationship with these siblings.

RECOMMENDATIONS

Residential Placement and Visitation Schedule

1. Primary residential placement of the child should now remain
   with the mother.

2. The visitation schedule for Mr. D. should remain as stated in the current temporary order, until the conditions set forth below are completed.

Decision Making

1. Day-to-day decision making should be by the parent with whom the child is residing.
2. In light of the domestic violence and documented inability of Mr. D. to work well with Ms. M., all decision-making authority should rest with Ms. M.

Treatment

1. Mr. D. should enroll in and complete domestic violence treatment at [one of three named agencies] that has respected programs for ending domestic violence while protecting potential victims.
2. Mr. D.'s visitation with A. should remain supervised until he has completed the above program.
3. When Mr. D. has completed the domestic violence program successfully, the summer and vacation schedule for A.'s visitations should change as follows: Mr. D. will have visitations with A. for 8 of the 10 summer weeks, which will include 2 weeks of vacation time. During that period, Ms. M. will have visitations the 1st, 3rd, and 5th weekends of the month, from Friday after the day's activities until Sunday evening, or Monday evening if it is a holiday weekend. This visitation schedule also remains contingent on A. being involved in at least 6 hours a weekday of summer enrichment programming that is approved by Ms. M. Mr. D. must specify the weeks of the summer visitation and the summer enrichment programming by April 1 of every year.
4. Ms. M. should provide A. with at least three visits to one of the three child psychologists [three child psychologists who have agreed to meet with this child, along with their office telephone numbers listed here] to finish processing concerns she may have about remaining primarily with her mother.
5. Once Mr. D. has successfully graduated from the domestic violence treatment program, Mr. D. and Ms. M. should seek counseling with a qualified coparent counselor and follow treatment recommendations about remediating communication and parenting deficits: [three names and telephone numbers of professionals]. All counseling should occur in separate

sessions with each parent and A. Continuity of care will more likely occur if one coparent counselor is working on the issues of both parents on separate occasions. The issues the coparent counselor and parents should address include (a) coming to terms with differences in parenting style; (b) developing appropriate parenting skills for dealing with difficulties with A.; (c) ending rancor; (d) avoiding use of the child against each other; (e) integrating lessons learned in treatment with parenting; (f) providing mutual respect for positive differences in the separate households; and (g) monitoring and counseling of stepparent (or significant other) interactions.

6. Ms. M.'s fiancé, Mr. J., if he remains involved with Ms. M., must attend coparent counseling to focus on the age range of A. and help him develop age-appropriate expectations for a stepparent relationship with her. If Mr. J. refuses to enter counseling, an impasse should be declared by the coparent counselor (see dispute resolution section below), and an arbitrator should determine whether residential placement of A. with Ms. M. should continue.

Communication With the Child and Other Parent

1. Neither parent shall discuss the details of any aspect of the dispute with A. This includes but is not limited to legal action, visitation, placement, child support, and parental allegations. Each parent shall convey positive support regarding visitation and placement with the other parent. Both parents shall exhibit a positive attitude regarding the plan when communicating with their daughter.

2. Neither parent shall limit the telephone contacts between the child and the parent with whom she is not currently residing.

3. To minimize opportunities for conflict, the parents shall communicate solely in writing.

4. They are to use fax, certified mail, or electronic mail to provide verifiable receipt.

5. Each message shall address one issue only, no more than 50 words per message.

6. The parent receiving the message shall respond to the issue within 72 hours.

7. Should the coparent counselor declare an impasse, the parents will provide information and all correspondence about the issue to the arbitrator.

Dispute Resolution Process

1. The parents should bring disputes between them to the co-parent counselor. If the coparent counselor declares an impasse, the parties shall bring the matter to mandatory arbitration. The parents should select one of the three following arbitrators: [names and telephone numbers here].

2. We recommend that the parents begin the arbitration process by sending notification by certified mail. The arbitration process shall give preference to carrying out the approved parenting plan and prepare a written record of any agreement the parties reach and any arbitration award.

3. If the arbitrator finds that either party has used or frustrated the process in bad faith, the arbitrator should award attorney fees and financial sanctions to the other party. The arbitrator should distribute the costs between the parties at his or her discretion. To deter abusive use of the process, the cost should be assessed in a way that places financial responsibility on the person who uses the process inappropriately. In addition, if an arbitration decision is appealed to the trial court, the moving party must pay the retainer fees for the lawyer of the nonmoving party. Unless the moving party substantially improves his or her legal position, the moving party must also pay the entire cost of the arbitration.

This report is written to the best of my ability and has been reviewed by _____. I can be contacted at the following telephone number for future correspondence [add telephone number.]

_____   _____
Evaluator   Date

12

SAMPLE B. REPORT OF *MR. D. v. MS. M.*, EVALUATION FOR PERMANENT PARENTING PLAN ACTION

All of the facts are the same. The sections that are different for a permanent parenting plan action are altered to fit the legal criteria of the two different types of actions (an action calling for the modification of an existing permanent parenting plan and a permanent parenting plan action), and these sections follow. Readers of this book, please note that the statutory criteria are set out in italics below so that the lawyers and judge can easily find how the evaluation evidence leads to the recommendations.

PARENTING EVALUATION

Referral Source and Purpose

This evaluation was ordered by Judge Z. on September 2, 2000, who directed [name of evaluator] to investigate and report on the issues related to the development of a permanent parenting plan about physical custody, issues of visitation, and decision-making allocation. The parents in this case, Mr. D. and Ms. M., agreed in 1999 to a temporary parenting plan organized by a court-appointed mediator. When their child, A. (DOB: _____), visited Ms. M. on the weekend of October 10, 1998, her mother reported that she saw red welts on A.'s back, thighs, and buttocks. Ms. M. reported this to the police, which prompted A.'s transition from her father's care into her mother's home. Mr. D. maintained regular visits with A., per his compliance with certain conditions. The purpose of this evaluation and report is to assess all parties in the matter, evaluate the parenting circumstances for A., and offer recommendations to the court for developing a permanent parenting plan. Mr. D., the petitioner, is represented by Mr. P. The defendant, Ms. M., is representing herself *pro se*.

Discussion

Each parent has made several accusations against the other. Each of these allegations, as well as other relevant issues, will be discussed in the context of the Washington State Parenting Act and the criteria for establishing a permanent parenting plan (RCW 26.09.187, .191).

Residential Provisions [RCW 26.09.187(3)]:

1. The relative strength, nature, and stability of each child's relationship with each parent, including whether a parent has taken greater responsibility for performing daily parenting functions relating to the daily needs of the children.

In this section, the findings about the allegations that might affect the relative strength, nature, and stability of the child's relationship with each parent are discussed. In addition the relative parental capabilities are delineated.

A. PARENTAL ALLEGATIONS

1. **Allegations regarding Mr. D. using physical punishment in an abusive manner against A. when he struck her several times with a belt, and has acted in a similar fashion prior to this incident; that he is a threat to physically mistreat the child; and that he is a threat to physically mistreat Ms. M.:**

   Although he had never denied that he was the one who left the welts and bruises on his daughter, he has never admitted it to anyone in this ongoing matter; neither to the police, nor to me, nor to the other professionals involved in this case. He did, however, in the closing interview, deny having made the marks on her. Yet A.'s consistent answers when asked about the marks have been that her father "whupped me." The other children in his household have reported, when asked, that their father, on occasion, has "whupped" them. Indeed the eldest reported that his father had "whupped" A., as he heard the story, and that his father used the belt sometimes and sometimes his hand to whip the children.

Furthering this stance of obfuscation, the Children's Services report of June 15, 1999, stated that Ms. S. had left a voice mail message for a detective saying that she had hit the child, a statement which, however intended, belies the direct statement of the child. Still further, Mr. D.'s defense counsel in his pleadings for Mr. D. makes the argument that the marks resultant of a beating did not cause her caretaker, the mother in this case, to seek medical attention. Because no medical attention was required, he argued, the marks are not the result of child abuse. The point to focus on is not the savagery nor barbarism of the archaic practice of corporal punishment of children, nor again its legality. Rather a pattern of reinforcing Mr. D.'s denial and avoidance of responsibility has arisen, and this pattern permits the process of pressure-cooking his anger to result inevitably in the eruption of violence.

In an incident in December of 1993, Mr. D. was involved in physical acting out in a confrontation with Ms. M. Although the assault charges were dismissed, the physical striking, shoving, and pushing are on record as admitted to by Mr. D., although he minimized the extent of the violence. Ms. M. gave a detailed account in which she described him grabbing her by the back of her hair and trying to bash her face into the hood of the car. Further, legal declarations attested to by two witnesses corroborated that the violence as described by Ms. M. occurred. On another occasion, Mr. D. struck his domestic partner, Ms. S., with a baseball bat and pulled her hair such that the investigating detective found a clump of her hair. As part of this incident, Ms. S. reported that Mr. D. tried to burn the apartment, an accusation charged to him by the arresting officer.

Demonstrating the pervasive pattern of household denial, Ms. S. later wrote a letter in which she attempted to justify the presence of a gasoline smell. She took responsibility for Mr. D.'s eruption, suggesting she stirred up the fight (out of jealousy about a current issue) and that Mr. D. was acting in self-defense. The other evidence suggested attempted arson by Mr. D. At the time of the police investigation, she admitted to calling attention to the smell in a way to arouse the suspicions of the police and fire department. Again, the charges were dropped. But the bruises and marks on Ms. S. were real, and Mr. D. clearly caused them as indicated in the police reports in which Mr. D. admitted to striking Ms. S. but explained that the bruises occurred because she bruised easily.

The domestic violence assessment found him a candidate likely to benefit from treatment. In response to the assessment, Mr. D. has denied his need for treatment.

During the pendency of this evaluation, Mr. D. was easily frustrated. For instance, he appeared to stifle his upset with sarcasm when he found himself ready for an observed play session with his daughter and discovered he had come unprepared. Although he did not erupt, he was visibly shaken by the dearth of toys and other materials to occupy his hour with his daughter. During the closing interview, he denied hearing the instruction to come prepared to play for an hour. When the videotape was replayed to show the instruction was given at that time, he commented that the instruction was given in "too quiet a manner."

The results of Mr. D.'s psychological assessment, and specifically the findings of the MMPI–2, appear to place Mr. D. squarely in that population of people who harbor chronic, intense anger. Although such people appear overcontrolled, occasions arise when they are unable to inhibit violent outbursts. This is what happened when Mr. D., after a period of pressure-cooking in the stressful situations mentioned, erupted without thinking through the consequences of his actions. He acted out violently, purposefully causing physical pain and harm. Subsequently to the violent acts, he either denied or minimized the events.

Deepening the level of concern that his constant denial arouses is how devoid of psychological insight Mr. D. possesses. He truly believes his statement that he was not the cause of A.'s injuries, (nor of Ms. M.'s, nor Ms. S.'s). He believes that his temper is always in control and never flares. He insisted on this stance, repeatedly, in the closing interview. Such denial when faced with such overwhelming evidence to the contrary makes his tendency toward violent eruptions even more egregious. He often doesn't even know that he has been out of control or can remember when he has lost control. A grave concern exists then, based on past behaviors and psychological test results, as well as his present denial, that Mr. D. is likely to erupt in violence given stressful circumstances.

2. **The allegations that Mr. D. emotionally mistreated A. by unilaterally deciding to take her to his home as her primary residence; blaming Ms. M. for his children's upset at A.'s transfer to visit her mother; discussing the likely outcome of this examination with A.; and his use of conflict in an abusive way:**

Although their stories about A.'s move to East Coast city do not overlap, both Ms. M. and Mr. D. have said that it was a decision Mr. D. took on himself, alone, as the one with the authority to make that decision. In his social history narrative, Mr. D. fondly described his grandmother as "very firm, direct, structured, orderly, loving." His grandfather, too, was "orderly and structured . . . disciplined."

Speaking of his current covenanted relationship, he remarked about the order and structure in his family. In the questionnaire screening for battering, he checked that he was the one who made final decisions in the household. (It was a religious conviction.) He complained about Ms. M.'s parenting lacking environmental structure and a standard of discipline.

In play, Mr. D., although asked to first let the child direct the play, directed the play from the beginning and did not cede that role to his daughter at any time. He began that session by rearranging the furniture in the playroom while he fretted over the lack of materials to suit him. Throughout the remainder of the observation he remained in absolute control.

In another instance of rigidity, Mr. D. failed to follow the standard instructions of the evaluation process given at the beginning to all participants. He was to provide copies of pertinent legal documents. Only after several prompts, including calls to his attorney, did Mr. D. bring the legal documents with a note attached asking my staff to make copies of the originals that he brought. He failed to provide copies of the legal documents in a timely manner as instructed repeatedly.

Several times Mr. D. was asked to make copies of allegation forms provided to him. He was instructed to use a separate sheet for each allegation. As chronicled above he was afforded repeated opportunities to complete this task. On finally receiving the completed work, he had included four allegations on each of two sheets originally provided him rather than making copies of the sheets for one allegation per each sheet as instructed.

In the closing interview, after hearing about the findings related to his behavior, Mr. D. was told that he had 72 hours to present any additional evidence. It took to the end of the week for Mr. D. to obtain the police records that he left under the door of the evaluation offices. He made an un-announced visit to A.'s school, arousing consternation in the school officials about how to accept his visit.

In a letter on his behalf, his supervisor at his current job site praised his effectiveness with children but described his style as authoritarian. Ms. S. concurred with this view. In my closing interview with her she acknowledged that Mr. D. is rigid and authoritarian. She described him as wishing to ap-pear aloof and complex, acknowledging that he often inspires fear by his silent demeanor. She said he often walks away when she is confronting him. This behavior is another in-dicator of his controlling behavior and inability to engage in reasonable conflict resolution on many occasions.

Ms. S. raised further alarm when she described Mr. D.'s plan for raising A. from infancy (as well as his other chil-dren). She said he saw the children as an experiment, some-one whom he could train to be "his ideal women." He sees himself as training the children with perfect discipline. She said he can say something "one time" and then (she snapped her fingers) he gets an instant response. In developing this description, she said of him that he is a strict, stern parent. He has convinced Ms. S. that adults cannot play that much with children; they have to remain adults and keep the dis-tance.

Concerns about his controlling parenting grew even stronger after witnessing the three children Mr. D. and Ms. S. brought to the closing interview. While Ms. S. had sug-gested to him at home earlier that day that it might not be appropriate to bring the children, he insisted, hungry though they were (by Ms. S.'s report.) The children, beautiful and immaculate, lined up, ranging from age 2 to 9, with Ms.. S. on one side, Mr. D. on the other. Not a peep. No giggling, no looks toward one another, no jostling, pinching, mild shoving, or whispering. In a word, the children were drasti-cally subdued. They remained this way throughout the 2 hours they were present at my office until they left with their parents at 9 p.m.

Mr. D. has shown himself incapable of the level of reci-procity parenting calls for. By both his and Ms. S.'s descrip-tions of parenting goals and methods to strive for them, the children repeatedly serve as his chattel. The matter he constantly referred to throughout the evaluation is how his parenting appeared, how the children's demeanor and behavior redounded to his glory. This focused gaze on oneself depicts a sense of ownership and the children being in his life to meet his needs rather than a focus on the development of autonomy of his children in a child-centered approach to parenting.

These examples support and flesh out the MMPI–2 findings that describe him as defensive, argumentative, rigid, moralistic, and authoritarian. It appears from the evidence of this evaluation that he has developed a controlling approach to others in his current life. His need for control and to control is an aspect that furthers opportunities for him to erupt.

3. **Allegations that Ms. M. created or used conflict in an abusive way; that she withheld access to A. from the father:**

Indeed the record of both parties describes the same incidents, with differing flavors. Ms. M. was party to raising a ruckus over the baby bottle incident. Several times Ms. M. did not comply with the court-ordered visitations after the alleged child abuse by Mr. D. Before that, she caused Mr. D. to have to call the police so that he could pick up A. from her home and hand her the official copy of the new visitation schedule. The documentary evidence shows that Ms. M. did not, in fact, know that Mr. D. was arriving, nor did she know that he wanted to give her an official visitation schedule.

4. **Allegations that Ms. M. threatened to neglect or physically mistreat A.; that she has physically mistreated her:**

Mr. D. asserted and Ms. M. denied that she has struck A. or threatened to do so. The question had been raised and not answered whether Ms. M.'s mother spanked A. one time. Ms. M. denies that her mother has ever spanked a child. She said that physical punishment was a method her parents strenuously objected to. Ms. M. denied using physical punishment, and the testimony of the collaterals, including the therapist, Ms. C.; the day care provider, Ms. R.; and the teachers Ms. D. and Ms. Sa. have corroborated that Ms. M. does not use hitting or spanking as a means of discipline.

5. **Allegations that Ms. M. emotionally mistreats or neglects A. and that she is inadequate or incompetent to care for her:**

Mr. D. has complained that A. spends much of her time at her mother's house in her room, while her mother entertains her boyfriend. He further asserted that Ms. M. does not routinely allow her daughter to wear the nicer, new clothes he bought for her. He also said that A. often arrives dirty and unkempt at his house for weekend visits. Further, he said that her apartment is messy and dirty, and for this reason the mother seldom allows A. to bring playmates into the home.

No corroborating evidence exists that supports any of these allegations. In fact, those who made planned home visits to Ms. M.'s apartment described it as neat and clean. The collateral witnesses, to a person, commented on A.'s neatness and grooming. Nor is such behavior consonant with what Ms. M. demonstrated during the evaluation. Ms. M. always had A. when she arrived at the office with her. Both A. and she were well groomed. Her psychological profile suggests that she may likely find it difficult starting and following through on tasks, is likely to feel inertia, particularly when stressful conditions have made her tense and worried. However, this isolated test result is not corroborated by any other piece of independent evidence that emerged during the evaluation.

6. **Allegations that Ms. M. uses alcohol and drugs to excess:**

    Mr. D. furnished a declaration sworn by Mr. T. (a friend of Mr. D.'s) that he witnessed Ms. M. working in an adult entertainment establishment and thought he smelled alcohol on her breath at the time. Mr. D. suspected he smelled alcohol on her breath several times when he arrived at her apartment. However, Ms. M. never tested positive for any substances as a barkeep, nor did Mr. F. (her employer) ever observe Ms. M. intoxicated. None of the employees or customers had complained about Ms. M. in any respect.

    Ms. M. admitted to occasional use of alcohol while she denied using alcohol to excess or other illegal drugs. At the same time, Ms. M. admitted for a time dating and cohabitating with a Mr. R., who had a record of using and selling drugs and was on probation. She said she kicked him out of the house the very moment she heard from the police that he had drugs in his possession or was using drugs at the time.

7. **Concerns about Ms. M. exercising poor judgment:**

    During the closing interview, Ms. M.'s poor judgment was questioned in choosing to have a relationship with a man with a drug history, in selecting and working a job in the adult entertainment industry, and in ignoring court-ordered visitation times (for which she was cited for contempt on one occasion). Ms. M. responded in her defense that she was unaware of her ex-boyfriend's past and current drug-related behaviors; that she worked the bartending job because she could not find work that would pay her more money, money that she needed for the legal fees; and that she claims to have been unaware of the schedule as she unwittingly broke it. However, of greater concern is that Ms. M.'s current fiancé refused to accompany her to the closing interview, although I urged her, and she him, vehemently. His refusal raises yet another question about Ms. M.'s judgment at pursuing a relationship with a partner who would not help her in such an important matter.

Ms. M. also has a troubled driving record: Although never stopped for driving under the influence, she has been stopped for speeding, cited for not having insurance, and has had her license suspended. Again, each of these examples of poor judgment is of concern.

The weight of the evidence seems to point to Ms. M. as young, unworldly, and naïve in her pregnancy, birth, and early months with A. and her interacting with the father. However, every collateral recently interviewed spoke of her in terms of her making great efforts, listening and learning from guidance, seeking that guidance and feedback on the changes she was making in parenting A., and being open to hearing about weaknesses she might address. There is no doubt about her growing and developing as an open-minded mother. It appears that her poor judgment is changing with maturity and that she has made significant progress in this respect.

B. PARENTING CAPABILITIES

From observation of both parents with A., it was apparent that both parents are bonded with A., show her affection, and demonstrate a variety of parenting skills, including attending to her behavior and being able to supervise her. However, Ms. M. demonstrated superior parenting skills and many fewer deficits than Mr. D. This should carry substantial weight in determining A.'s primary residential placement.

It is of primary concern that Mr. D.'s difficulty regulating his emotions may interfere with his parenting abilities. In the parenting observation, he expressed frustration with the process in front of A. that affected A.'s experience. Ms. S., Mr. D.'s covenanted wife, readily admits to such an effect. Throughout the evaluation, Mr. D. has expressed very intense and negative emotions relating to Ms. M. and her parenting abilities. It is doubtful that

Mr. D. possesses the skills to contain his emotions without significant treatment. Mr. D. shows little insight into how his difficulty with emotional regulation may affect others, including his daughter.

The other central concern is Mr. D.'s basic distrust of Ms. M.'s parenting abilities. His proposal that he be the primary parent with no decision-making and no contact until A. develops "self-worth" and becomes a "modest and quiet young lady" represents a serious flaw in his capacity to understand A.'s developmental needs and the importance of A.'s relationship with her mother. His controlling and intimidating behavior appears to have had a significant impact on his daughter, as occurred in the parenting observation when he was overly directive and persistent with A. when she did not comply. Further, Mr. D.'s hostility toward Ms. M. has affected his ability to interpret her parenting behavior accurately.

II. Agreements of the parties, provided they were entered into knowingly and voluntarily.

There are no agreements; all parenting provisions have been court ordered.

III. Each parent's past and potential for future performance of parenting functions.

A significant strength of this family is that both parents appear to have the capacity and willingness to provide for their child's basic material needs, such as food, clothing, and shelter. In addition, both parents appear to care for A. and are very concerned about her welfare. However, a significant gap exists in the parents' skills. As described earlier, Mr. D.'s emotional volatility, pattern of control, and overreactions related to Ms. M. interfere with his parenting.

Both parents continue to distrust each other's parenting abilities, and this is interfering in their fulfilling the needs of their child. To have positive impacts on their child, they must stop dwelling on past injustices by the other parent and concentrate on improving their own parenting practices. This especially applies to Mr. D. This is difficult, in that both parents appear to genuinely believe that they are fighting to protect their child from the negative effects of the other's parenting.

Particularly concerning is Mr. D.'s level of denial and refusal to take responsibility for his actions. He repeatedly blamed the judicial process and saw himself as a "victim" of it and of Ms. M.'s "exaggerated claims." He is also resistant toward following through with long-term therapeutic services. Mr. D. denies that his level of hostility toward Ms. M. is interfering with his parenting. He seems so consumed with his battle with her that his behavior is detrimental to his child. His high need for control and reactivity when emotionally overloaded clearly interferes with his parenting. He will require professional assistance to extinguish this pattern, move on with his life, and learn to parent in a nonreactive, reality-based manner.

Ms. M. would also benefit from intervention. She has displayed bad judgment in relationships and may continue to do so if she does not receive help. However, she demonstrated a good level of insight during the judicial and evaluation process and was willing to take responsibility for her actions. She was aware of her relationship problems and expressed willingness for treatment. She has responded very positively to treatment in the past. Ms. M. has expressed that she wants Mr. D. to continue to be a part of A.'s life. Of the two parents, she is the more likely to cooperate in establishing a workable parenting plan.

IV. The emotional needs and developmental level of the children.

A paramount concern for A. is that she be shielded from her parents' discord and helped to develop a positive relationship with each parent. Postdivorce conflict is one of the major risks to children's emotional and behavioral health. In addition, research suggests a correlation between postdivorce conflict in high-conflict families and the amount of shared decision making that requires direct communication. Thus, the custody arrangement should ideally allow these parents to disengage from their conflict with each other and develop parallel and separate parenting relationships with their child.

A. needs to learn how stress can be managed in a healthy manner. She needs to learn how to appropriately express her feelings, to know she should be treated with respect, and to be respectful with others. Both counseling and school interventions have assisted in her developing these skills. Further intervention will help her continue becoming a healthy adolescent.

V. The children's relationship with siblings and with other significant adults, as well as the children's involvement with their physical surroundings, school, or other significant activities.

Both Mr. D. and Ms. M. have indicated that A. should spend time with her half-siblings. Since leaving her father's home she has made a successful transition to her new school and begun a number of extracurricular activities that she enjoys. Every effort should be made to maintain consistency for A. with her half-siblings, in school, and her extracurricular activities.

VI. The wishes of the parents and the wishes of the children who are sufficiently mature to express reasoned and independent preferences as to residential schedules.

Mr. D. has requested primary residential placement, no contact between Ms. M. and A., and sole decision-making with any possibility of dispute resolution. He indicated that he would want Ms. M. to "visit or spend time with him during the holidays" after A. develops "self-worth" and becomes a "modest and quiet young lady." At that point, Mr. D. believes that she will have developed sufficient ability to understand the behavior of her mother. Ms. M. stated, "It's important for children to have both parents in their lives. As long as both parents are a healthy part of the children's lives." She reported being "happy" with the current temporary parenting plan, although "I do feel we might want to re-evaluate the visitation." She indicated that she does not want Mr. D. having overnight visits with A. She requested that most holidays be spent with each parent on alternate years, except she wanted to spend Mother's Day and her birthday with A. and have Mr. D. spend his birthday and Father's Day with A. She requested that the parents make joint decisions and undergo dispute resolution through court order.

A. is not old enough to express an informed preference regarding the parenting plan.

VII. *Each parent's employment schedule.*

Mr. D. reported that his work schedule is from Friday until Tuesday from 7 a.m. to 5:30 p.m. He anticipates a potential change in residence in the near future due to "management opportunities" that would require relocation out of the state [that Ms. M. and A. live in]. He requested that A. move with him if he relocates out of state. Ms. M. works between 7:30 a.m. and 4 p.m., Monday to Friday.

IV

AFTERWORD

AFTERWORD

In this book we endeavored to describe a step-by-step evaluation protocol for generating comprehensive custody evaluations. This allegation-focused method is embedded squarely in current clinical research across mental health disciplines and from practical experiences derived from hundreds of cases. The method is also the result of evolving legal doctrines in the United States, as well as ethical perspectives developed by the American Psychological Association.

Divorcing parents, because of their heightened sensitivity, will make allegations that may not be wholly accurate. High-conflict custody cases are commonly infused with highly charged allegations of domestic violence and child abuse or neglect. These types of allegations require complex judgments about personal credibility, family relationships, and true parenting abilities. Of all the professionals involved with high-conflict families in the legal arena, a trained mental health expert is the best candidate to evaluate the allegations, arrive at findings about the parties, and offer recommendations about how to reorganize family relationships to promote healthy child adjustment. This evaluative form of alternative dispute resolution is thorough, efficient, and less emotionally and financially costly than trial.

It is important to remember that custody evaluations are particularly conducive to errors in clinical judgment. Further, the vagaries of the best interests standard allow for a range of clinical judgments regarding parenting ability that may in fact have little to do with true parenting abilities. In our view, trained forensic mental health professionals can learn to make these difficult judgments about credibility but should maintain reliance on converging evidence and use a cautious approach in their conclusions and interpretations. In short, the error rates for clinical judgment are high enough to create a level of uncertainty that should inspire a cautious approach to generating conclusions in custody evaluations. Our proposed allegation method will result in substantially reduced risks of evaluator errors that would result in ethical or malpractice complaints.

The allegation method involves reviewing and analyzing massive, complicated puzzles. To understand and arrange the puzzle pieces to create a representative and realistic picture, the evaluator's mandate is to accomplish the following: (a) to clarify the limits of confidentiality and explain the nature of evaluation; (b) to write about and speak with respect to each party, focusing on descriptions of the relevant behaviors, not diagnoses, and to operationalize how the behavior may affect parenting; (c) to acknowledge subjective opinion while upholding the objective facts; (d) to reveal only that which is relevant and not make recommendations about unrelated issues; (e) to use all available data to ensure that findings result from multiple measure corroboration to obtain convergent validity; (f) to accept no contingency fees; and (g) to withdraw from cases when countertransference interferes with objectivity.

The evaluator should always be aware that this work takes place in the legal arena, which is an adversarial forum. As a result, the evaluator must expect and be prepared for routine and special challenges. There will be attempts to blame the evaluator, hold him or her liable, or place him or her in an adversarial position. The evaluator may also feel buffeted by an imbalance of power, when one party is better represented and better prepared than the other. Despite the challenges that arise, the evaluator should avoid being drawn into adversarial conflict. The evaluator's prevailing focus throughout the process is to maintain an objective point of view and produce a comprehensive evaluation.

Throughout this book we described our step-by-step approach to performing comprehensive family law evaluations, which focuses specifically on the well-being of children in postdivorce adjustment. By conducting evaluations in the manner described, we believe that the interests of the children caught in these family law cases will best be served and protected. We encourage, however, each evaluator to continue studying and considering the emerging clinical, legal, and ethical information. This commitment to learning will not only assist each evaluator to eventually adapt and extend our procedures, but will also raise the standard for our services. It is, in our opinion, the best way to honor the forensic evaluator's dual commitment to our professional discipline and to the persons whose lives it is designed to enhance. We hope this book results in a better future for all children evaluated and the communities in which they live.

V

APPENDIXES

APPENDIX A: AGREEMENT TO PARENTING EVALUATION

In this agreement, I address common issues that arise in parenting evaluations. Please take the time to read through this document, review it with your attorney, and then ask questions in your initial meeting with the evaluator.

It is important that you understand in advance that this is an evaluation for legal purposes and that your children are our only clients. There is a possibility that our impressions, conclusions, and recommendations may not be what you desire and may be unfavorable to your legal position. It is a very difficult and, at times, a painful task to make recommendations concerning parent–child relationships. But this is my job and that is why you are here by court order or through stipulated agreement of all the parties in this case.

Psychological questionnaires, personality assessments, and other tests may be administered before the interviews. The evaluation itself will consist of the results of these psychological tests, interviews with each parent, observations of each parent with their children, and collateral interviews with third parties (e.g., other professionals involved with members of your family). This allows me to collect a wide range of data and organize the issues while minimizing the cost to you. During the interviews, you have the right to refuse to answer a question or line of questions. You also can ask to take a break from the interview, if necessary. The interviews and observations will be videotaped. All videotapes will be destroyed before the end of the evaluation process and you agree that none of the tapes will be released to any party, attorney, or court. At the end of the evaluation, a typed report with specific recommendations will be provided to your attorney.

I recognize that my findings about the allegations and impressions are very important to you. However, please do not ask me to give you an opinion until I have had an opportunity to hear all sides, review the psychological test results, and fully review the file of documents provided by both parties. Once the report is written, reviewed, and approved, a written report will be discussed and given to the attorneys. If you would like to hear about the results of your evaluation, you may schedule an additional appointment when the legal matter is completed, and I will answer questions about the results that you might have. It is an additional opportunity to learn more about yourself and your child.

Once the evaluation has begun, I cannot be a resource to you or anyone else involved in the case for advice, therapy, or support. These activities conflict with my role as a nonpartisan (e.g., neutral) evaluator. However, both parties should seek therapy if they would find it beneficial. Some people refrain from doing this for fear it will reflect badly on them during the evaluation process. I do not feel that this reflects badly on anyone, especially given the stresses of divorce and custody situations.

You enter into this evaluation process by waiving confidentiality and releasing me from any and all liability for damages that might result from the release of information. You do so fully recognizing that my impressions, statements, reports, testimony, and other actions might be adverse and detrimental to you personally, financially, and to your legal position. I shall consider each child's interests ahead of any adult's interests. Anything discussed between any child and I shall remain confidential at my sole discretion, unless a court of law determines otherwise.

You will pay a $_____ fee before the evaluation is begun. This is the charge for the evaluation up to discovery or courtroom testimony. It includes all face to face contact, phone calls, test scoring, consultation with lawyers and other professionals involved with the case, as well as report preparation time. Your charges may be considerably higher than this amount if discovery and courtroom testimony occur. The reason the fee is paid up front does not reflect on you but on the reality that I could not go into court with one party owing a large bill. This would leave me open to a question as to whether the financial situation had influenced my judgment. This is not an acceptable situation for you and I will adhere strictly to this policy in order to avoid it.

The cost of providing an opportunity for your lawyer to review the records, answering interrogatories, and providing testimony at a deposition or in court is often high and difficult to predict. I will charge an additional fee for record review, responding to interrogatories or providing deposition or court testimony. Such a fee will include all travel, waiting and professional service. The cost varies widely with the number and complexity of the issues, the number of children involved, and the degree of attorney and court involvement. An estimate of the time involved will be given and payment is expected before I will engage in any of these additional services.

The policies and procedures described in this form have been developed to help assure that I am able to direct the evaluation toward recommendations that are in the best interests of the child or children involved. If after reviewing this information you have questions, please be sure to discuss them at your initial interview, when I will more fully explain the evaluation procedure you are about to begin.

This information and the procedures of a parenting evaluation have been explained to me, and I agree to abide by these policies and have received a copy of this agreement.

DATE: _____ SIGNATURE OF PARTY: _____

I have reviewed this information with the party and the party agrees with the policies as evidenced by his/her signature.

DATE: _____ SIGNATURE OF EVALUATOR: _____

APPENDIX B: EVALUATION TRACKING FORM

Docket Number _____ Appointment Date _____

Case Name _____

Appointing Judge _____ Wants Notification of Report   Y   N

(circle one)

Petitioner's Attorney	**Petitioner**
Address	Address
Telephone	Telephone
Fax	Fax
E-mail	E-mail
First Retainer	Date Paid
Second Retainer	Date Paid
Third Retainer	Date Paid

Respondent's Attorney | **Respondent**

Address | Address

Telephone | Telephone

Fax | Fax

E-mail | E-mail

First Retainer | Date Paid

Second Retainer | Date Paid

Third Retainer | Date Paid

Guardian *ad Litem*

Address | Telephone

Fax | E-mail

Probation Officer

Report Due Date | Extension Date

Date of Discovery Cutoff | Trial Date

APPENDIX C: DECLARATIONS OF PARTY NONCOMPLIANCE

A.   Declaration for No-Show

IN THE SUPERIOR COURT OF THE STATE OF WASHINGTON
FOR KING COUNTY

IN RE THE MARRIAGE OF:	)	
	)	
male party,	)	
	)	
Petitioner,	)	
	)	
and	) No. 00-0-0000-1SEA	
	)	
female party,	) DECLARATION OF	
	) G. ANDREW H. BENJAMIN	
Respondent.	)	
	)	

G. Andrew H. Benjamin declares the following:

1. As a lawyer and a clinical psychologist, part of my practice involves working half days as a clinical professor at the University of Washington Schools of Law and Medicine.

2. I direct the forensic training program for licensed or certified mental health professionals, entitled Parenting Evaluation Training Program (PETP); they are instructed and supervised to conduct parenting evaluations and to act as expert witnesses for legal cases involving family law and dependency cases.

3. The program is recognized for providing a detailed therapeutic assessment for all members of a family in conflict. It delineates a specific, practical plan to alleviate the issues that are injuring the children.

4. A parenting evaluation includes: psychological testing; at least three hours of clinical interviews per party; parent/child dyad assessments with home visits if relevant; independent interviews of adolescents as indicated; collateral interviews as necessary; interpretation of testing and interview findings; review of relevant party legal filings or prior evaluations or treatment notes; and closing interviews with the parties to provide an opportunity to explain the findings.

5. The parties were ordered on May 20, 2001, to be evaluated by PETP to provide additional evidence to the court about residential placement, visitation, decision making, and counseling needs for the children and the parties.

6. Ms. [Female party] has not complied with the PETP process. On two separate occasions, the last occurring as recently as today, she has refused to meet with the PETP evaluator and an interpreter for psychological testing and an interview.

7. After the first failed appointment, I contacted her lawyer, [lawyer's name], and was assured that Ms. [Female party] would proceed with the evaluation process. Despite the best efforts of her lawyer, Ms. [Female party] failed to attend the appointment of today. In fact, she called PETP and refused to ever proceed with the evaluation.

8. PETP cannot conduct an evaluation because of Ms. [Female party]'s noncompliance.

I declare under the penalty of the laws of the State of Washington that the foregoing is true and correct.

DATED at Seattle, Washington, this 28th day of May, 2001.

G. Andrew H. Benjamin, PhD, JD

B. Declaration for Non-Payment

IN THE SUPERIOR COURT OF THE STATE OF WASHINGTON
FOR KING COUNTY

IN RE THE MARRIAGE OF:	)
	)
male party,	)
	)
Petitioner,	)
	)
and	) No. 00-0-00000-1SEA
	)
female party,	) DECLARATION OF
	) G. ANDREW H. BENJAMIN
Respondent.	)
	)

G. Andrew H. Benjamin declares the following:

1. As a lawyer and a clinical psychologist, part of my practice involves working half days as a clinical professor at the University of Washington Schools of Law and Medicine.

2. I direct the forensic training program for licensed or certified mental health professionals, entitled Parenting Evaluation Training Program (PETP); they are instructed and supervised to conduct parenting evaluations and to act as expert witnesses for legal cases involving family law and dependency cases.

3. The program is recognized for providing a detailed therapeutic assessment for all members of a family in conflict. It delineates a specific, practical plan to alleviate the issues that are injuring the children.

4. A parenting evaluation includes: psychological testing; at least three hours of clinical interviews per party; parent/child dyad assessments with home visits if relevant; independent interviews of adolescents as indicated; collateral interviews as necessary; interpretation of testing and interview findings; review of relevant party legal filings or prior evaluations or treatment notes; and closing interviews with the parties to provide an opportunity to explain the findings.

5. The parties were ordered on April 25, 2001, to be evaluated by PETP

to provide additional evidence to the court about residential placement, visitation, decision making, and counseling needs for the children and the parties.

6. It is the policy of PETP that the evaluation process will not proceed until each party has paid $150 processing fee.

7. Both parties were notified of this requirement in July 2000 after Ms. [Female party] forwarded the court order to PETP.

8. On July 16, 2000, Ms. [Female party] complied with this process.

9. After several contacts with Mr. [Male party], including a formal demand letter sent by Ms. [Female party]'s attorney, Mr. [Male party] has failed to provide the processing fee.

I declare under penalty of the laws of the State of Washington that the foregoing is true and correct.

DATED at Seattle, Washington, this 8th day of May, 2001.

G. Andrew H. Benjamin, PhD, JD

APPENDIX D: PARENTING EVALUATION IN A LEGAL SETTING

The following describes the steps and the purposes of the procedures that are involved in this evaluation process. This description is being given so that you know what to expect as you decide to have an evaluation done and as you prepare for and go through this evaluation. This evaluation will follow a structured pattern to maximize the fairness and the objectivity of the report and to work toward the best interests of your child or children. The evaluator will not discuss details or factors of the evaluation outside of the clinical interviews. If further details arise between interviews, please submit the material in writing.

1. The first step of this process is for each side to agree to the evaluation. There must be a stipulated agreement or a court order that includes the following information:
   a. The precise nature and purpose of this appointment.
   b. An outline of the issues that are to be examined and addressed in the report. These issues need to be specific and framed in a manner so that they can be addressed clearly in the evaluation.
   c. A statement of who will pay for the evaluation that details the proportion that each party pays and that states that the payment is required in advance of each of the two stages of the evaluation.
   d. Permission to contact professionals and collaterals who have knowledge of the family.
   e. The expected due date or deadline for the completion and submis-

sion of the final report. This date must be more than 8 weeks from the date of the stipulated agreement or court order.

2. Payment for this evaluation must be made in advance. The first of two payments is required after the stipulated agreement is signed and before any other processing can take place. This first retainer fee covers the cost of the initial correspondence and the processing of a Parenting History Survey and of a Disclosure Form.

3. Once the first retainer is paid, then the Parenting History Survey and the Disclosure Form will be mailed to both parties.

4. The first clinical interview appointments will be scheduled after the Parenting History Survey and the Disclosure Forms are received back in the evaluator's office.

5. The first clinical interview will require at least a 4-hour block of time. Each party will be scheduled for a separate day.

6. Each party will be required to bring the balance of the evaluation fee to this first appointment. Failure to bring the retainer fee will cause the appointment to be delayed while the evaluator sends out a declaration of noncompliance to both attorneys so that the judge can decide whether the evaluation should proceed.

7. At the first appointment, you should bring any written documents that you might think would be relevant to the allegations that you are raising. Please highlight the segments of the documents that you think are noteworthy. Do not include documents from people who have not observed firsthand parenting behavior or alarming behavior that might affect parenting.

8. In the first part of the clinical interview you and the evaluator will go over the Disclosure Form, ask and answer any questions, and sign that document. If the Disclosure Form is not understood, agreed to, and signed, then the clinical interview will have to be delayed while the evaluator sends out a declaration of noncompliance to both attorneys so that the judge can decide whether the evaluator should proceed.

9. In the second part of the clinical interview you will complete the MMPI–2 in the office. This psychological test is the most researched and standard test in use today.

10. When the testing is completed, then an elaborate structured psychosocial interview will be conducted.

11. Following the structured interview, releases of information will be signed so that relevant records may be obtained and so that third-party individuals can be contacted who may be able to help with the evaluation. **It is most likely that only collaterals who can provide firsthand information about the allegations or about parenting strengths or weaknesses will be contacted.**

12. If you request that a nonprofessional collateral be contacted, then that individual must submit a legal declaration that is specific about relevant evidence from firsthand witness of parenting behavior or behavior that could affect parenting.

13. Each party will be asked to produce records that become apparent during the first interview. These records might include police incident reports, criminal history reports, juvenile court records, mental health records, medical records, school attendance and grade reports, achievement and standardized testing records, social services agency records, and psychological and educational testing reports. Once each party has offered permission to access records, that party is to ask the agency to mail the unredacted records directly to the evaluator. Each party has 2 weeks in which to obtain all of the records, or both lawyers will be informally informed of the failure to produce the records. If either party still fails to produce the records, then the evaluation is stopped, a declaration of noncompliance is sent out, and the evaluation will not resume until the records are returned.

14. At the end of the first interview, each party will be given a set of allegation forms. A significant allegation will be used as an example of how to fill out these forms. The individual will fill out these forms for each allegation so that there are three specific examples of each allegation. There will be 1 week in which to return the completed allegation forms. If either party delays in completing the forms, then both lawyers will be informed about the delay. If either party fails to comply, then the evaluation is stopped, a declaration of noncompliance is sent to both lawyers, and the evaluation will not resume until the forms are returned.

15. The interview ends with the scheduling of a parent–child observation in the evaluator's office. The parent will be instructed "to be prepared to play with the children" for about an hour at the next appointment.

16. If a party has a new life partner who is involved with the children, then that new partner will be required to take the MMPI–2.

17. The psychosocial section of the report for each individual and the allegations that he or she raised about the other party will be sent to that individual for review and additions.

18. A parent–child observation session will take place for each parent.

19. A final clinical interview is scheduled for each parent at the end of his or her parent–child session.

20. A draft of the report will be written before the collateral contacts are made. This is so that the collaterals are used to support or disconfirm allegations and so that they do not unduly influence the objectivity and the balance of the report.

21. Collaterals will be interviewed, and a written summary of the interview will be sent to the respective collateral for additions.

22. All of the documents will be reviewed.

23. Typically, a young child is not interviewed individually or asked about his or her preferences for placement or visitation. This is to protect the child from feeling responsible for any outcome associated with the evaluation.

24. Some adolescents might be interviewed individually. If so, that interview will take place in the hour preceding the final interview of one of the parents. The timing of this interview is intended to minimize the child feeling or being held responsible for the outcome of the evaluation.

25. The closing clinical interview will consist of two parts. The first part is to clarify any details that are missing or that are inconsistent with the findings of the evaluation. The second part allows the party the opportunity to examine how each of the findings was formed and to comment about the details that led to the finding.

26. A meeting to go over the report is scheduled with both attorneys and the guardian ad litem, if one is appointed. The parties do not attend this meeting unless one or both of the parties are pro se. Both sides must be able to attend the review meeting, or it will not be held.

27. The attorneys are able to ask questions about the recommendations in the report. The attorneys are given a copy of the report for their later review.

28. If there are any further questions that arise about the report, then a conference call will be arranged with both attorneys and the guardian ad litem, if one is appointed.

29. If the evaluator is to serve as an expert witness during discovery or trial because the settlement process has failed, then an additional retainer will be required.

APPENDIX E: SEMISTRUCTURED INTERVIEW FOR ADULTS

Name of Party and relation to children: _____

Date: _____ Interviewer: _____

Time Interview Began: _____ Time End: _____

Warning of nonconfidentiality of this proceeding has been issued to the party _____ (yes or no)

Identifying Data

The party's name, current residential address, phone numbers, age, marital status, and occupation.

Mental Status Exam

[Describe the following: appearance and overall impression as reflected by posture, poise, clothing, and grooming; behavior and motor activity; attitude toward the examiner; mood, neuro-vegetative symptoms for depressive disorders; manic syndrome criteria; affect (e.g., emotional responsiveness in the interview); perceptual disturbances; thought process; content of thought; suicidal and homicidal intent; orientation; attention, concentration, memory, and cognition; fund of knowledge; abstract thought (also obtained through proverb interpretations and explaining similarities); and review of physical symptoms.]

Family History

Where were you born? Are you from this area originally?

Tell me who was in your family. Did your parents marry? Divorce?

How many siblings did you have? Any step-siblings? What is your birth order?

What was it like growing up in your family? What was your childhood like?

What kind of person was your mom? How about your dad? Stepparents?

What was their relationship like with each other? How about with their families?

Were there any difficulties while you were growing up in the family?

Was there any drug or alcohol abuse among family members or friends?

Did you ever experience physical, emotional, and/or sexual abuse or other problems when you were younger?

Did anyone know? How did this affect the family? How did this affect you?

What did your mom and dad do for a living? Why were they unemployed?

How far did your parents get through school?

How were things financially in your family while you were growing up?

Do you remember experiencing any situations or events that made you sad or upset? Anything that was stressful?

How much contact do you have with your immediate and extended family members? How would you describe your relationships with your family now?

Social History

Where do you live now? How long have you been living there? What is the neighborhood like?

Describe your home and environment, especially facilities for kids.

School History

Where did you go to school? What grade did you finish?

Do you have any degrees or professional/specialty training?

Any significant events happen during your time in school?

How did you do academically in school? What was your GPA?

Did you have any learning problems, including difficulties with attention or concentration?

Did you have any disciplinary problems? Behavioral problems with teachers or peers?

What would people remember about you in school?

What would people who knew you then say to describe you?

Back then, did you have as many friends as you wanted to?

Extracurricular activities?

Did you work during high school?

Did you leave school before graduating? For what reasons? What year did you graduate?

Employment History

What did you do after you finished school?

What was your first job after school?

   Repeat the same questions for each job the client has held:

What year was this?

How satisfied were you with the job?

Why did you leave the job?

What would a boss say about you?

Current job:

Where do you work now? What is your position?

What do you do?

How much are you paid?

Do you like this job?

How is this job distinguishable from the other jobs you have held?

How long have you been doing this work?

What do you think of your boss?

What would this boss say about you?

Would you like to stay there?

Medical History

Have you had *past* medical problems? Past operations or hospitalizations?

Do you have any *current* medical problems? Do you have any physical disabilities?

Are you currently taking any medications for your health? How about over-the-counter medications? Do you take vitamins or herbs?

Do you have a family doctor? When was your last physical checkup?

Do you worry about your physical health? How come?

Do you smoke? Have allergies?

Psychiatric/Psychological History and Treatment

Have you ever experienced psychiatric/psychological problems?

Have you ever been diagnosed with a psychiatric/psychological illness?

Have you ever participated in counseling or psychotherapy of any sort?

Are you currently in therapy or counseling? Who is your counselor? At what clinic?

When did you start, and how often have you attended therapy?

In general, what kinds of issues do you focus on or talk about in therapy?

How has your participation in therapy worked for you? How has it helped your parenting?

Substance Use History and Treatment

Have you ever used, or do you currently use, any of the following: beer, wine, hard liquor, marijuana, heroin, cocaine, amphetamines (uppers), benzodiazepines (e.g., downers), and other prescription or other drugs that you bought without a prescription?

When did you use these substances?

Has your use of any of these substances caused problems for you?

Have you ever neglected your friends, family, or children because of your use of substances?

Has anyone ever objected to your use of these substances?

Have you received treatment for your substance use? What was the name of your counselor?

What kinds of treatment did you participate in, and for how long? What agency?

Are you in a 12-step program? What is the name of your sponsor? Do you have a home group? How often do you attend AA, NA (etc.) meetings?

Are you required to have drug testing of any kind?

Criminal History

Have you ever been arrested, charged, or convicted of a crime?

What happened? How was it resolved? Did you serve time? Parole or probation?

Dating and Relationship History

Did you date while you were in school? When did you start?

How many significant relationships have you had? Have you ever been engaged or married?

Any children? (get name, sex, age, where they live and are they in contact with the party)

Who and where are the other biological parents of your children?

How often do you see the children? What is the visiting arrangement?

For each significant relationship ask the following:

What was the nature of the problems with the relationship?

How did you resolve the problems until the relationship ended?

How long did your relationships last?

Who left whom? How long between relationships?

How did you decide to have children?

Both wanted them?

Did one want children more than the other did?

How was the course of the pregnancy and deliveries?

What was the relationship like after each child was born?

What was the crux of the matter? The main issue you had? Any other issues?

What led to the breakup?

What was said about the custody of the children?

How did you decide visitation rights and who would have the kids?

Did you have any issues about parenting with any of your relationships?

Please give three examples of the toughest issues you attempted to fix that have led to the worst of your allegations about the other party. (Use the allegation form questions; see Appendix F. While party is answering questions let them hold the forms so that as you model specificity they can see what you expect.)

Present Romantic Relationship

Are you dating presently? In what capacity? How did you meet?

What attracted you to her/him? How long have you been together?

What has the course of this relationship been like for you?

How did you decide to stay together?

Are you living together, engaged, or married? How did you make each of these decisions?

Do you have children together? Are you planning to have children together? How many?

How will you blend your families together?

How will you both support those children?

Parenting History

How many children do you have?

What are their names, genders, and ages?

Where is each of your children now?

Who is their guardian? How was that determined?

Do they see their other parent? Do they get to see each other?

Where is the other parent? Do they have contact with their children? In what capacity?

How do the children respond to this arrangement? Do they seem distressed?

Why are your children living where they do?

How often do you see each child?

How long has this been the arrangement for your kids? How was this arrangement planned?

Why don't you have your kids right now?

Do you want your children back?

All of them?

How will you support them?

If you were on your own, would you still be able to support all of them?

What has prevented you from having all of your children living with you?

Are all your children living and healthy?

Concerning your deceased or injured child, what were the circumstances surrounding the death or injury of that child?

How were you involved in caring for the child at that time?

Where is that child buried? Where were they treated for their injuries?

How do you explain this death or injury to your other children?

What do they think about the death or injury?

Developmental Status and Needs of the Children
What is the stage of development each child is in?

How mature is each of your children? How would you describe their personality and temperament?

What are their sibling relationships like? How do they get along with peers and adults?

How strong is their relationship to you? What is the strength of their relationship with the other parent?

What is each child's specific daily schedule and routine?

Does your child require special attention or guidance in particular areas of their routine?

What does your child like to do for fun? How much quiet time do they need in the course of the day? How much time do you spend with your children each day?

Has your child experienced any difficulties with their attention, language, behavior?

Does your child currently experience any physical or medical disabilities?

Do they speak a language other than English? In what contexts do they speak this language?

Are your children in school? Where do they attend school? What grades are your children in?

Who are their teachers? When have you met with them?

Did you ever attend parent–teacher conferences? How many per year?

What do they say about your child?

Have you spoken with other school professionals? What do they say about your child?

How are their grades? Do they complete their homework?

Do they like school? What aspects of school do they like and dislike?

When they are with you, do you help them with their homework?

In what ways have you helped your children with their school work and grades?

Have any of your children had any problems or bad experiences at school?

Have any of your children been abused, bullied, or harassed while at school?

Has your child experienced disciplinary problems at school? How have you responded to these problems?

Has your child attended after-school programs or enriched learning programs?

Whom do your children play with? What kinds of games do they select?

How often do they play with other children? Any problems or concerns?

Trauma

Please describe the worst instance of physical, sexual, emotional, or verbal abuse that each child has endured. (Use the allegation form questions; see Appendix F. While party is answering questions let them hold the forms so that as you model specificity they can see what you expect.)

Financial Status (only ask if allegations about financial manipulations arise in PHS or interview)

How do you support yourself? Other than your job, do you get additional money?

Does your family help you out?

How much do you get on a monthly basis from all sources?

Does your partner contribute to your income?

How much is your rent?

Who pays this?

What other monthly expenses do you have?

How long have you lived at this address?

Who is your landlord?

Later I will ask you to sign a release to contact your landlord.

How many rooms do you have?

Do you have a car?

Who owns it?

Who pays for the car insurance?

Do you have a valid driver's license?

Did you ever lose your driver's license? If so, for what reason?

What other kinds of transportation do you use?

How do you pay for your groceries?

Pay your bills?

Buy clothes?

How will you do this for your children?

Will their other parent help you?

General Questions

What has happened since your children have moved away?

What are your strengths/weaknesses as a parent?

What are the other parent's strengths and weaknesses?

How involved are they in the lives of their kids?

Did they give you money for the children?

Do they continue to help out with money?

What are your current partner's strengths and weaknesses?

Please give me some examples of the worst allegation you have raised about the other parent.

"Before we end today, you have identified a number of people, ranging from doctors, therapists, teachers, and friends, who know you and your children. I may want to learn more from these people, both by talking with them and getting their records and reports. Could you please list the people that you think may be able to tell me more about your situation? It is important to remember that this information will be revealed to the court and in that sense, the evaluation will not be held confidential." [Have filled out Release of Information Forms ready for the party to sign in black ink (red and blue ink do not photocopy well). For any persons who are nonprofessionals, state to party that you will not talk with them at all unless they submit a legal declaration about what they have witnessed first hand about the behavior of the other party.]

Provide an appointment time for parent–child(ren) observation and give the instruction that the parent "should be prepared to play for one hour." Thank the party for working hard during the interview today. Remind the party that they can write down additional information or explanations and send them to you in the next week or so. Remind them as much as possible to please submit the additional information on a copy of the allegation forms: "Remember: the more specific you are, the more likely that the truth about this entire situation will emerge."

End of Interview

APPENDIX F: ADULT AND CHILD-FOCUSED ALLEGATION FORMS

LIST OF ALLEGATIONS ABOUT PARENTS OR CARETAKERS

Adults involved in custody disputes often express strong concerns about the welfare and behavior of other adult parents and caretakers. This questionnaire asks you to do three things: First, read the list of divorce-related allegations below. Second, please write down the name of the adult caretaker you are referring to and check off one allegation. *Please choose one person and check one allegation per sheet.* If you think the same allegation applies to two or more adults, then fill out separate sheets for each adult. Writing one allegation per adult, per sheet helps the evaluator track your specific concerns.

NAME OF PARENT OR ADULT: _____

TYPE OF ALLEGATION: Check *one* of the allegations below.

_____ Threatens to mistreat or harm me
_____ Physically mistreats or harms me
_____ Emotionally mistreats or harms me
_____ Sexually mistreats or harms me
_____ Tries to control me through finances (e.g., withholding child support)
_____ Tries to control or scare me through damaging property

_____ Invades my privacy or monitors my whereabouts
_____ Uses alcohol to excess
_____ Uses drugs to excess
_____ Uses alcohol or drugs in my presence
_____ Threatened to harm him- or herself in front of me
_____ Physically harms him- or herself in front of me or the children
_____ Creates or uses conflict in a way that creates distress for my child
_____ Withholds contact or access to the children
_____ Refuses to comply with the court order regarding adult issues
_____ Refuses to coparent with me (e.g., will not talk with me about parenting issues)
_____ Says negative things about me that make me confused, upset, or sad
_____ Has a long-term emotional impairment (e.g., mental illness)
_____ Does not have parenting skills or experience, which makes it hard for me to parent
_____ Other A: _____ .
_____ Other B: _____ .

EVIDENCE TO SUPPORT ALLEGATION: Please write down brief and specific descriptions of the situation that supports the allegation that the other adult or parent has affected you. Please try to include factually correct and detailed information about the event that supports your assertion. Please describe the _two most recent examples and the worst example_ (e.g., most troubling) for each allegation on three separate sheets. If you have questions, please ask your evaluator for more explanation. Remember: Use one sheet per allegation. You may use the back of a sheet if you need more space.

Date, Time, and Place of Event or Situation:

Who was present? (Include name, phone number, relationship to the child)

What happened exactly?

What did you do before, during, and after this event or situation?

What did the other adult do before, during, and after the event or situation?

Did you talk with anyone about the event or situation? Did anyone witness the event? (Include name, phone number, and date of conversation)

If we were to talk to these witnesses, what would they say about what happened?

What were the negative effects of this specific event or situation on you?

LIST OF CHILD-FOCUSED ALLEGATIONS

Children involved in custody disputes may experience problems as a result of the behavior of their parents or caretakers. This questionnaire asks you to do three things: First, read the list of child-focused allegations below. Second, please write down the name of the parent or caretaker you are concerned about, and check off one allegation. *Please choose one person and check one allegation per sheet.* If you think the same allegation applies to two or more adults, then fill out separate sheets for each adult. Writing one allegation per adult, per sheet helps the evaluator track your specific concerns.

NAME OF PARENT OR ADULT: _____

CHILDREN WHO HAVE BEEN HARMED: _____

TYPE OF ALLEGATION: Check *one* allegation.

_____ Threatens to mistreat or harm my children
_____ Physically mistreats or harms my children
_____ Emotionally mistreats or harms my children
_____ Sexually mistreats or harms my children
_____ Tries to control my child through finances (e.g., bribes or withholding allowance)
_____ Tries to control or scare my child through damaging property
_____ Invades my children's privacy or monitors my child's whereabouts
_____ Uses alcohol to excess in front of the children
_____ Uses drugs to excess in front of the children
_____ Uses alcohol or drugs or both while responsible for parenting
_____ Threatened to harm him- or herself in front of the children
_____ Physically harms him- or herself in front of the children
_____ Creates or uses conflict in a way that creates distress for my child
_____ Withholds contact or access to the children
_____ Refuses to observe the court order regarding parenting (e.g., misses child visits)
_____ Refuses to coparent with me (e.g., will not talk with me about parenting issues)
_____ Says negative things about me that make my child confused, upset, or sad
_____ Has a long-term emotional impairment (e.g., mental illness)
_____ Does not have parenting skills or experience, which impacts my child's well-being
_____ Other A: _____.
_____ Other B: _____.

EVIDENCE TO SUPPORT ALLEGATION: Please write down brief and specific descriptions of the event or situation that supports your allegation. We are interested in how this event affected your child. Please try to include factually correct and detailed information about the event that supports your assertion. Please describe the *two most recent examples and the worst example* (e.g., most troubling) for each allegation on three separate sheets. If you have questions, please ask your evaluator for more explanation. Remember: Use one sheet per allegation. You may use the back of a sheet if you need more space.

Date, Time, and Place of Event or Situation:

Who was present? (Include name, phone number, relationship to the child)

What happened exactly?

What did you do before, during, and after this event or situation?

What did your child(ren) do before, during, and after the event or situation?

What did the other adult do before, during, and after the event or situation?

Did you talk with anyone about the event or situation? Did anyone witness the event? (Include name, phone number, and date of conversation)

If we were to talk to these witnesses, what would they say about what happened?

What were the negative effects of this specific event or situation for your children?

APPENDIX G: RELEASE FORMS

Parenting Evaluation Treatment Program (PETP)
4045 Brooklyn Avenue NE
Seattle, WA 98105

Phone: 206.616.6220   Fax: 206.685.2388

Consent For Release Of Information

To: Name _____

      Address _____

      City, State, Zip _____

Consent

I hereby request that the above-named person or institution furnish the University of Washington School of Law's Parenting Evaluation Treatment Program with all information requested, including all records requested, for the purpose of a court ordered evaluation:

Name: _____

Birth date: _____

Today's date: _____

Signature (of patient or person who voluntarily gives consent):

_____

Relationship to patient, if signed by person other than patient:

_____

Please return one copy of this form with all records to the above address, attention to:

Name: _____

Information To Be Disclosed

[X] All information requested by the court-ordered parenting evaluation.

State and federal law protects information disclosed by this consent (42CFR Part2). These laws prohibit making any further disclosure of this information without the specific written consent of the person to whom it pertains, or as otherwise permitted by state law.

This consent is subject to revocation at any time except to the extent that the program that is to make the disclosure has already taken action in reliance on it. This consent expires on _____ or in 90 days unless otherwise specified.

APPENDIX H:
ADOLESCENT INTERVIEW

STRUCTURED ASSESSMENT QUESTIONS FOR
INTERVIEW WITH TEEN

Questions for Interview

Name of child: _____

Date: _____ Interviewer: _____

Time Interview Began: _____ Time Interview Ended: _____

Warning of nonconfidentiality of this proceeding has been issued to the child _____ (yes or no)

School History

Where do you go to school?

What grade are you in?

Who are your teachers?

Do you like school?

211

What aspects do you like and dislike of school?

How do you do academically in school? What is your GPA?

Do you complete your homework?

In what ways has each parent helped you with your school work and grades?

What would people in school who knew you say to describe you?

Do you have as many friends as you like?

Extracurricular activities?

Do you work after school?

Any significant events happen during your time in school?

When have your parents met with your teachers?

What do they say about you?

Have you spoken with other school professionals?

What do they say about you?

Do you have any learning problems, including difficulties with attention, concentration?

Have you had any problems or bad experiences at school?

Have you been abused, bullied, or harassed while at school?

Do you have any disciplinary problems?

Behavioral problems with teachers or peers?

How has each parent responded to these problems?

Family Questions

How well are the current living arrangements with your parents working in your view?

What works? What doesn't work?

What are your specific daily schedule and routine in both of your parents' homes?

Does either parent give different attention or guidance in the particular areas of your routine?

What do you do for fun?

How often do you play with your siblings?

Any problems or concerns?

How much quiet time do you need in the course of the day? What type?

What kind of activities do you do with each parent?

How much time do you spend with your parent each day?

What kind of play do you engage in with each parent?

What kinds of games do you select?

How has your relationship changed with each parent since they separated?

What works? What doesn't work?

Where and when do you make transitions from one house to another?

What works? What doesn't work?

What kinds of behavior does each parent engage in to make you mad? Sad? Happy?

How about your behaviors that make each parent mad? Sad? Happy?

What kinds of topics does each parent talk to you about, either in person or by phone?

What are the hot issues that usually produce arguments between your parents?

Please discuss the worst fight you saw them in (use the allegation form in Appendix F).

For each of the child-related and adult-related allegations raised by each party, ask the teen to describe two of the worst examples of each allegation he or she may have witnessed or endured (use the allegation form in Appendix F).

Mental Status Exam

[Describe the following: appearance and overall impression as reflected by posture, poise, clothing, and grooming; behavior and motor activity; attitude toward the examiner; mood, neuro-vegetative symptoms of depressive disorders; manic syndrome criteria; affect (e.g., emotional responsiveness in the interview); perceptual disturbances; thought process; content of thought; suicidal and homicidal intent; orientation; attention, concentration, memory, and cognition; fund of knowledge; abstract thought (also obtained through proverb interpretations and explaining similarities); and review of physical symptoms.]

APPENDIX I: DECLARATION TO ENFORCE AGREEMENT TO PARENTING EVALUATION

IN THE SUPERIOR COURT OF THE STATE OF WASHINGTON
FOR KING COUNTY

IN RE THE MARRIAGE OF:)
)
male party,   )
)
        Petitioner,   )
)
and   ) No. 00-0-00000-1SEA
)
female party,   ) DECLARATION OF
) G. ANDREW H. BENJAMIN
        Respondent.   )
)

G. Andrew H. Benjamin declares the following:

1. As a lawyer and a clinical psychologist, part of my practice involves working half days as a clinical professor at the University of Washington Schools of Law and Medicine.

2. I direct the forensic training program for licensed or certified mental health professionals, entitled Parenting Evaluation Training Program (PETP); they are instructed and supervised to conduct parenting evaluations and to act as expert witnesses for legal cases involving family law and dependency cases.

3. The program is recognized for providing a detailed therapeutic assessment for all members of a family in conflict. It delineates a specific, practical plan to alleviate the issues that are injuring the children.

4. A parenting evaluation includes: psychological testing; at least three hours of clinical interviews per party; parent/child dyad assessments with home visits if relevant; independent interviews of adolescents as indicated; collateral interviews as necessary; interpretation of testing and interview findings; review of relevant party legal filings or prior evaluations or treatment notes; and closing interviews with the parties to provide an opportunity to explain the findings.

5. The parties were ordered on March 19, 2001, to be evaluated by PETP to provide additional evidence to the court about residential placement, visitation, decision making, and counseling needs for the children and the parties.

6. In the PETP "Agreement to Parenting Evaluation" that both of the parties signed, record review, deposition and expert witness testimony procedures are established.

7. Mr. Male party's lawyer, Mr. Lawyer received further notice at meeting with both counsel for the parties that PETP must receive its expert witness testimony fee in advance of any testimony as called for by the PETP "Agreement to Parenting Evaluation."

8. Although Ms. Evaluator, PETP's evaluator in the Party's name case, received notice of deposition, no fee was attached.

9. Ms. Evaluator will not be present at the deposition unless Mr. Male party's lawyer or his client provides a money order for $900 which represents the fee for two hours of preparation and four hours of testimony.

10. In addition, Ms. Evaluator is only available to testify in the afternoons, during the PETP office hours, where the deposition can be videotaped.

11. I have instructed Ms. Evaluator that if Mr. Male party's lawyer acts in

an abusive manner by yelling, engaging in unprofessional innuendo, harassing her by asking questions already asked and answered, or incorrectly stating the facts of the case during the deposition, Ms. Evaluator is to leave the deposition with the videotape and seek a protective order from Judge Z where she can view the tape and rule appropriately about Mr. Male party's lawyer's behavior.

12. In prior interactions with Ms. Evaluator as an expert witness on an earlier case, Mr. Male party's lawyer has acted in an abusive manner by yelling, engaging in unprofessional innuendo, harassing the expert witness by asking questions already asked and answered, and incorrectly stating the known facts of the case during his questioning.

I declare under penalty of the laws of the State of Washington that the foregoing is true and correct.

DATED at Seattle, Washington, this 2nd day of July 2001.

_____

G. Andrew H. Benjamin, PhD, JD

REFERENCES

Achenbach, T. M. (1979). The Child Behavior Profile: I. Boys aged 6–11. *Journal of Consulting and Clinical Psychology, 46,* 478–488.

Achenbach, T. M. (1991a). *Manual for the Child Behavior Checklist/4-18 and 1991 Profile.* Burlington: University of Vermont, Department of Psychiatry.

Achenbach, T. M. (1991b). *Manual for the Teacher's Report Form and 1991 Profile.* Burlington: University of Vermont, Department of Psychiatry.

Achenbach, T. M., & Edelbrock, C. S. (1979). The Child Behavior Profile: II. Boys aged 12–16 and girls aged 6–11 and 12–16. *Journal of Consulting and Clinical Psychology, 47,* 223–233.

Achenbach, T. M., & Edelbrock, C. S. (1981). Behavioral problems and competencies reported by parents of normal and disturbed children aged four through sixteen. *Monographs of the Society for Research in Children Development, 46,* 82.

Ackerman, M. J. (1994). American Psychological Association *Guidelines for Child Custody Evaluations in Divorce Proceedings. American Journal of Family Law, 8,* 129–134.

Ackerman, M. J., & Ackerman, M. C. (1997). Custody evaluation practices: A survey of experienced professionals (Revisited). *Professional Psychology: Research and Practice, 28,* 137–145.

Ackerman, M., & Ackerman, M. (1999). Custody evaluation practices: A survey of experienced professionals (revisited): Notice of clarification to Ackerman and Ackerman (1997) article. *Professional Psychology: Research and Practice, 30,* 599.

Amato, P. R., & Keith, B. (1991). Parental divorce and the well-being of children: A meta-analysis. *Psychological Bulletin, 110,* 26–46.

American Academy of Psychiatry and the Law. (1995). *Ethics guidelines for the practice of forensic psychiatry.*

American Psychological Association. (1990). *Guidelines for providers of psychological services to ethnic and culturally diverse populations.* Washington, DC: Author.

American Psychological Association. (1991). Specialty guidelines for forensic psychologists. *Law and Human Behavior, 6,* 655–665.

American Psychological Association. (1992). Ethical principles of psychologists and code of conduct. *American Psychologist, 47,* 1597–1611.

American Psychological Association. (1993). Record keeping guidelines. *American Psychologist, 48,* 984–985.

American Psychological Association, Committee on Professional Practice and Standards. (1994). *Guidelines for child custody evaluations in divorce proceedings. American Psychologist, 49,* 677–680.

American Psychological Association. (2002). *Ethical principles of psychologists and code of conduct.* Washington, DC: Author.

American Psychology Law Society, Committee on Ethical Guidelines for Forensic Psychologists. (1991). Specialty guidelines for forensic psychologists. *Law and Human Behavior, 15,* 655–665.

Appel, A. E., & Holden, G. W. (1998). The co-occurrence of spouse and physical child abuse: A review and appraisal. *Journal of Family Psychology, 12,* 578–599.

Ash, P., & Guyer, M. (1986). The functions of psychiatric evaluations in contested child custody and visitation cases. *Journal of American Academy of Child Psychiatry, 25,* 554–561.

Association of Family and Conciliation Courts. (1994). *Model standards of child custody evaluations.* Madison, WI: Author.

Association of Family and Conciliation Courts. *Guidelines for court connected child custody evaluations.* Madison, WI: Author. (Available from 329 Wilson Street, Madison, WI 53703.)

Azar, S. T., & Benjit, C. (1994). A cognitive perspective on ethnicity, race, and termination of parental rights. *Law and Human Behavior, 18,* 249–269.

Azar, S. T., & Cote, L. R. (2002). Sociocultural issues in the evaluation of the needs of children in custody decision making: What do our current frameworks for evaluating parenting practices have to offer? *International Journal of Law and Psychiatry, 25,* 193–217.

Bagby, M. R., Nicholson, R. A., Buis, T., Radovanovic, H., & Fidler, B. J. (1999). Defensive responding on the MMPI–2 in family custody and access evaluations. *Psychological Assessment, 11,* 24–28.

Bathurst, K., Gottfried, A. W., & Gottfried, A. E. (1997). Normative data for the MMPI–2 child custody litigation. *Psychological Assessment, 7,* 419–423.

Beck, C. J. A., & Sales, B. D. (2001). *Family mediation: Facts, myths, and future prospects.* Washington, DC: American Psychological Association.

Bennett, B. E., Bryant, B. K., VandenBos, G. R., & Greenwood, T. K. (1990). Professional liability and risk management. Washington, DC: APA Press.

Block, J. H., Block, J., & Gjerde, P. F. (1986). The personality of children prior to divorce: A prospective study. *Child Development, 57,* 827–840.

Borum, R., Otto, R., & Golding, S. (1993). Improving clinical judgment and decision making in forensic evaluation. *Journal of Psychology and Law, 21,* 35–76.

Bow, J. H., & Quinnell, F. A. (2001). Psychologists' current practices and procedures in child custody evaluations: Five years after American Psychological Association Guidelines. *Professional Psychology: Research and Practice, 32,* 261–268.

Bramlett, M. D., & Mosher, W. D. (2001, May 31). First marriage dissolution, divorce, and remarriage: United States. *Advance Data Report, 323.*

Bray, J. H. (1991). Psychosocial factors affecting custodial and visitation arrangements. *Behavioral Sciences and the Law, 9,* 419–437.

Briere, J. N. (1992). *Child abuse trauma: Theory and treatment of the lasting effects.* Newbury Park, CA: Sage.

Buchanan, C., Maccoby, E., & Dornbusch, S. (1991). Caught between parents: Adolescents' experiences in divorced homes. *Child Development, 62,* 1008–1029.

Butcher, J. N., Dahlstrom, W. G., Graham, J. R., Tellegen, A., & Kaemmer, B. (1989). *Manual for the administration and scoring of the MMPI–2.* Minneapolis: University of Minnesota Press.

Camera, K. A., & Resnick, G. (1989). Styles of conflict resolution and cooperation between divorced parents: Effects on child behavior and adjustment. *American Journal of Orthopsychiatry, 59,* 560–575.

Castro Martin, T., & Bumpass, L. (1989). Recent trends and differentials in marital disruptions. *Demographics, 26,* 37–51.

Ceci, S. J., & Bruck, M. (1993). Suggestibility of the child witness: A historical review and synthesis. *Psychological Bulletin, 113*(3), 403–439.

Ceci, S. J., & Crotteau Huffman, M. L. (1997). How suggestible are preschool children? Cognitive and social factors. *Journal of the American Academy of Adolescent Psychiatry, 36,* 948–958.

Centers for Disease Control and Prevention. (1995). *Monthly Vital Statistics* (Report 43, No. 13). Washington, DC: U.S. Public Health Service.

Deed, C. (1991). Court-ordered child custody evaluations: Helping or victimizing vulnerable families? *Psychotherapy, 28,* 76–84.

Deutsch, R., Rotman, A., & Ward, M. (2001, May). *Developmentally appropriate parenting plans.* Paper presented at the Massachusetts Conference for Guardians ad Litem, Boston.

Ehrenberg, M. F., Hunter, M. A., & Elterman, M. F. (1996). Shared parenting agreements after marital separation: The roles of empathy and narcissism. *Journal of Consulting and Clinical Psychology, 64,* 808–818.

Emery, R. E. (1982). Interparental conflict and the children of discord and divorce. *Psychological Bulletin, 2,* 310–330.

Emery, R. E. (2001). Changing the rules for determining child custody in divorce cases. *Clinical Psychology: Science and Practice, 6,* 323–327.

Emery, R. E., Matthews, S. G., & Kitzmann, K. M. (1991). Child custody mediation and litigation: Parents' satisfaction one year after settlement. *Journal of Consulting and Clinical Psychology, 62,* 124–129.

Famularo, R., Fenton, T., & Kinscherff, R. (1994). Maternal and child posttraumatic stress disorder in cases of child maltreatment. *Child Abuse and Neglect, 18*(1), 27–36.

Federal Rules of Evidence for United States Courts. (1992). West Publishing.

Fortstrom-Cohen, B., & Rosenbaum, A. (1985). The effects of parental marital violence on young adults: An exploratory investigation. *Journal of Marriage and the Family, 47,* 467–472.

Frost, A., & Pakiz, B. (1990). The effects of marital disruption on adolescence: Time as a dynamic. *American Journal of Orthopsychiatry, 60,* 544–555.

Garb, H. N. (1989). Clinical judgment, clinical training, and professional experience. *Psychological Bulletin, 105,* 387–396.

Garb, H. N. (1998). *Studying the clinician: Judgment research and psychological assessment.* Washington, DC: American Psychological Association.

Gindes, M. (1995). Competence and training in child custody evaluations. *American Journal of Family Therapy, 23,* 273–280.

Glassman, J. B. (1998). Preventing and managing board complaints: The downside risk of custody evaluation. *Professional Psychology: Research and Practice, 29,* 121–124.

Gould, J. W. (1998). *Conducting scientifically crafted child custody evaluations.* Thousand Oaks, CA: Sage.

Gourley, E., & Stolberg, A. L. (2000). An empirical investigation of psychologists' custody evaluation procedures. *Journal of Divorce and Remarriage, 33,* 1–29.

Greenberg, S. A., & Humphreys, L. (1998). *Parenting history survey.* (Available for a nominal fee from Dr. Greenberg, PhD, ABPP, 2815 Eastlake Avenue East, Suite 220, Seattle, WA 98102)

Greenberg, S. A., & Shuman, D. W. (1997). Irreconcilable conflict between therapeutic and forensic roles. *Professional Psychology: Research and Practice, 28,* 50–57.

Grillo, T. (1991). The mediation alternative: Process dangers for women. *Yale Law Review, 100,* 1545.

Grove, W. M., & Meehl, P. E. (1996). Comparative efficiency of informal (subjective, impressionistic) and formal (mechanical, algorithmic) prediction procedures: The clinical–statistical controversy. *Psychology, Public Policy, and Law, 2,* 293–323.

Guidubaldi, J., & Perry, J. (1985). Divorce and mental health sequelae for children: A two-year follow-up of a nationwide sample. *Journal of the American Academy of Child Psychiatry, 24,* 531–537.

Hagen, M. A., & Castagna, N. (2001). The real numbers: Psychological testing in custody evaluations. *Professional Psychology: Research and Practice, 32*(3), 269–271.

Hall, A. S., Pulver, C. A., & Cooley, M. J. (1996). Psychology of best interests standard: Fifty states and their theoretical antecedents. *American Journal of Family Therapy, 24,* 171–180.

Halon, R. L. (1990). The comprehensive child custody evaluation. *American Journal of Forensic Psychology, 8,* 19–46.

Halon, R. (2000). The comprehensive child custody evaluation, ten years later. *University of Arkansas Little Rock Review, 481,* 491.

Hazelton, R., Lancee, W., & O'Neil, M. (1998). The controversial long-term effects of parental divorce: The role of early attachment. *Journal of Divorce and Remarriage, 29,* 1–17.

Heilbrun, K. (1992). The role of psychological testing in forensic assessments. *Law and Human Behavior, 16,* 257–272.

Heinze, M. C., & Grisso, T. (1996). Review of instruments assessing parenting competencies used in child custody evaluations. *Behavioral Sciences and the Law, 14*, 293–313.

Henning, K., Leitenberg, H., Coffey, P., Bennett, R., & Jankowski, M. K. (1997). Long-term psychological adjustment to witnessing interparental physical conflict during childhood. *Child Abuse and Neglect, 21*, 501–515.

Henning, K., Leitenberg, H., Coffey, P., Turner, T., & Bennett, R. (1996). Long-term psychological and social impact of witnessing physical conflict between parenting. *Journal of Interpersonal Violence, 11*, 35–51.

Herman, K. D. (2001, April). *The parenting coordinator: The needs for role development/clarification.* Paper presented at the Massachusetts Continuing Legal Education Conference, Boston.

Hetherington, E. M. (1989). Coping with family transitions: Winners, losers, and survivors. *Child Development, 60*, 1–14.

Hetherington, E. M. (Ed; 1999). *Coping with divorce, single parenting, and remarriage: A risk and resiliency perspective.* Mahwah, NJ: Erlbaum.

Hetherington, E. M., Cox, M., & Cox, R. (1985). Long-term effects of divorce and remarriage on the adjustment of children. *Journal of the American Academy of Child Psychiatry, 24*, 518–530.

Hysjulien, C., Wood. B., & Benjamin, G. A. H. (1994). Child custody evaluations: A review of methods used in litigation and alternative dispute resolution. *Family and Conciliation Courts Review, 32*, 466–489.

Jaffee, P., Wolfe, D., & Wilson, S. (1990). *Children of battered women.* Newbury Park, CA: Sage.

Johnston, J. R. (1994). High-conflict divorce. *Future of Children, 4*, 165–182.

Johnston, J. R., Gonzalez, R., & Campbell, L. E. G. (1987). Ongoing postdivorce conflict and child disturbance. *Journal of Abnormal Child Psychology, 15*, 493–509.

Johnston, J. R., & Roseby, V. (1997). *In the name of the child: A developmental approach to understanding and helping children of conflicted and violent divorce.* New York: Free Press.

Kalter, N., Kloner, A., Schreier, S., & Okla, K. (1989). Predictors of children's postdivorce adjustment. *American Journal of Orthopsychiatry, 59*, 605–618.

Keilin, W. G., & Bloom, L. J. (1986). Child custody evaluation practices: A survey of experienced professionals. *Professional Psychology: Research and Practice, 17*, 338–346.

Kelly, J. B. (2000). Children's adjustment in conflicted marriage and divorce: A decade review of research. *Journal of the American Academy of Child and Adolescent Psychiatry, 39*, 963–973.

Kendall-Tackett, K. A., Williams, L. M., & Finkelhor, D. (1993). Impact of sexual abuse on children: A review and synthesis of recent empirical studies. *Psychological Bulletin, 113*, 164–180.

Kirkland, K., & Kirkland, K. (2001). Frequency of child custody evaluation complaints and related disciplinary action: A survey of the Association of State and Provincial Psychology Boards. *Professional Psychology: Research and Practice, 32*, 171–174.

Kolbo, J. R., Blakely, E. H., & Engleman, D. (1996). Children who witness domestic violence: A review of empirical literature. *Journal of Interpersonal Violence, 11*(2), 281–293.

Krauss, D. A., & Sales, B. D. (2000). Legal standards, expertise, and experts in the resolution of contested child custody cases. *Psychology, Public Policy, and Law, 6*, 843–879.

Kropp, P. R., Hart, S. D., Webster, C. W., & Eaves, D. (1995). *Manual for the spousal assault risk assessment guide* (2nd ed.). Vancouver, British Columbia, Canada: British Columbia Institute on Family Violence.

Kropp, P. R., Hart, S. D., Webster, C. W., & Eaves, D. (1998). *Spousal assault risk assessment: User's guide.* Toronto, Ontario, Canada: Multi-Health Systems.

Long, N., Slater, E., Forehand, R., & Fauber, R. (1988). Continued high or reduced parental conflict following divorce: Relation to young adolescent adjustment. *Journal of Consulting and Clinical Psychology, 56*, 467–469.

Luvera, P. N. (1981). How to take depositions. *Personal Injury Annual*, 866–879.

Maccoby, E. E., Mnookin, R. H., Depner, C. E., & Peters, E. H. (1992). *Dividing the child: Social and legal dilemmas of custody.* Cambridge, MA: Harvard University Press.

Magana, H. A., & Taylor, N. (1993). Meyer Elkin Essay Contest Winner: Child custody mediation and spousal abuse: A descriptive study of a protocol. *Family and Conciliation Courts Review, 31*, 50–64.

Mason, M. A., & Quirk, A. (1997). Are mothers losing custody? Read my lips: Trends in judicial decision-making in custody disputes—1920, 1960, 1990, and 1995. *Family Law Quarterly, 31*, 215–236.

McEwen, C. A., Rogers, N. H., & Maiman, R. J. (1995). Bring in the lawyers: Challenging the dominant approaches to ensuring fairness in divorce mediation. *Minnesota Law Review, 79*, 1317–1411.

Medoff, D. (1999). MMPI–2 validity scales in child custody evaluations: Clinical versus statistical significance. *Behavioral Sciences and the Law, 17*, 409–411.

Meehl, P. E. (1954/1996). *Clinical versus statistical prediction: A theoretical analysis and review of the evidence.* Northvale, NJ: Jason Aronson.

Melton, G. B., Petrila, J., Poythress, N. G., & Slobogin, C. (1987). *Psychological evaluations for the courts.* New York: Guilford Press.

The Mental Measurements Yearbook. (2001). Gryphon Press: Highland Park, NJ.

Montemayor, R. (1984). Picking up the pieces: The effects of parental divorce on adolescents, with some suggestions for school-based intervention programs. *Journal of Early Adolescence, 4*, 289–314.

Myers, J. B., & Erickson, R. (1999). *Legal and ethical issues in child custody litigation.* In R. M. Galatzer-Levy & L. Kraus (Eds.), *The scientific basis of child custody decisions* (pp. 12–32).

National Center for Health Statistics of the United States. (2001). Table 1. Provisional number of marriages and divorces, 1997–1999. *Monthly Vital Statistics Report, 48,* 1–2.

Otto, R. K., & Collins, R. P. (1995). Use of the MMPI–2/MMPI–A in child custody evaluations. In Y. S. Ben-Porath, J. R. Graham, G. C. N. Hall, & M. S. Zaragoza (Eds.), *Forensic applications of the MMPI–2* (pp. 222–252). Thousand Oaks, CA: Sage.

Pagelow, M. D. (1990). Effects of domestic violence on children and their consequences for custody and visitation agreements. *Mediation Quarterly, 7,* 347–363.

Pagelow, M. D. (1992). Adult victims of domestic violence: Battered women. *Journal of Interpersonal Violence, 7,* 87–120.

Pappas, E. H. (1987). Preparing your witness for deposition. *For The Defense, 29,* 8–9.

Pearson, J., & Thoennes, N. (1985). Mediation versus the courts in child custody cases. *Negotiation Journal, 1,* 235–244.

Roll, S. (1998). Cross-cultural considerations in custody and parenting plans. *Child and Adolescent Psychiatric Clinics of North America, 7,* 445–454.

Saywitz, K., & Camparo, L. (1998). Interviewing child witnesses: A developmental perspective. *Child Abuse and Neglect, 22,* 825–843.

Scott, E. (1992). Pluralism, parental preference, and child custody. *California Law Review, 80,* 615–672.

Shaw, D. S., Emery, R. E., & Tuer, M. D. (1993). Parental functioning and children's adjustment in families of divorce. *Journal of Abnormal Child Psychology, 21,* 119–134.

Sheets, V., & Braver, S. (1996). Gender differences in satisfaction with divorce settlements. *Family Relations, 45,* 336–342.

Shuman, D. W., & Sales, B. D. (1999). The impact of Daubert and its progeny on the admissibility of behavioral and social science evidence. *Psychology, Public Policy, and Law, 5,* 3–15.

Siegel, J. C. (1996). Traditional MMPI–2 validity indicators and initial presentation in custody evaluations. *American Journal of Forensic Psychology, 14,* 55–63.

Simons, Grossman, & Weiner. (1990). A study of families in high conflict custody disputes: Effects of psychiatric evaluation. *Bulletin of the American Academy of Psychiatry and the Law, 18,* 85–97.

Sonkin, D. J. (1987). *Domestic violence on trial.* New York: Springer.

Sorenson, E. D., & Goldman, J. (1990). Custody determination and child development: A review of the current literature. *Journal of Divorce, 13,* 53–67.

Straus, M. A. (1979). Measuring intrafamily conflict and violence: The conflict tactics (CT) scales. *Journal of Marriage and the Family, 41,* 75–88.

Straus, M. A., Hamby, S. L., Boney-McCoy, S., & Sugarman, D. B. (1996). The revised Conflict Tactics Scales (CTS2): Development and preliminary psychometric data. *Journal of Family Issues, 17,* 283–316.

Strausburger, L. H., Gutheil, T. G., & Brodsky, A. (1997). On wearing two hats: Role conflict in serving as both psychotherapist and expert witness. *American Journal of Psychiatry, 154,* 448–456.

Sue, D. W., & Sue, D. (1999). *Counseling the culturally different: Theory and practice* (3rd ed.). New York: Wiley.

Wah, C. R. (1994). Mental health and minority religions: The latest weapon in custody battles. *International Journal of Law and Psychiatry, 17,* 331–345.

Wah, C. R. (1997). Evaluating "nontraditional" religious practice in child custody cases. *Family and Conciliation Courts Review, 35,* 300–316.

Wallerstein, J. S. (1986). Women after divorce: Preliminary report from a ten-year follow-up. *American Journal of Orthopsychiatry, 56,* 65–77.

Wallerstein, J. S. (1991). The long-term effects of divorce on children: A review. *Journal of American Academy of Child and Adolescent Psychiatry, 30,* 349–360.

Wallerstein, J. S., & Lewis, J. (1998). The long-term impact of divorce on children. A first report from a 25-year study. *Family Conciliation Courts Review, 36,* 368–383.

Watkins, B., & Bentovim, A. (1992). The sexual abuse of male children and adolescents: A review of current research. *Journal of Child Psychology and Psychiatry, 33,* 197–248.

Watson, A. S. (1978). On the preparation and use of psychiatric expert testimony: Some suggestions in an ongoing controversy. *Bulletin American Academy of Psychiatry and the Law, 6,* 226–246.

Wexler, D. B., & Winick, B. J. (1996). *Law in a therapeutic key.* Carolina Academic Press.

Whiteside, M. E. (1998). The parental alliance following divorce: An overview. *Journal of Marital and Family Therapy, 24,* 3–24.

Ziskin, D., & Faust, D. (1995). *Coping with psychiatric testimony* (5th ed., Vol. 1).

TABLE OF AUTHORITIES

Bruce v. Bryne-Stevens & Associates Engineers, Inc., 113 Wash. 2d 123, 776 P.2d 666 (1989).

Commonwealth of Massachusetts v. Lamb, 365 Mass. 265, 270 (1974).

Daubert v. Merrill Dow Pharmaceuticals, 509 U.S. 579 (1993).

Frye v. United States, 292 F.1013 (D.C. Cir. 1923).

Hernandez v. Thomas, 50 Fla. 522 (1905).

Kumho Tire v. Carmichael, 119 S. Ct. 1167 (1999).

Revised Code of Washington, § 26.09.187 (1993).

Uniform Marriage and Divorce Act, 9 A.U.L.A. 197 § 402 (West, 1979).

INDEX

Attorneys
  communication with, 44
  meeting with, 94–97, 190–191
    preparing for, 93–94
  See also Discovery
Audiotapes, of clinical interviews, 35
Authority to conduct evaluation, 41–43

Baseline parenting behaviors, 68–70
Best interests of the child standard, 6,
    19–21
  in Agreement to Parenting Evaluation,
    178, 179
  and clinical judgments, 27–28
  and domestic violence, 58
  and evaluation parameters, 54
  and mediation, 22
  vagaries of, 173
Bruce v. Bryne-Stevens & Associates Engineers, Inc., 42

Case of D. *vs.* M., 117–118, 159–160
  allegations and perceptions in, 119–
    121, 147–154, 160–167
  child's environment in, 154
  clinical findings in, 133–135
  collateral contacts in, 119
    interviewing of, 85–86
    questions for, 76, 77–78
  collateral information in, 80, 142–146
  discussion on, 146–147
    of parental allegations, 147–154
  documents in, 119
  evaluation procedures in, 118
  and factual inconsistencies, 84
  interviews and observation sessions in,
    118
  parent-child observations in, 135–142
  parenting capabilities in, 167–170
  psychological measures in, 118
  recommendations in, 154–157
  social histories in, 122–133
Case manager, for high-conflict cases, 33
Child custody assessment protocol, 6
Child custody cases or disputes. *See* Custody cases or disputes
Child custody evaluations. *See* Custody evaluation
Child-harming behaviors
  in evaluation report, 112

in sample evaluation report, 125, 130–
    131
Child interviews, 86–88
Child neglect or abuse
  as allegation in custody disputes, 13,
    173
  in sample evaluation report, 148
  See also Physical abuse; Sexual abuse
Child protection cases, 6
Children, impact of divorce on, 13–16
Child's environment, in sample evaluation report, 154
Clinical findings, 113
  in sample evaluation report, 133–135
Clinical interviews
  first, 49–64
  in evaluation report, 111
  in Parenting Evaluation in Legal Setting, 190
Clinical judgment, 27–28
  errors of, 27, 47, 173–174
  and hypotheses, 134
Closing interviews, 83–91
  and trial testimony, 103
Code of ethics, 29–31
Collateral information or evidence
  in evaluation report, 83, 114
  example of, 73–74
  in sample evaluation report, 80–81,
    142–146
Collateral reporters, 71
Collaterals (collateral contacts), 62, 73
  documents from, 80
  in evaluation report, 110
  and hypotheses about allegations, 74–
    76
  interviewing of, 73, 78–79, 85–86
  in Parenting Evaluation in Legal Setting, 189
  questions for, 75, 76, 77–79
  in sample evaluation report, 119
  in semi-structured interview, 204
Collateral summaries, 79–80
Common law, 17
Commonwealth of Massachusetts v. Lamb,
    51
Communication
  with attorneys, 44
  with child and other parent (sample
    evaluation report recommendations), 156
Communication skills, need for, 32–33

Competence
  cultural, 56–57
  of custody evaluators, 34
Compound questions, during meeting
      with attorneys, 96–97
Computer, laptop, 60
Conducting evaluations, 3
  evaluator's demeanor during, 52, 90,
      94–95
  and legal rules, 18 (*see also* Law)
  Phase 1 of (pre-evaluation procedures),
      41–48
  Phase 2 of (first clinical interviews),
      49–64
  Phase 3 of (observation of parents and
      children), 65–72
  Phase 4 of (contacting collaterals),
      73–81
  Phase 5 of (closing interviews and data
      integration), 83–91
  Phase 6 of (presentation to court), 93–
      104
Confidentiality, absence of. *See* Nonconfi-
      dentiality warnings
Confidentiality, waiving of, 178
Conflicting factual details, 84–85
Conflict Tactics Scale, 58
Consent agreement, 52
Consent to release of information. *See*
      Release-of-information forms
Constraints of legal rules, 18
Consultants, 35, 43–44
Contempt motion, 45
Contingent fees, professional guidelines'
      prohibiting of, 32, 174
Coparenting counseling
  estimates of time for, 97
  for high-conflict cases, 33
Court-appointed or -stipulated evalua-
      tions, 3. *See also* Custody evalua-
      tions
Court(s)
  and evaluator's competence, 35
  presentation to, 93–104
  See also Law
Criminal history, in semi-structured inter-
      view, 197
Cultural competence, in semi-structured
      interview, 56–57
Current relationship
  in evaluation report, 112

in sample evaluation report, 123–125,
      129
in semi-structured interview, 199
Custody cases or disputes, 4
  and best-interests standard, 6, 19–21
      (*see also* Best interests of the
      child standard)
  and dependency or child protection
      cases, 6
  differences in family environments of,
      13
  mental health professionals in, 4–5
  See also Case of *D. vs. M*
Custody and divorce law, 19
Custody (parenting) evaluation, 4, 5, 12
  and allegations, 13, 16, 107, 173 (*see
      also* Allegations)
    as method, 173, 174
  and clinical judgment, 27–28, 47, 134,
      173–174
  continued learning needed on, 174
  and dissatisfaction of party, 64
  ethical guidelines for, 29–31, 89, 173
      (*see also* at Ethical)
  and legal standards, 18 (*see also* Law)
  overall description of (Parenting Evalu-
      ation in a Legal Setting), 46,
      187–191
  parental weaknesses delineated in, 15–
      16
  professional guidelines for, 31–34
  as prone to errors in clinical judgment,
      173–174
  referrals for, 41–42
  as therapeutic jurisprudence, 6
  time period for, 44
Custody evaluation, conducting of. *See*
      Conducting evaluations
Custody evaluation report. *See* Evaluation
      report
Custody evaluators
  licensing board complaints concerning,
      6
  neutrality of, 33–34, 42, 95
  role(s) of, 174
  selection of, 34, 41
  training of, 5, 34–35

Data collection, 17–18
Data integration, 63–64, 83–91
  in writing after party contact, 48

and allegations, 64, 107, 110 (*see also* Allegations)
annotated structure of, 109–115
collateral summaries in, 79–80 (*see also* Collaterals)
discussion section of, 33, 64, 74, 80–81
preliminary, 71–72
review of, 64, 97, 190
samples of
for modification of parenting plan, 117–158
for permanent parenting plan action, 159–170
writing of immediately after evaluation sessions, 47, 48, 60, 63, 71, 91
Evaluations, conducting of. *See* Conducting evaluations
Evaluation Tracking Form, 181–182
Evidence
scientific (rules of admissibility), 23–26
in support of allegation, 206, 208
Evidentiary standards, 17
and evaluation report, 75
Ex parte communication, 44. *See also* Out-of-court statements
Expert witness, evaluator as, 95, 97–104
additional retainer for, 97
Extended families, 57–58

Fact finder, and best-interests standard, 20
Family forensic evaluation, 5. *See also* Custody evaluation
Family history
in evaluation report, 111
in sample evaluation report, 122, 125–127
in semi-structured interview, 194
Family questions, in adolescent interview, 212–214
Federal Rules of Evidence, 23
Fee retainers, 45–46, 98, 102, 178–179, 188, 191
Fees, contingent, prohibition of, 32, 174
Financial status, in semi-structured interview, 202
First clinical interviews, 49–64
Forensic evaluation. *See* Custody evaluation
Frye standard or test, 23, 24

Greenberg, Stuart, 47
Guardian ad litem (GAL), 30, 44
in discussion of report, 97
for high-conflict cases, 33
interviewing of, 79
and waiving of child's psychotherapy privilege, 52
Guidelines for Child Custody Evaluations in Divorce Proceedings (APA), 30, 31, 42, 43, 47, 50, 51, 72, 89, 107
Guidelines for Providers of Psychological Services to Ethnic and Culturally Diverse Populations (APA), 56–57

Hedrick, Marsha, 50
Hernandez v. Thomas, 19
Home visits, 71
for observation, 63
Hypotheses, 64
about allegations, 74–76, 80
clinical judgment in selecting of, 134
and psychological testing, 53

Inappropriate cases, screening for, 43
Inferences, from data of case and expert knowledge, 96, 100
Informed consent agreement, 52
Interparental conflict. *See* Parental conflict
Interrogatories, 94, 98–99
Interview(s)
with adolescents, 85, 190, 211–214
with children, 86–88
clinical, 111, 190
first, 49–64
closing, 83–91, 103
with collaterals, 73, 78–79, 85–86
in sample evaluation report, 118
semistructured, 50, 53–61, 193–204
with third parties easily influenced, 85

Jurisprudence, therapeutic, 6, 22

Kumho Tire v. Carmichael, 26

Language barrier, 58

United States v. Frye, 23

Validity, 25
Victimization, 15
  therapy for, 33
Videotapes
  in Agreement to Parenting Evaluation,
    177–178
  of clinical interviews, 35
  of parent-child interaction, 67
Violence
  extended family history of, 15
  See also Domestic violence; Physical
    abuse

Voir dire, 102

Warning of nonconfidentiality, 50–52,
    109
  in sample evaluation report, 118
Work (employment) history
  in evaluation report, 111
  in sample evaluation report, 123, 127–
    128
  in semi-structured interview, 55, 195–
    196
Writing, report, 71
  immediate vs. retrospective, 48

ABOUT THE AUTHORS

G. Andrew H. Benjamin, PhD, JD, has exceptional career features that are distinguished by the breadth of his professional activities and the strength of his commitment to combining the best resources of psychology and law for the benefit of adults and children enmeshed in family conflicts. While working with families engaged in high-conflict litigation, he was named "Professional of the Year" by the Washington State Bar Association's Family Law Section. He was elected to serve as president of the Washington State Psychological Association, and later his colleagues created an award named after him for "outstanding and tireless contributions." He was honored by the Puyallup Nation's Health Authority for serving as a "modern-day warrior fighting the mental illnesses, drug–alcohol addictions" of the people served by the nation's program. He has published 36 articles in psychology, law, and psychiatry journals and is the author of *Law and Mental Health Professionals: Washington* published by the American Psychological Association. Andy lives in Seattle with his wife of 25 years and two children. His hobbies include extensive family travel and watching his son's and daughter's soccer teams.

Jackie K. Gollan, PhD, received her PhD with Distinction in 2000 from the University of Washington with training in both clinical research and forensic psychology. She finished her internship training in 2000 at Brown University Medical School and received the A.T. Beck and Brown University Medical School Award for original research in major depression, and was offered a National Institute of Mental Health F-32 grant funding to investigate the development of depression during divorce. To complement her Parenting Evaluation Treatment Program training, Jackie completed a Harvard Medical School Postdoctoral Fellowship in Pediatric Forensic Psychology at Massachusetts General Hospital, with emphasis on custody/visitation disputes and child dependency/protection issues. In 2001, she became a faculty member in the Department of Psychiatry at the University of Chicago and obtained funding via a Young Investigator Award from the American Foundation of Suicide Prevention. As director of the Center for Cognitive Therapy, her clinical research focuses on social and biological underpinnings of depression and the impact of both child-hood adversity and divorce on adult adjustment.